COGNITIVE PSYCHOLOGY

THE BASICS

Cognitive Psychology: The Basics provides a compact introduction to the core topics in the field, discussing the science behind the everyday cognitive phenomena experienced by us all. The book considers laboratory and applied theory and research alongside technological developments to demonstrate how our understanding of the brain's role in cognition is improving all the time.

Alongside coverage of traditional topics in the field, including attention and perception; learning and memory; thinking, problem-solving and decision-making; and language, the book also discusses developments in interrelated areas, such as neuroscience and computational cognitive science. New perspectives, including the contribution of evolutionary psychology to our understanding of cognition, are also considered followed by a thoughtful discussion of future research directions. Using real-world examples throughout, the authors explain in an accessible and student-friendly manner the role our human cognition plays in all aspects of our lives.

It is an essential introductory text suitable for all students of cognitive psychology and related disciplines. It will also be an ideal read for any reader interested in the role of the brain in human behaviour.

Sandie Taylor is an experienced lecturer and author. Her DPhil in cognitive psychology focused on memory, in particular face recognition, and applied memory approaches to facilitate recognition of faces. She has previously published four books and many peer reviewed articles and book chapters.

Lance Workman is Visiting Professor of Psychology at the University of South Wales. He was formerly Head of Psychology at Bath Spa University. Lance has published widely in psychology including over 100 articles and nine books. For seven years he was interviews editor for *The Psychologist* and regularly appears in the media.

The Basics

The Basics is a highly successful series of accessible guidebooks which provide an overview of the fundamental principles of a subject area in a jargon-free and undaunting format.

Intended for students approaching a subject for the first time, the books both introduce the essentials of a subject and provide an ideal springboard for further study. With over 50 titles spanning subjects from artificial intelligence (AI) to women's studies, *The Basics* are an ideal starting point for students seeking to understand a subject area.

Each text comes with recommendations for further study and gradually introduces the complexities and nuances within a subject.

Town Planning
Tony Hall

Women's Studies (second edition)
Bonnie G. Smith

English Grammar
Michael McCarthy

Pragmatics
Billy Clark

World Prehistory
Brian M. Fagan and Nadia Durrani

For a full list of titles in this series, please visit www.routledge.com/The-Basics/book-series/B

COGNITIVE PSYCHOLOGY

THE BASICS

Sandie Taylor and Lance Workman

Routledge
Taylor & Francis Group

LONDON AND NEW YORK

First published 2022
by Routledge
2 Park Square, Milton Park, Abingdon, Oxon OX14 4RN

and by Routledge
605 Third Avenue, New York, NY 10158

Routledge is an imprint of the Taylor & Francis Group, an informa business

British Library Cataloguing-in-Publication Data
A catalogue record for this book is available from the British Library

Library of Congress Cataloging-in-Publication Data
A catalog record has been requested for this book

ISBN: 978-0-367-85686-1 (hbk)
ISBN: 978-0-367-85685-4 (pbk)
ISBN: 978-1-003-01435-5 (ebk)

DOI: 10.4324/9781003014355

Typeset in Bembo
by MPS Limited, Dehradun

For Dafydd

CONTENTS

ACKNOWLEDGEMENTS

We would like to acknowledge Professor Ray Bull. Also to Sandie Taylor for 92 per cent of the figure work.

WHAT IS COGNITIVE PSYCHOLOGY?

Cognitive psychology is concerned with how we process information. It has been eloquently defined by the American Psychological Association (APA) in 2020 as "the branch of psychology that explores the operation of mental processes related to perceiving, attending, thinking, language, and memory, mainly through inferences from behavior". The exploration of mental processes is not new. For a very long time, philosophers and 'scientists' have been fascinated by the connection between our mind, mental processes and the brain. Studying the brain using 'scientific' methodology began during the Renaissance period; a time in European history arguably between 1400 and 1700. It was during this period that scholars became interested in studying nature, which included the mechanics of the human body. Great thinkers such as René Descartes pondered over the philosophical approach of 'dualism' to understand the difference between mind and body. He believed the two were separate from each other such that our body (including the brain) represented a physical entity while the mind represented a spiritual one. The implication of this is that the mind can exist independently of the body. Conversely, monism described the mind and body as coexisting. With the development of scientific technology used to map the brain, the notion of the mind existing separately from the physical brain became very unlikely. Nevertheless, Descartes helped expand our way of thinking about the mind and body interface. Even today with our extensive explorations inside the working brain, finding direct connections between structure and function is not always straightforward (see Chapter 2). It could be argued that ideas from dualism and monism

DOI: 10.4324/9781003014355-1

spurred questions about whether it is possible to replicate a model of how the mind works. For example, a sub-group of researchers in Information Technology (IT) have sought to develop a robotic brain based on a series of inputted commands and algorithms. This is designed in such a way as to emulate the connections of neurons (nerve cells) in the human brain. This type of neural networking comes out of research in computational modelling, which aspires to imitate cognitive functioning in humans. Despite this, development of a 'brain' that is able to learn independently of further human instruction is still beyond our reach.

The reason for this short history lesson is to provide us with a context of how cognitive psychology has developed. Not only this, but how the different disciplinary routes of science and philosophy have found their way as sub-disciplines into modern cognitive psychology. In this chapter, the objective is to outline these different contributory disciplines, and their contributions towards an understanding of how our brain processes information. The four main areas of contribution include: cognitive psychology; cognitive neuroscience; cognitive neuropsychology and computational cognitive science.

COGNITIVE PSYCHOLOGY

The development of cognitive psychology was, in part, a reaction to the focus on overt behaviour advocated by 'Behaviourism'. The behaviourist movement was concerned with only what you can see and not that which is hidden from scientific scrutiny. In other words, aspects of brain function, such as how we think and remember, were off limits. For behaviourists, such brain activity was encapsulated in a 'black box' that could not be researched objectively. Nevertheless, even as behaviourism maintained its hold over academic psychology, there were key scholars who contributed towards developing a method for studying mental processes. George Miller is one such scholar who, in 1956, introduced an experimental method for studying memory. Alongside Miller, there were others who devised ingenious experiments to understand mental processing. Also, with the popularisation of **information processing** during the 1970s, an all-encompassing approach for understanding mental (or cognitive) processing was introduced. The information processing approach helped cognitive psychology to develop further. It enabled cognitive psychologists to formulate models to represent, for example, how attention, perception and memory might operate. There were many types of information processing models, some of which highlighted the similarities in function between the human brain and a computer. As we will see in Chapter 3, information processing models have helped cognitive psychologists understand the transition from sensory pick-up of stimuli in our environment to forging meaning in the brain. Models of attention have brought with them new terminologies such as bottom-up *versus* top-down processing, and serial *versus* parallel processing (see Chapter 3). Different types of memory storage have been introduced such as short-term *versus* long-term memory (see Chapter 4).

So how are cognitive information processing models derived? A succinct answer to this is by collating participant scores from cognitive-related tasks. This appears to be simple, but these cognitive-related tasks have to be controlled such that they test the same aspect of cognition under the same conditions. This means that to test problem-solving, for example, the same conditions of the study must be applied to all participants. Often two groups are compared where only one variable is changed. In this context, the term variable is used to denote something that can be changed or manipulated. An example of this might be that one group is given more time to complete the task or that they have to do so in the presence of a distraction. In this way we can compare the performance of the two groups for the effect of time or distraction on problem-solving. Different cognitive tasks are designed to test specific aspects of performance; such as, how many items participants recall within a set period of time, after memorising them for one minute. For each group of participants, it is possible to derive an average score of performance for the specific task in question. This average score can be considered as representative of how a particular population sample performs on the task studied (under each condition). The average performance of each group is known as a normative score. This is important as it can be added to existing knowledge about how people perform on such a task but under slightly different conditions. In our problem-solving example, it could be that resolution of the task fails when the time allowed is halved or when distracted. This information can then be added to existing theory or a model of problem-solving (see Box 1.1).

Cognitive tasks can be used as an objective method of exploring mental processes. Moreover, by adopting such a method, cognitive

BOX 1.1   HOW ARE COGNITIVE INFORMATION PROCESSING MODELS DERIVED?

An interesting way of developing scientific knowledge was outlined by philosopher Karl Popper (1959). He provided a protocol for devising experiments in his Deductive Model of Science. Not only was this embraced by cognitive psychologists, but by the scientific community as a whole. It describes a number of stages which should be followed as a means of building knowledge based upon existing knowledge. Sometimes the existing knowledge becomes extended, but it can also be refuted. The key element is to test and retest using the same variables and method; the experimental method. He described how it is important to make predictions or hypotheses about the phenomenon under investigation. For example, 'Faces presented twice during learning are more likely to be recognised in a test than those faces shown once'. This hypothesis is making a statement of prediction and prescribes the best way of investigating this. The experimental method should have two conditions, one where participants see a series of faces, some of which are repeated and some of which are not. In the other condition, participants are shown the same faces but all of them are shown once only. The test should include the target faces with a set of new unseen faces. This means that all participants have the same test. If the hypothesis holds true, then participants shown the faces twice should recognise more of the faces than those participants who saw one presentation only. Results supporting the hypothesis are added to existing theories about memory for faces; in this case showing faces more than once improves facial memory. Hence, the hypothesis is supported, and findings are added to the general theory of memory for faces. We could devise a simple model based on this hypothesis (see Figure 1.1).

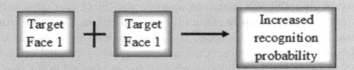

Figure 1.1 Fictitious model based on collated performance results

This example shows how it is possible to develop models based on participant scores from a cognitive task (face recognition). It makes sense, however, to include scores that are similar. If scores are 'all over the place', then the hypothesis will not be confirmed. Scores have to be evaluated carefully because it is possible that there are one or two scores that are odd, in that they fail to fit the majority pattern. These scores are considered as outliers and can be above or below the average score. Hence, most scores that are similar are considered the average (norm or mean) while other scores are distributed away from mean. The distance from the mean is calculated as standard deviations and these scores can still be included. Outliers that are 'many' standard deviations from the mean, fail to represent a normative population and can be excluded. Unless we are interested in the extreme scores (which we can be), the exclusion of 'outliers' is important if we want to obtain a consensus on individuals' performance for specific cognitive tasks. This type of scoring fits with the bell-shaped Yerkes-Dodson curve (see Figure 1.2). Such results help cognitive psychologists under-stand how the brain processes information and enables the tweaking of existing models.

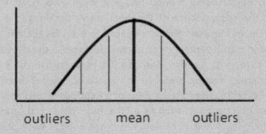

Figure 1.2 Yerkes–Dodson curve
Soutce: Adapted from Yerkes and Dodson (1908)

psychologists have a means of opening the 'black box' that behaviourists so vehemently argue cannot be accessed. There are many examples of where cognitive tasks have helped progress our understanding of cognition. One interesting area is mental imagery. Mental imagery is considered to be a series of pictures in the mind's eye without input from the outside world. One study examined the hypothesis that mental imagery uses visual representations (see Box 1.2).

Cognitive psychology has contributed to how we study and understand mental processing. It has introduced a successful methodological ethos. It has, however, introduced limitations to how cognitive tasks are designed and who comprises the participant population. Most research is conducted within the walls of a laboratory using university students. This, it has been argued, can result in findings that are divorced from the 'real' world; findings which lack ecological validity. Another problem

BOX 1.2 MENTAL IMAGERY

The study of mental imagery is attributed to Stephen Kosslyn, who devised an experiment in 1973 to examine how we can 'see' images in our mind, without actually receiving input from our visual system. He argued that we scan images introspectively in our mind, and that this is a cognitive process. Kosslyn found that when participants were instructed to imagine moving from one location to another, it took them longer to achieve this when the distance between the two points was further away. He also demonstrated that when asked to scan an object using mental imagery, such as a boat, the more distant the components of the boat were, the longer it took to 'reach' them. For example, when asked to scan for the anchor from the motor, participants moved in real time across the deck and bow to find it. In 1978, Kosslyn, Ball and Reiser wanted to know whether these mental images preserve the spatial distances between the parts of objects. They used a map of a fictitious island which had a series of objects on it, such as a lake, hut, rock, sand, grass and a well. The spatial distances between these objects were pre-defined and set in a way that some objects were closer together than others (see Figure 1.3).

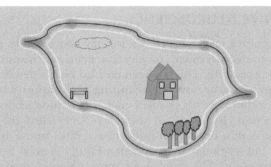

Figure 1.3 Fictitious island map
Source: Adapted from Kosslyn, Ball and Reiser (1978)

Participants learnt the objects on the map, their locations and relative positions. The map was removed, and participants were told that they would hear the name of one of the objects on the map, at which point they had to mentally image the whole map and focus on the object. Participants effectively scanned their mental image of the map and pressed a button when they arrived at the location of the object. From this object's location they had to travel mentally to the next object and so on. The length of time it took to travel from one object to the next was consistent with the spatial distances on the map. Hence, the further the distance between two objects, the longer it took to scan the mental image. They concluded that the content of a picture, including the spatial properties, are preserved in our mental imagery. In 2005, Kosslyn calculated that there is a two thirds overlap of areas activated in the brain during mental imagery and during visual processing.

concerns the level of interpretation of the findings. For instance, measures taken, including the correctness and speed of task performance, can be interpreted as providing evidence of specific cognitive function. Mental processes involved in task completion are often more complicated and operate on an interdependent basis. In recent years this latter problem has been addressed by the development of scanning technology provided by cognitive neuroscience.

COGNITIVE NEUROSCIENCE

When cognitive neuroscience was initially conceived its remit was to study the involvement of physical brain mechanisms during cognitive processing. This has been enabled by the development of technological advances such as **scanning techniques**. Using brain scanning technology has enabled cognitive neuroscientists to map brain function. By doing so they have unravelled the intricate complexities of a brain with multi-neural links (some 100 billion neurons) and seemingly independent areas of the brain that operate interdependently. The brain is far more complex than they had originally envisaged over 30 years ago. Cognitive neuroscience has contributed towards our understanding of individual differences, cognitive intervention and rehabilitation, and theoretical neuroscience. Of interest here, however, are the different scanning techniques available and how these have been used to map the brain. There are many different scanning (or imaging) techniques used in cognitive neuroscience (see Table 1.1).

Table 1.2 provides some examples of how these three different imaging techniques can be used to investigate cognitive processing.

Scanning techniques have provided detailed pictorial information about the structure and function of the brain (as discussed in Chapter 2). For example, in Figure 1.4, the basic structure of the brain can be seen.

An interesting case of the woman who has no fear due to serious damage to the amygdala (see Box 1.3) has shown the important role that brain imaging has as a diagnostic tool.

This confirms the mapping of the brain produced by neurologist, Korbinian Brodmann (1868–1918). Scanning techniques such as fMRI have helped cognitive neuroscientists to understand how the different areas of the brain are interconnected while, at the same time, maintaining some function specificity.

COGNITIVE NEUROPSYCHOLOGY

While cognitive neuroscientists highlight how intricately the brain is interconnected, another relatively new field – cognitive neuropsychology – has developed the concept of **modularity**. Ellis and Young (1988) defined modularity as 'the orchestrated activity

Table 1.1 Different scanning techniques commonly used by cognitive neuroscientists

Scanning techniques	How it works
Single unit recording	The activity of a single neuron can be studied through the insertion of a micro-electrode into the brain. This is very sensitive and can pick up the activity in a single cell.
Event related potentials (ERPs)	Many electrodes are placed in several areas on the scalp. These record brain activity while the individual is performing a cognitive task. The recordings are averaged to produce a single continuous waveform.
Positron emission tomography (PET)	This indirectly measures neural activity by using radioactive substances that release atomic particles known as positrons. When the released positrons are detected by this scanner, a spatial image is created.
Functional magnetic resonance imaging (fMRI)	Changes of blood oxygenation and flow are indicators of neural activity. Active areas in the brain consume more oxygen and it is this that fMRI detects and images.
Event related functional magnetic resonance imagining (efMRI)	A measure known as BOLD (blood oxygen level-dependent) is used to detect the amount of deoxyhaemoglobin in the capillaries and veins of the brain. This provides a measure of the amount of oxygen used (OEF: oxygen extraction fraction) by areas active in the brain. This measure provides information regarding areas active during specific cognitive tasking.
Magnetic encephalography (MEG)	Electrical activity of neurons generates a magnetic field. It is this magnetic field that is measured by sensors called magnetometers. This is then translated into images of structure and function.
Transcranial magnetic stimulation (repetitive transcranial magnetic stimulation: rTMS)	Magnetic pulses are applied to the brain. A non-invasive coil is placed against the head which delivers an electric current. When this is repeated in quick succession it is known as rTMS. This helps to stimulate areas of the brain where applied.

Table 1.2 Different scanning techniques commonly used to investigate cognitive phenomenon.

Scanning techniques	When is it used
Event related potentials (ERPS) from Electroencephalography (EEG)	EEG is often used as part of a 'bio-pack' for undergraduate biological and cognitive laboratory experiments. An averaged single waveform can be recorded from a series of electrodes placed on the scalp. ERPS are produced from EEG recordings which can provide useful information about reaction times. Reaction time is a useful behavioural measure indicating how quickly participants respond to cognitive tasks. This also provides information about the speed of brain activation once the task has been given. For example, if the task is to detect a face amongst other non-face stimuli, then ERPS can provide information regarding the general area of brain activation. This method has limitations such as teasing out 'noise' from brain tissue itself, as this can distort the brain's electrical fields during task performance. Also, ERPS can only be used for simple cognitive tasks that draw upon basic processes and rely on a single measure like reaction time. Jutai and Hare (1983) considered differences of focused (or selective) attention among criminal psychopathic and non-psychopathic inmates. They listened to a series of tone pips through headphones while playing a video game. Their performance on the video game was used as a measure of their attention deployed to playing. Psychopaths had small N100 (measure on the ERPS) readings suggesting that they suppress the distractor tone pips. It was concluded that psychopaths show altered deployment of attention in comparison to non-psychopathic inmates.
Positron emission tomography (PET)	This scanning technique can obtain images of areas of brain activity while participants perform a cognitive task. A clear structural image is obtained of an active area of the brain within 5-10 mm. This clarity, however, does not extend to the amount of activity in

(*Continued*)

Table 1.2 (Continued)

Scanning techniques	When is it used
	specific areas of the brain. PET scans have been used to investigate how murderers perform on a task requiring focused attention (Raine, Buchsbaum, Stanley, Lottenberg et al. 1994). PET scans made it possible to see the brain in action. Raine et al. found that the murderers in comparison to the controls, had processing deficits to the area of the brain called the prefrontal cortex. This area has a controlling influence on evolutionary older parts of the brain such as the amygdala which itself is involved in the processing of fear and feelings of aggression. Deficits in the prefrontal cortex have repercussions for a host of behaviours (aggressive outbursts, argumentative, rule breaking). This, in turn, influences cognitive thinking styles such as how focused attention is used.
Functional magnetic resonance imaging (fMRI)	There are two types of MRI scans: structural and functional. Of interest to psychologists is functional MRI scans. The clarity of fMRI far exceeds that of PET scans. Using fMRI, cognitive psychologists have discovered why specific words are forgotten in comparison to the remembered words. It has been found that remembered words receive more processing during learning (Wagner, Schacter, Rotte, Koutstaal et al. 1998). Furthermore, Kiehl, Smith, Hare, Mendrek et al. (2001) found the fMRI scans of psychopaths demonstrate reduced amygdala activity for the processing of negative emotional words such as angry or frightened.

of multiple cognitive processors (modules)'. It is these that make our mental life possible, they argued. There are different modules, each processing its own specific stimuli independently of other modules. For example, one module might be responsible for processing faces; another for the recognition of written words and

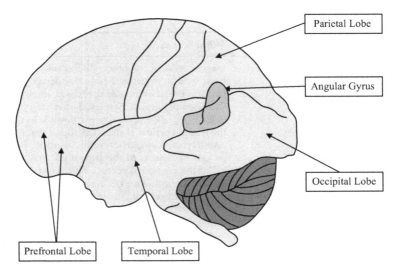

Figure 1.4 Lobes of the brain and the position of the angular gyrus (the junction point between the different lobes)

Source: Taken from Taylor (2015) *Crime and Criminality: A multidisciplinary approach* (p. 156)

BOX 1.3   THE STRANGE CASE OF THE WOMAN WHO KNEW NO FEAR

A 44-year-old woman from Kentucky in the US, known as SM, became famous for being fearless when wandering around the 'haunted' Waverly Hills Sanatorium showing tourists the spooky empty corridors. During Halloween when the building was decorated to scare the tourists and was littered with 'monsters' who leapt out when least expected, SM showed no fear. Her behaviour has been described as fearless and, even when faced with a dangerous situation, she laughs. Once she was held at knifepoint but talked her attacker out of it and then just walked away from him as if nothing had happened. She now handles snakes and spiders even though she claims she dislikes them. But why does SM behave this way? What has gone wrong? By all accounts she wasn't always like this. She was scared of the dark as a child. She screamed and ran away when her brother jumped unexpectedly out of a tree and showed extreme fear when a Doberman trapped her in a corner. It was discovered that SM has a rare genetic condition called Urbach-Wiethe disease. This disease slowly causes areas of the brain to harden and waste away.

SM underwent an MRI brain scan which showed severe damage to her amygdala (Adolphs, Tranel, Damasio and Damasio 1994). These almond-shaped structures reside in each hemisphere of the brain and play a major role in recognising and experiencing fear. SM epitomises an individual with problems to the amygdala. Her difficulty discerning fearful facial expressions and recognising fear in others and feeling fear herself, has not interfered with her ability to experience other emotional states. Interestingly, despite being an accomplished artist, she is unable to draw a face showing a scared expression. Despite her dislike of spiders and snakes, she shows excitement at holding large snakes and had to be reminded not to provoke the dangerous snakes and tarantula by poking them. To this she replied, 'Why' and was filled with curiosity! Even her own children are bemused by the contradiction of disliking snakes but happily approaching them. Her son describes an event where they saw a huge snake on the road. 'Well mom just ran over there and picked it up and brought it out of the street, put it in the grass and let it go on its way... She would always tell me how she was scared of snakes and stuff like that, but then all of a sudden, she's fearless of them. I thought that was kind of weird' (Yong 2010).

Without a working amygdala, it appears that the long-standing evolutionary advantage of experiencing fear becomes lost.

yet another engaged in stimuli concerning spatial orientation. Modules therefore process stimuli within their own domain but can be in direct communication with closely linked modules. The way in which these modules function is sometimes referred to as domain specificity; simply because they are receptive to specific types of stimuli. Jerry Fodor introduced the notion of cognitive modules as a way of understanding how the mind works in relation to language (see Figure 1.5). In 1983, he argued in his book, *The Modularity of Mind*, that the mind should be understood as comprising a set of related, and yet independent 'organs' which function together, thereby resulting in behaviour. A simple analogy is

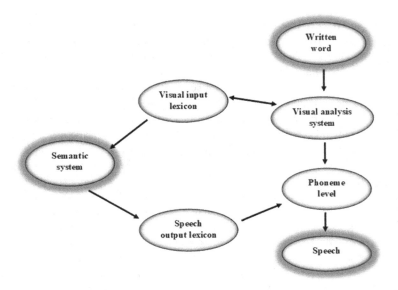

Figure 1.5 Modular system of language
Source: Adapted from Fodor (1983)

to consider the physiological example of digestion. Different organs which function within the alimentary canal help convert food into energy givers. The stomach, for instance, churns partially digested food amongst a mix of enzymes and hydrochloric acid, while the liver detoxifies harmful molecules from broken down food particles and the small intestine releases specific enzymes for protein digestion. Each organ has its own function but collectively they combine to digest food. Fodor argues that our cognition is the product of a multi-tiered processing system. Within this are independent sub-processes receiving distinct inputs and producing distinct outputs that are communicated to other relevant modules. The notion of cognitive modularity is at the heart of the work of many cognitive neuropsychologists. Much of their research has come from studying the workings of the brain in clinical populations; in other words, individuals who have sustained brain damage that has led to deficits of brain function. Using the cognitive modularity notion, it is possible to isolate deficits of behaviour and cognitive processing in relation to the location of brain damage.

Taking our example of Fodor's language modularity, it can be seen that there are different cognitive processors responsible for understanding what is written on paper (i.e. being able to read the written word) and for producing speech (i.e. being able to pronounce words). Although the system works as a whole, the individual components have segregated roles. Therefore, it is possible to ascertain the focal point of damage within the semantic system. To do this, cognitive neuropsychologists study individuals with specific cognitive deficits resulting from brain damage. The underlying assumption of modularity is that a deficit on one specific cognitive task will not extend to other tasks. Hence, cognitive neuropsychologists look for dissociations across different types of cognitive tasking. An individual with a brain injury might only have problems recognising faces while object recognition is spared. Likewise, a patient known as HM had amnesia regarding long-term memory but an intact short-term memory. The problem was pinpointed to the hippocampus which was considered to play an important role in the laying down of long-term memories.

There are obvious problems with the assumption that different cognitive tasks rely on different modules, just because performance on one is good but poor on the other. The idea that a dissociation of performance can be traced to an area of brain damage might be rather simplistic. Differences in performance across cognitive tasks can be a consequence of varying levels of task difficulty rather than one module not functioning as well as another. Hence, both tasks could be processed by the same module, but one task is harder to resolve. The solution? Cognitive neuropsychologists have introduced the concept of double dissociation across two cognitive tasks. This means the performance on two cognitive tasks in two differentially brain-damaged individuals is compared. For example, one of the individuals might perform normally on a task of linguistic understanding but simultaneously show a deficit in mathematical ability while the other individual might demonstrate an opposite pattern. The conclusion here is that these two tasks are processed by separate regions of the brain and cannot be explained away by differences of task difficulty. Research from clinical populations has in the past typically relied on single case studies. The case-series method, however, is more commonly used in cognitive neuropsychology today (see Box 1.4).

BOX 1.4   CASE-SERIES METHOD

In cognitive psychology, the emphasis is on testing a large sample of participants so that performance scores can be averaged, and outliers excluded from the analysis (see Box 1.1). When studying clinical populations, it is difficult to find individuals with damage to the same areas of the brain. Furthermore, it is difficult to assume that, despite the same brain damage, their cognitive performance would be similarly affected. This is why the emphasis is on testing for similar cognitive impairments. Performance data are then compared for variations between all brain-damaged participants. This method provides a richer data base and allows cognitive neuropsychologists to assess the level of variation across the participants. Moreover, it is possible to formulate theoretical explanations based on these performances and exclude the outliers. This is not possible when using single case studies. Nor can it be established in single case studies whether the participant makes for a representative and reliable source of explanation for other brain-damaged individuals who may or may not perform similarly.

While cognitive psychology, cognitive neuroscience and cognitive neuropsychology rely on data generated through testing individuals, computational cognitive science does not.

COMPUTATIONAL COGNITIVE SCIENCE

This approach to understanding human cognitive processing uses computational models based on theoretical assumptions. Bechtel and Graham (1998) claim that most models can be categorised as being computational, mathematical or verbal-conceptual. Whereas computational models use algorithms and mathematical models use equations, verbal-conceptual models apply an informal lexicon to describe relations, processes and entities. While simple mathematical modelling, for instance, can be useful in making predictions about behavioural outcomes, these are generally a 'number-crunching' exercise devoid of reliable explanation. They are based on limited inputted details. An example of their application can be for insurance companies wanting to predict which drivers are likely to be a high risk. One aspect of this prediction might be based on a driver's record of traffic transgression. If there are many, then car insurance could feasibly be declined. Needless to say, such models have a limited use if we want to understand and explain human cognitive performance. Computational models are of more interest to cognitive psychologists because they provide the explanations that simple mathematical ones fail to do.

Computational models are tools for generating theories about human cognitive performance. Such models can also provide cognitive architectures; in other words, a framework in the guise of a computer program designed to understand cognition. Sun (2008) described cognitive architecture as a "comprehensive, domain-generic computational cognitive model, capturing the essential structures, mechanisms, and processes of cognition" (p. 7). It should be noted that Sun, in contrast to Fodor (who espouses domain-specific processing), is referring to domain-generic processing. This means that processing covers many domains or areas of cognition. In other words, Sun is describing a general-purpose computational model which oversees the function of many modules. Furthermore, it allows for cross-module analysis of cognition *per se*.

There are many computational models. Of interest to cognitive psychologists, however, are those that consider interconnected networks of units; hence the label connectionist models. (For further discussion of connectionist models see Chapter 2.) Cognitive psychologists have also made use of production systems. Young (2001) defined a production system as: "a model of cognitive processing, consisting of a collection of rules (called production rules, or just production)". Production systems consist of a series of 'if' and 'then' statements. There is a working memory buffer that stores information. This information is compared with the content of the 'if-then' statement. When there is a match in working memory with the 'if' part of the statement, the production system executes the 'then' component. The production system operates by following these statement rules. It is, however, only as good as the information inputted into the system. The General Problem Solver introduced by Newell and Simon (1972) was one of the early production systems designed to identify the cognitive processing used to solve problems. Another example is the Adaptive Control of Thought–Rational (ACT–R) system (see Box 1.5).

BOX 1.5   ADAPTIVE CONTROL OF THOUGHT-RATIONAL (ACT-R) SYSTEM

Anderson and Lebiere (1998) developed ACT-R as a demonstration of how the brain might be organised to coordinate the processing of individual modules. The combined processing of these modules produces cognition *per se*. Anderson and Lebiere found, by using the ACT-R model, that they could simulate how neurons in the brain process information while individuals try to solve a difficult problem. This model enabled them to see how specific areas of the brain would be activated during such problem-solving. Once such problems were solved, the level of activation in these brain areas would be reduced during future solving of the same type of problem.

They outline the ACT-R modules associated with specific areas of the brain as follows:

- Inferior ventrolateral prefrontal cortex houses the retrieval module. This uses retrieval cues to access data.
- Posterior parietal cortex houses the imaginal module. This makes a problem easier to solve by making it more user-friendly.
- Anterior cingulate cortex houses the goal module. This monitors intentions and controls how data are processed.
- Basal ganglia houses the procedural module. This decides the action as a result of following the 'if-then' rules.

The information from these modules is integrated, so that the most appropriate response can be made. ACT-R is a profound model and perhaps a simpler example by way of applying 'if-then' statements is seen in Figure 1.6.

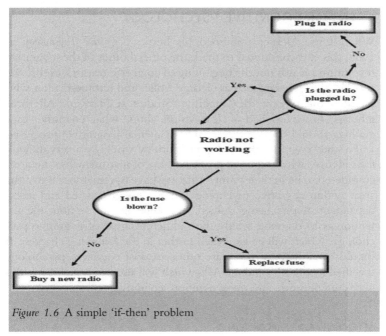

Figure 1.6 A simple 'if-then' problem

Thus far, we have learned that cognitive psychology, as a discipline, has benefited from:

- brain scanning techniques used by cognitive neuroscientists
- theoretical assumptions of modularity by cognitive neuroscientists
- computational models such as connectionist and production systems, adopted by computational cognitive scientists.

The influence from these other disciplines can be clearly seen when we consider the core and sub-areas researched by cognitive psychologists. The British Psychological Society (BPS) has highlighted areas which cognitive psychologists should study.

These include the four core-areas: perception, memory, thinking and language; and

the sub-areas: attention, learning, problem-solving and communication.

AREAS OF COGNITIVE PSYCHOLOGY

When Ulric Neisser published his book, *Cognitive Psychology* in 1967, this was considered to mark the official onset of the 'cognitive revolution'. It was not the beginning of cognitive research as this was accredited to scholars such as George Miller and Jerome Bruner who founded the Centre for Cognitive Studies at Harvard. All three scholars, however, had a clear vision about what cognitive psychology should be about; the study of mental [cognitive] processes.

To study cognitive processes in its entirety would be a very difficult feat. Hence, why cognitive psychologists compartmentalise the areas considered to be in their remit. What we have to remember is that the areas within cognitive psychology are all interconnected and interdependent despite being studied separately. In this section, the intention is to describe briefly these different areas of cognitive psychology, which will be explained further in the following chapters. It should be noted that there are other areas of cognitive psychology specified by the BPS and the APS which will also be considered in this text: consciousness and metacognition; cognitive neuropsychology.

ATTENTION AND PERCEPTION

By attending to stimuli in our environment, it is argued that we can then process them. Hence, our ability to attend to what we see, hear, smell, taste and feel allows us to process the information further, and to understand what is occurring around us. Our sensory organs (such as eyes, ears and nose), are designed to pick up light, sound and pressure waves and molecules, all comprising the process of sensation. By attending closely to these inputs, we are able to process these further for meaning. The brain interprets these inputs based mainly on experience which is the process of perception. In Chapter 3, William James' early work of passive and active modes of attention is considered and how this is still used today as a basis for the division of focused and divided attention. Models are helpful in the understanding of attention and their applications to visual and auditory phenomena. Attention and perception are clearly inter-dependent. We perceive what goes on in our environment and try to make sense out of potential chaos. Our brain is responsible for making sense out of potential chaos by interpreting, for example, object form and movement as well as face familiarity. Our interactions with our environment are important for helping the brain to learn and remember events, so that we can put meaning to them.

LEARNING AND MEMORY

Learning can occur when we interact with our environment. Being able to attend and perceive connections with stimuli is an important factor in learning. But learning is of no consequence unless we can store and retrieve information when and as required. There are many models of memory but perhaps the two most popular are the multi-store model and working memory (as will be discussed in Chapter 4). Studies have focused on how these models operate in learning, storing, retrieving and forgetting information. The processes involved in learning new information and how this is eventually retained in long-term storage have been examined. The most popular of these over the years have been levels of processing and implicit learning. The understanding of how these play a role in the consolidation of information in long-term storage continues to expand and develop. There are many other types of memory studied such as episodic and semantic memory (known as declarative). And with the increasing interest in everyday memory, credence has been given to autobiographical, flashbulb and prospective memory. Theories of memory have played an important role in how we remember and recall criminal events (known as eyewitness memory) and faces.

THINKING: DECISION-MAKING AND PROBLEM-SOLVING

Thought processing consists of a multitude of activities such as problem-solving and decision-making. When we consider thinking, it is hard not to regard it as some type of reflective process. We think about a book we read and make a judgement about it; such as its quality of writing or script. Thinking, however, is so much more than this (see Chapter 5). How do we do it and what form does it take? Reasoning is required for hypothesis testing, such as that needed in order to solve the classic Wason task. When doing such tasks deductive reasoning serves us better than inductive for instance. Theories of deductive reasoning include mental models and dual-system models which give insight to how we use information to problem-solve. There are different strategies used in problem-solving such as means-ends analysis, progress monitoring and planning; all of which can be successful when applied appropriately to the task at hand. Judgements are made in decision-making and can often require a quick analysis using rules of thumb known as heuristics. Heuristics can be reliant on statistical inductive thought but are, for the best part, the antithesis of deductive thought used in problem-solving.

LANGUAGE AND COMMUNICATION

Reading, writing and speech are all considered as part of language (see Chapter 6). Various models have been developed in order to help us understand how we do all three. Classic and contemporary theories of language comprehension focus on a multitude of aspects of language such as parsing, pragmatics and discourse. Phonological processes required in reading are linked with word recognition. The Dual-route cascaded and connectionist triangle modes models are used to illustrate how reading and speech are possible. Theories of speech production, perception and communication draw upon models to help understand how problems of language can occur. There is debate about whether we naturally develop language as our brain structure predisposes us to communicate using speech and writing. Hence, many of the theories of language development address how we learn language; in other words, the acquisition of language. Some theories focus on whether language acquisition is innate; hence driven by nature. Other theories view this as a learning process taught by those who influence us most such as our caregivers; hence driven by nurture. The consensus is very much that language acquisition is driven by both nature and nurture. While language is a means to communicate with others, it is also a subset of communication. Communication can be non-verbal. Animals communicate but, as yet, there is no evidence that they are able to produce something akin to human language!

SUMMARY

Cognitive psychology is concerned with the study of mental (cognitive) processing. It concerns itself with understanding the core areas of cognitive processing such as perception, memory, thinking and language. Other important sub-areas include attention, learning, decision–making, problem–solving and communication. One way of investigating these processes is to devise cognitive tasks, the success of which can be measured using variables such as response time and correct *versus* incorrect responses. There are many types of cognitive tasks, but more often than not these are laboratory based and require large numbers of participants in order to reduce outliers. Knowledge about how we process information and the involvement of the brain has increased by including other disciplines such as cognitive neuroscience and cognitive neuropsychology. Both disciplines have contributed towards how the brain is structured and functions. Cognitive neuroscience has developed brain scanning technology which has provided evidence of which areas of the brain are involved in specific types of cognitive processing. In the case of cognitive neuropsychology, theoretical notions of modularity have helped us to understand how areas of the brain are involved in specific processes such as face recognition. It also provides information about module-specificity, and cognitive deficits incurred when a module is structurally and functionally impaired. Computational cognitive science has offered another way of representing cognition via use of modelling. Technological advancements here have also enabled the development of connectionist models (i.e. networking) and production systems (i.e. ACT-R). These have provided cognitive psychologists with ideas of how neurons are interconnected in the brain.

FURTHER READING

Farrell, S. (2018) *Computational Modelling of Cognition and Behavior*. Cambridge: Cambridge University Press.

Heyes, C. (2018) *Cognitive Gadgets: The cultural evolution of thinking*. Harvard: Harvard University Press.

Shallice, T. and Cooper, R.P. (2011) *The Organisation of the Mind*. Oxford: Oxford University Press.

Wilshire, C. (2014) *Cognitive Neuropsychology: Exploring the mind through brain dysfunction*. Hove: Psychology Press.

RELATIONSHIP BETWEEN BRAIN STRUCTURE, FUNCTION AND COGNITIVE MODELLING

It was during the latter period of the Renaissance that scientists were exploring how the human body and brain are structured. Leonardo da Vinci in the early fifteenth century drew the anatomy of the human brain. He even considered the inter-connection between the brain, olfactory and optic nerves. His intention, however, was to find where the human soul resided in the brain; needless to say, he failed to locate it. Understanding the macro-structure of the brain relied on observations made during autopsies by the eminent anatomists of the time. Thomas Willis, an English physician, outlined the brain's structure in his text, 'Anatomy of the Brain' in 1664. Based on the understanding of the circulatory system examined by William Harvey, Willis highlighted how circulation in the brain occurred by using animals which he injected with India ink. Furthermore, he classified the ten cranial nerves, distinguished sympathetic nerves and documented the interaction between localised areas of the brain with function. In 1669, Nicolaus Steno, a Danish anatomist, put pen to paper to create his 'Lecture on the Anatomy of the Brain'. Mapping the macro-structures of the brain was undertaken by noting the various divisions of the brain such as there being two halves (or hemispheres) largely connected by numerous neural fibres known as the corpus callosum. Areas that were easily defined structurally were referred to as lobes. These lobes appeared to be segregated by ridges and inward folds, labelled gyri and sulci respectively. The Renaissance era certainly revived interest in the human brain, and in contrast to

DOI: 10.4324/9781003014355-2

previous eras, this revival was driven by science and not religion. As the anatomy of the brain became increasingly explored by scientists, the macro-structure was comprehensively mapped before the arrival of twentieth-century technological developments. With the developments of brain imaging techniques, however, micro-structures of the brain can now be seen, and their functioning observed in real time (see Chapter 1). Such developments in brain imaging now allow for cognitive psychologists to make connections between brain structure and function, through experimentation.

Although cognitive psychologists have a framework of how the brain is structured and how it functions, there is still much to be discovered. The interface between brain structure and function is still an enigma. This can be demonstrated when we consider individuals who have sustained brain damage. Among younger individuals with brain damage, clinical cognitive psychologists have discovered how resilient the brain can be. Functions that would normally be processed by certain areas can often be performed by different areas of the brain following brain damage. This is an example of **plasticity** in the brain and demonstrates how the brain can reconfigure itself for function. Eric Lenneberg (1967) observed that there is a timeframe when the brain shows particular resilience and plasticity. In his example of language acquisition, Lenneberg suggests, this occurs before the brain becomes fully lateralised for function at about the age of 12 years. Being able to perform cognitively to the same level prior to sustained brain damage, is far more difficult in older individuals. From cognitive neuropsychology, the notion of modularity (see Chapter 1) has helped us to understand that there are areas of brain localisation. Hence, individuals with damage to one area of the brain, are very likely to show a specific deficit of function that is controlled by this area (especially when the damage is sustained later in life). It is possible to identify the connection between the damaged area and cognitive deficit using double dissociation (see Chapter 1). The early observations from anatomists and physicians have helped to highlight the relationship between brain structure and function. This interface has proven to be extremely complex, as modern technology has shown. It is worth us studying the structure of the brain and outlining the interconnectiveness between the different areas and connecting neural pathways. Understanding how the structure of the brain and its interconnectiveness is related to function, is important in the development of accurate cognitive psychological theories. These theories after all should sing to the hymn sheet of brain science.

STRUCTURE OF THE HUMAN BRAIN

MICROANATOMY

At birth a healthy human brain is 25 per cent of its adult weight, reaching 75 per cent at two years of age. The gross structure of the brain is largely formed by the end of prenatal development. The inter-connections between these structures, however, are immature as the nervous system, consisting largely of neurons, is still developing. Although neurons develop during the embryonic stage of gestation as elongated shapes, these information processing units are very limited in their transmission but are ready to make new connections. The elongated shape allows for quick transmission of an electrochemical message called an impulse. This impulse travels down the length of the neuron (i.e. axon) which tapers into a series of **synapses** that produce a chemical called a neurotransmitter. The neurotransmitter enables the impulse to cross the synaptic gap and excite (or inhibit) another neuron (see Figure 2.1). In the brain there are numerous types of neurotransmitter: acetylcholine, noradrenaline, serotonin, dopamine and GABA to name but a few. According to Azevedo, Carvalho, Grinberg, Farfel et al. (2009) our brain contains 86 ± billion neurons. Sixteen billion (19 per cent) of these neurons are found in the outer layer of the brain called the **cerebral cortex** (Azevedo et al. 2009; Bigos, Hariri and Weinberger 2015). These neurons communicate via synapses, of which there are believed to be some 10,000 synaptic connections for each neuron – this translates to 86 million, million synapses in the brain (see Figure 2.1).

GROSS ANATOMY

The architecture of the human brain is very complex. For our pur-poses the majority of the human brain consists of the two enlarged cerebral hemispheres. These are connected by bundles of axons which make up the commissures ('bridges'), the largest being the corpus callosum. Both hemispheres divide further into the frontal, temporal, parietal and occipital lobes (see Figure 1.4; Figure 2.2). There are

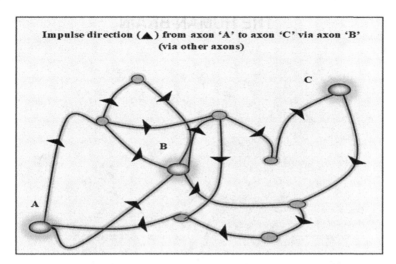

Figure 2.1 A representation of neurons in the brain showing activity among connecting synapses

other structures that lie beneath the cerebral cortex, some of which will be considered when addressing specific cognitive functions of the brain in future chapters. Figure 2.2 also shows an area of the brain, the cerebellum and the medulla [oblongata]. The medulla is part of the lowest portion of the brainstem and continues with the spinal cord. The cerebellum itself is divided into three lobes: anterior, posterior and flocculonodular. The brainstem consists of three main structures: midbrain, pons and medulla. Information is transmitted to and from the cerebral cortex to the rest of the body, across the brainstem through the many nerve tracts. An important structure (not shown in Figure 2.2) is the hippocampus. The hippocampus projects out in each hemisphere where it connects with the amygdala. It plays an important role in the consolidation of short-term memories into long-term memories (see Chapter 4).

In addition to the neurons present in the brain, there is cerebrospinal fluid which cushions the brain and acts as a drainage route of waste products from brain tissue. Two circulatory systems supply oxygenated blood to the front and back of the brain while another drains the deoxygenated blood away. There are areas of the brain which process

THE HUMAN BRAIN

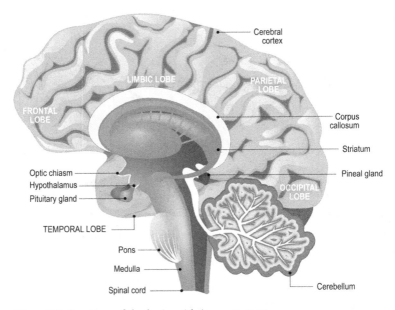

Figure 2.2 Structure of the brain with its many parts

sensory information from our sensory organs such as our eyes and ears. Given the importance of interpreting signals from our sensory system as a means of surviving and navigating our environment, the structure of the most commonly researched sensory organs in cognitive psychology (the eye and ear) will be considered later.

Neural pathway activation in the brain

Neural activity occurs throughout the structures of the brain. There are neural pathways, packaged as bundles of fibres, that connect areas of the brain involved in passing specific information. For example, in Chapter 3, two neural networks involved in passing specific visual information are considered in relation to attention. These neural networks become activated by information from the primary visual cortex of the occipital lobes of the brain. This part of the brain processes information received from our eyes via the optic nerve. In the case of the ventral attention network, activation is driven by the components of stimuli (such as the vertical lines comprising a tree trunk). These components are pieced together by the brain. For the dorsal attention network, however, activation occurs in response to the intact stimulus (such as the whole tree). Other areas of the cortex draw on the information processed in these two neural networks in order to help decision-making (see Figure 2.3).

SENSORY ORGANS: THE EYE AND EAR

The eye and ear have layers of cells that are receptive to specific visual shapes / patterns or sounds and their frequencies. When these cells become activated, neural impulses travel down neural axons and across their synapses. These neural axons eventually synapse with connecting cells which then change their pattern of activation (i.e. 'firing rate'). Where there are masses of synaptic connections and cells, a ganglion is formed which acts as a way station for sending signals to higher ordered cells in the brain. This is clearly seen where

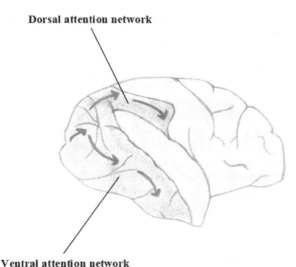

Dorsal attention network

Ventral attention network

Figure 2.3 Brain showing the locations of the dorsal and ventral attention networks

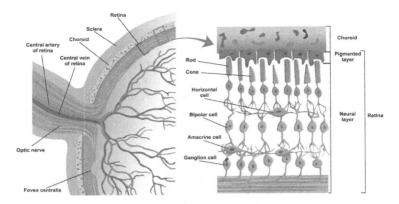

Figure 2.4 Structure of the eye and the layers of cells in the retina

the hierarchical structure of cells in the retina of the eye passes fragmented bits of visual information to the optic nerve (see Figure 2.4). Figure 2.4 shows how the ganglion cells collect information and forward feed this to the optic nerve.

Figure 2.5 shows the route taken from the eye to the area of the brain concerned with initial processing of visual stimuli (the primary visual cortex). This area of the brain then begins to decode and attribute meaning to the incoming visual stimuli due to the collective activation of the neurons. In the case of the ear, there are different structures operating. The principle of passing information on via the auditory nerve to the brain is the same, however. The mechanism involved with the ear is to decipher sound waves, hence, the outer ear is shaped to funnel sound into the auditory canal. Once inside there are a series of bones which vibrate as a sound wave enters. The more sound, the more these bones vibrate causing neurological activation. This activation continues from the auditory nerve to the auditory cortex of the brain (Hall 2011). This is where sensations become perceptions.

Neuron activation in the retina

The 1950s saw pioneering research on feature detectors in the retina of frogs and cats. Researchers such as visual neuroscientist, Horace Barlow; cognitive scientist, Jerome Lettvin and neurophysiologists, Hübel and Wiesel were at the forefront of understanding how the

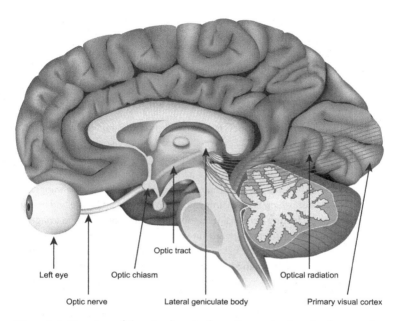

Optic track

Left eye   Optic chiasm   Optical radiation

Optic nerve   Lateral geniculate body   Primary visual cortex

Figure 2.5 Mapping of the visual route from the eye to the visual processing area of the brain

eyes of frogs and cats could so easily detect their prey. Barlow (1953) provided evidence of retinal cells in frogs having a limited receptor field. Some cells were responsive to light and some to the dark such that they would be inhibited if the opposite conditions were present. He argued that certain cells in the retina could be feature detectors. Lettvin, Maturana, McCulloch and Pitts (1959) identified four classes of ganglion cells in the retina that served the frog's ability to detect, strike and catch its prey successfully. He labelled these cells as: sustained contrast detectors; bug detectors; moving edge detectors and net dimming detectors. Hűbel and Wiesel (1959) studied cats' eyes in the context of feature detection (see Chapter 3). Through electrophysiological recordings these researchers were able to unravel the workings of visual cells and their sensitivity to certain types of stimuli. As we saw in Figure 2.4, the human eye is structured such that specific cells are receptive to specific types of stimuli. When these cells are activated, their firing-rate is altered in order that impulses are sent to other higher ordered cells. These also become activated (i.e. their firing–rate alters) and in so doing pass information to the optic nerve. The sequencing of this activation can be compared to the 'Pandemonium Model' introduced by Selfridge (1959; see Box 2.1).

BOX 2.1   THE PANDEMONIUM MODEL METAPHOR

The Pandemonium Model is a useful way of representing how information coded by individual cells (in this case visual) is passed on to the next layer of higher ordered cells. Although rarely referred to in modern cognitive psychology, it is a model that provides a simplistic metaphor of how particular stimuli are processed further for meaning. It is a model describing how an 'image demon' detects an image and how a network of 'feature demons' recognise different aspects of the image. These 'feature demons' operate in a bottom-up pattern recognition modus. This means in the case of visual processing information comes in a piece-meal fashion and is reconstructed to form an image. The term 'demons' is used to account for how stimuli are passed on from basic feature detectors to the next level of processing referred to as 'cognitive demons'. The 'cognitive demons' can be regarded as ganglion way stations where many stimuli are received but only those that 'shout' the most and loudest are transmitted to the 'decision demon' – the point of perception. Although the terms used appear far from scientific, the processing mechanism of neural activation or inhibition are accounted for (see Figure 2.6).

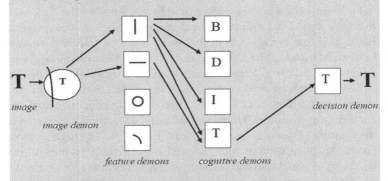

Figure 2.6 Selfridge's Pandemonium Model

FUNCTION OF THE HUMAN BRAIN

How the brain functions is dependent on its gross structure and micro-infrastructural mechanisms. These micro-infrastructural mechanisms, as we have seen, operate by way of passing information forward and sometimes backward (i.e. a **feedforward-feedback neural processing mechanism**). Hence, both gross and micro-structures are at the interface with brain function. Early experimental research on mapping the brain for function was undertaken by neurosurgeon Wilder Penfield, who in the 1930s developed a method called the Montreal Procedure. This involves probing the brain's cortex using a small electrode and observing bodily reactions when specific areas received electrical impulses (in other words, these areas were stimulated). Interestingly, this procedure was undertaken on conscious patients under local anaesthetic since the brain does not feel any pain. Penfield was interested in pinpointing the origins of a seizure in the brain of individuals with debilitating epilepsy. By using this method, Penfield was able to map the architecture of the brain and link sensation with areas of the brain including the gyri and sulci (singular, gyrus and sulcus; see Figure 2.7). He found that specific areas would induce sensations such as numbness in the fingers when stimulated while others evoked memories or flashes of light. Penfield concluded that brain circuits involved in the sensation and perception of stimuli, could be activated or deactivated by using electrodes to transmit electrical impulses. By using a numbering system, he was able to map the areas causing a specific action. For example, in the case of No.8, a sensation of thumb movement was reported by individuals (despite there being no movement) undergoing the Montreal Procedure.

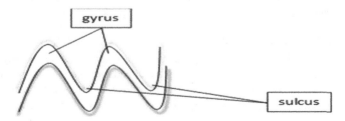

Figure 2.7 Diagram showing the gyrus and sulcus folds of the cortex of the brain

Interestingly, when personal memories were recalled, Penfield believed that he found evidence of physical structures for memory residing in the brain. Penfield, however, is famous for developing a 'homunculus' depicted as an exaggerated cartoon image of the human body. This representation showed how various parts of the body were oversized in accordance to the proportionate amount of brain-space devoted to each body part. Hence, the hands and mouth look extremely oversized because a large amount of our brain is used for controlling dexterity and speech.

Much of our understanding of the interface between the brain's structure and function has come from clinical cases of individuals with specific brain injuries and observations of their cognition and behaviours. One classic example of such a case study is Phineas Gage (see Box 2.2). Developments within cognitive neuroscience and cognitive neuropsychology have also contributed to understanding this interface. By studying the different lobes of the brain using scanning techniques, cognitive neuroscientists have developed the 'locationist' perspective. This refers to how different areas

BOX 2.2 THE FACT AND FICTION OF PHINEAS GAGE: THE MAN WITH A HOLE THROUGH HIS HEAD

Prior to 1848 Phineas Gage was a well-respected man and considered to be reliable, thoughtful and industrious by both his peers and colleagues. But in that year, he suffered a serious accident which apparently altered his personality beyond recognition. Gage helped in the construction of one of the new railroads running across North America as a foreman in charge of a team of workers. This involved the laying down of new tracks through a terrain of large boulders that often blocked the planned route of the railway. To remove such obstacles, holes were drilled into the rock so that a bundle of dynamite could be ignited to explode the rock into tiny pieces. In 1848, Gage had drilled a hole and used a tamping rod to push the dynamite into place which inadvertently caused enough friction to ignite the dynamite. The sheer force caused by the explosion catapulted the tamping rod into his left cheek exiting through the top-front area of his skull. The tamping rod exited his skull in one piece and was found some 300 feet away. Gage surprised the doctors of the time as he survived the accident and was able to walk to a carriage which took him for medical attention. Despite surviving and making a recovery, he was no longer Phineas Gage; he had changed. He was now childish, thoughtless and irritable (Harlow 1848; Ratiu and Talos 2004). Harlow went on to report that Gage was capricious, impulsive, foul-mouthed and lazy. A number of reports from the archives suggest that Gage became a changed man who drifted from one town to another as a fairground attraction who could no longer look after himself. This suggests that the brain damage had seriously altered his personality in detrimental ways. But is this really true? To help uncover the nature of his brain injury, various neuroscientists and neuropsychologists have been involved in studying Gage's skull using modern scanning techniques. Damasio, Grabowski, Frank, Galaburda et al. (1994) reconstructed the damage to the front of Gage's brain using high-power computer modelling. They located this to the orbitofrontal cortex of both hemispheres. Ratiu and Talos (2004), however, concluded that it was not possible for the tamping rod to cross over to the right hemisphere. Jack Van Horn (2012) used neuroimaging to explore millions of possible trajectories of the tamping rod and concurred with Ratiu and Talos that the rod did not enter the right hemisphere but instead some of the neural networks connecting both hemispheres might have endured damage; hence quite profound injuries. We might ask did Phineas Gage ever recover some of his personality from these severe brain injuries? Were his post-behaviours due to his brain injuries or as a result of the fungal infection to his brain that nearly killed him? Harlow performed emergency surgery 14 days into the fungal infection by puncturing Gage's tissue inside his nose to drain his wound. It was then Gage lost sight in his left eye which was sewn shut. It is difficult to know the impact of the fungal infection on his behaviour, but records of his later life can inform us if any recovery to normality had occurred. Harlow's report of Gage post-accident provides little guidance of timeline. There were unusual speculations of what had become of Gage. Some reported how his skeleton was sold to a medical school, while others claimed he lived for 20 years with the tamping rod still impaled in his skull. But evidence of Gage's later years shows that he was employed to drive horse and cart coaches along rugged mountainous tracks in Chile during the gold rush of 1852 (Harlow 1868). When doing such a job, the driver (Gage) requires intricate rein-work when controlling the horses and a good memory of the route. An impulsive and uncontrolled driver would have been a great risk. After seven years of doing this Gage travelled to San Francisco and worked as a farm labourer but in 1860 had a series of seizures after immense ploughing. He died, aged 36, nearly twelve years post his accident. His story tells us that he lived as normal a life as possible as his driver's job for seven years after his accident shows. Moreover, this suggests that the brain can relearn lost skills in some circumstances thereby demonstrating brain plasticity (Kean 2014).

of the brain process specific types of information; this means different locations are associated with specific function.

FRONTAL LOBES: THE ORBITOFRONTAL CORTEX (OFC)

The OFC is part of the prefrontal cortex within the frontal lobes and sits above the orbits of the eyes (see Figure 1.4; Figure 2.2). The frontal lobe is very much in control of our cognitive processing for decision-making, memory and language. The OFC is an important component of this processing, and in addition to having connections with other frontal lobe regions, also has connections with sensory systems and the limbic system (see Figure 2.2). This means it is very much informed about both the external and the internal world. The orbitofrontal cortex is made aware of planned behaviours through the connections it has with these regions which can be an advantage in regulating the activity of the limbic system especially the amygdala (see Table 1.2; Box 1.3). For this reason, it has been associated with the processing of emotion (Toates 2014; Workman and Reader 2021). Ray (2013) found that while the left OFC processes positive emotions (such as happy and pleasantly surprised), the right OFC focuses on negative emotions (such as anger and disgust). Ray further suggests that this supports the notion of there being lateralised function of emotion. Damage to this region of the frontal lobe can cause profound alterations to emotional perception and response. Moreover, damage to the OFC can change an individual's personality (see Box 2.2). This can be externalised as extreme euphoria and irresponsibility (Kringelbach and Rolls 2004).

CORPUS CALLOSUM

The left and right hemispheres are known to operate independently and interdependently (that is working together due to complementary specialisation). This ability to work together on many tasks is made possible due to interhemispheric transfer of information through commissures such as the corpus callosum. Hence, the corpus callosum is involved in sharing information between each hemisphere. This function of the corpus callosum has been demonstrated in cognitive research using 'split-brain' individuals who have endured a corpus callosotomy (that is a procedure to sever the fibres joining the hemispheres; see Box 2.3). Similarly, the different lobes of the brain are connected by neural pathways criss-crossing the brain (see Figure 2.3 as an example).

BOX 2.3   THE CASE OF 'VICKI' LIVING WITH A 'SPLIT-BRAIN'

Whether we can live with a brain whose halves have been separated by a corpus callosotomy is an interesting question. This is particularly so given what we know about the sharing of information between two brain hemispheres via the corpus callosum. The succinct answer is 'yes we can'. But what impact would this have on everyday cognition for individuals with a divided brain? In 1979, Vicki underwent a ten-hour procedure where her corpus callosum was severed thus disconnecting her two hemispheres. Vicki suffered severe epileptic seizures prior to the operation. These seizures were extreme and often put her life in danger. There was one occasion where she collapsed onto an old-fashioned oven and burnt her back. It was her neurologist in 1978 who suggested a radical procedure involving the severance of the corpus callosum to relieve her of the *grand mal* fits that often traversed across one hemisphere to the other. After the corpus callosotomy, Vicki's fits were greatly reduced, suggesting the operation was a complete success. Her life, however, had changed in a number of ways. Activities such as shopping and choosing clothes to wear became a challenge as the left and right arm had to reconcile their differences of action. Vicki claimed that, 'I'd reach with my right for the thing I wanted, but the left would come in and they'd kind of fight.' She claimed that she would end up wearing three outfits at the same time and would have to put all the clothes on the bed and start all over again. There were improvements after a year where Vicki's difficulties of conflicting conscious thought and control over movement subsided (see Chapter 7). She could now perform the mundane things that we normally take for granted such as tying shoelaces and slicing vegetables. Vicki was even able to coordinate her body for water-skiing. Vicki's plight is similar to other individuals who have had a corpus callosotomy. Michael Gazzaniga, a cognitive neuroscientist, has continued the early work of Roger Sperry who was a pioneer in performing corpus callosotomies in cats, monkeys and humans in the 1950s. Gazzaniga's early studies demonstrated how the left hemisphere is dominant for speech and language while the right specialises in visuospatial skills. Through studying split-brain individuals, it is apparent, however, how both hemispheres are competent at most tasks but offer two different perspectives of the world. Gazzaniga, Volpe, Smylie, Wilson et al. in 1979 studied a boy of 14 known as P.S. who had a corpus callosotomy. He was interested in whether the boy's right hemisphere could process written words. In writing, presented to the right hemisphere, Gazzaniga asked what the boy's favourite girlfriend's name was. He shrugged and shook his head indicating he didn't know. Moments later he giggled and blushed and used his left hand to select Scrabble tiles that spelled the girl's name as LIZ. Hence, there was some language processing occurring in the right hemisphere. Vicki also demonstrated this right hemisphere capacity for speech (Gazzaniga 2000). On a final note, there is still much to learn about split-brain individuals. When Vicki was presented with two stories one involving intentional harm and one involving accidental harm and asked which of the two is more morally reprehensible, she reasoned that there was no difference between the two scenarios. This demonstrates a failure of being able to understand the intentions of the protagonist in the two scenarios. Her friends and family, however, vouched that she was able to perform such tasks outside of a laboratory setting. Perhaps in everyday life other reasoning mechanisms compensate for the divided brain.

TEMPORAL LOBES

The temporal lobes comprise about 17 per cent of the cerebral cortex (see Figure 1.4; Figure 2.2). They are involved in the processing of sensory stimuli such as olfactory, visual, auditory and vestibular (sense of balance and bodily posture) and linguistic information. It has been suggested that one of the major functions of the temporal lobes is the ability to listen and convert sounds to pictures. The temporal lobes enable us to anticipate words in utterances and to express thoughts using lexemes. A lexeme is defined as "a minimal meaningful unit of language, the meaning of which cannot be understood from that of its component morphemes. *Take off* (in the senses to mimic, to become airborne, etc.) is a lexeme, as well as the independent morphemes *take* and *off*" (Collins English Dictionary 2020). Furthermore, the temporal lobes are involved in recognising speech intonation and facial expression used in communication as well as emotional and memory management (Jeneson and Squire 2011).

By studying individuals who have had damage to the temporal lobes, the important role in integrating linguistic with visual information becomes obvious. In the case of right temporal lobe damage, individuals often show deficits in non-verbal auditory stimuli recognition (such as music). Damage to the left temporal lobe, however, leads to deficits in the recognition, memorisation and formation of speech. Individuals with damage to the temporal lobes often report dysfunctional perception of auditory stimuli, such as that coming from oral speech, and problems of analysing and forming speech sounds. This can also be confounded by problems with memory and the organisation of complex mental processing. There is a region at the back of the left temporal lobe known as Wernicke's area. (Note that even though there is still some controversy over its exact location, it is generally agreed that it is in the temporal lobe.) Wernicke's area is considered to be associated with language comprehension. When there is damage to this area of the temporal lobe, verbal communication can be severely compromised (hence, this is known as Wernicke's aphasia; see Box 2.4). Other symptoms from temporal lobe damage have been reported such as dizziness, mental disorders and extreme unprovoked irritation.

BOX 2.4   CASE OF INCOMPREHENSIBLE SPEECH: LENIN?

There have been some interesting historical cases of language disruption technically known as aphasia . One example is Vladimir Ilyich Ulyanov, known as Lenin, the Bolshevik leader who led the communist party during the Russian Revolution. Lenin was 52 years of age in 1922 when he suffered a series of strokes leaving sensory deficits to the right side of his body and language impairment (Volkogonov 1994). His neurologist Professor Kramer claimed Lenin had a clinical profile of an aphasic individual; one who made incomprehensible sounds every time he tried to speak. Kramer also described Lenin as suffering from complete motor aphasia as he was conscious but could not respond verbally (see Chapter 7). Volkogonov (1994) claimed that there were reports at the time of Lenin responding "Vot-vot" to all questions put to him. On further investigation, Volkogonov found secret archives of Lenin using the expression 'vot-vot' as a means of communicating; this could be to agree or disagree, complain or to initiate conversation. Today Lenin would be diagnosed with a language impairment known as Wernicke's aphasia. This form of aphasia was uncovered by German neurologist, Carl Wernicke in 1874. Wernicke discovered an area of the temporal lobe in the left hemisphere of the brain associated with the comprehension of speech. Wernicke described individuals with lesions to this area as being compromised in their ability to comprehend language. Hence, although Lenin was able to produce speech of a sort, he was unable to understand the utterances of others. It is likely that Lenin incurred damage to the left temporal lobe during the strokes he had suffered. In fact, this was the neurological assessment that Otfrid Foerster (a distinguished neuroscientist) suggested (Sarikcioglu 2007). Individuals with damage to the Wernicke's area exhibit sensory aphasia: they can speak fluently but often they are incomprehensible. They can also exhibit receptive aphasia where they make meaningless speech sounds (most likely the case with Lenin). The problem associated with diagnosing which aphasia a person has, is the complicated neural interconnections across the areas involved with language: damage can be to more than one area. Moreover, Harley (2013) highlights how those with the same form of aphasia can be very different in the way their symptoms are exhibited. Lenin never recovered from this aphasia and died in 1924 aged 54.

PARIETAL LOBES

The parietal lobes occupy the upper side of the hemispheres and form a large part of the cerebral cortex (see Figure 1.4; Figure 2.2). There are numerous functions that the parietal lobes perform. As is often the case, despite localised processing, the brain operates as a singular unit where the lobes are closely interconnected via neural pathways and commissures. Hence, the parietal lobes also perform functions in common with other areas of the brain, albeit differentially. The parietal lobes are considered to be a centre for the processing of sensory information, in particular the identification of objects in our environment. The parietal lobes interpret spatial relationships between objects and our own bodily position relative to our surroundings; in other words, our spatial awareness. There are different parts to the parietal lobes such as the primary somatosensory region which processes sensory stimuli involved with shape, weight and composition of objects. Within this area are zones that are receptive to pain, tactile contact, temperature as well as information from muscles, tendons and joints. In another area (posterolateral), visual and spatial information is processed in relation to object motion. It is here that information about the body's position is processed (this is known as proprioception). Writing, computing and perception of left-to-right orientation are processed in an area called Gerstmann while naming objects and word recognition occur in the angular gyrus. Interestingly, this area has connections with Wernicke's area due to a bundle of neural fibres known as the arcuate fasciculus which passes through the left parietal lobe. Musculoskeletal awareness and recognition of objects through touch are processed in the upper parietal gyrus. The posterior central gyrus area processes information about one's own bodily parts such as arms and legs and adds further data about proportionality and relative position. Damage to the parietal lobes can result in a diversity of problems given the different areas with different functions (see Box 2.5).

BOX 2.5 TWO CASES OF PARIETAL LOBE DAMAGE EXHIBITING VERY DIFFERENT PROBLEMS

Alan Burgess had a stroke which caused damage to the right parietal lobe. This left him ignoring friends and familiar objects to the left side of his body. Hemispatial neglect is one example of what can happen when there is damage to the parietal lobes (see Chapter 3). This commonly occurs after a stroke to either the left or right parietal lobe. If damage is to the right parietal lobe then anything occurring on the left side (which is what happened to Alan Burgess) is ignored and vice versa for damage to the left parietal lobe (see Box 3.3). Damage to the right parietal lobe can also lead to short-term memory impairments for visual features, including the colour, shape and location of objects (Berryhill and Olson 2007). There are problems with long-term memory also. For instance, neuroimaging of the brain during memory retrieval of personal experiences (e.g. episodic memory; see Chapter 4) shows how the parietal lobes are activated (Wagner, Shannon, Kahn and Buckner 2005). The posterior parietal area is more active when old rather than new items are correctly recognised (Konishi, Wheeler, Donaldson and Buckner 2000). Berryhill, Phuong, Picasso, Cabeza et al. (2007) studied episodic memory in individuals with damage to the parietal lobes. Patient EE555, a 39-year-old, suffered a third stroke in 2004. MRI scans revealed damage to specific areas of the parietal lobes. When shown a drawing of a scene, she found it difficult to interpret and understand the context of the whole scene depicted. Instead she described individual parts of the scene. Moreover, on tasks where items in a picture are crossed off as they are seen, she performed poorly as only the central items were acknowledged; all peripheral items were ignored. When subjected to a series of memory tests, deficits in the recollections of autobiographical events in her life lacked richness of depth and specificity of when they had occurred. Her recollections were scored as 'probably abnormal' although the descriptions she provided for events recalled were 'acceptable'. Berryhill et al. (2007) concluded that the parietal lobes have an important role in memory retrieval. Such patients, they argue, are not amnesic because when probed for more details they are able to recollect their personal experiences. They further suggest that these probes act as external pointers to help retrieve relevant information which become inaccessible when there is parietal lobe damage.

OCCIPITAL LOBES

The brain's smallest lobes, the occipital lobes, are positioned to the back of the cortex, under the parietal but above the temporal lobes (see Figure 1.4; Figure 2.2). The occipital lobes have an important role in making sense of what our visual system is seeing. And given how quickly we need to interpret our external world, for all sorts of reasons but primarily survival, rapid processing of visual stimuli is vital. Although the occipital lobes are primarily associated with processing visual stimuli, they perform a multitude of tasks:

1 By composing a visual map of the external world, the occipital lobes enable us to perform spatial reasoning and acquire visual memory that is needed to recall what was just seen.
2 By providing information about the colour, distance, depth and size of objects our visual experience is richer.
3 By identifying stimuli, we can make sense of our interactions with others and objects we come into contact with.
4 By sharing visual information with other lobes of the brain, information can be added such as responding using appropriate action or language or retrieving relevant episodic memories.
5 By receiving and processing stimuli from our eyes, the occipital lobes are the first locations for understanding our external world.

There are different structures operating within the occipital lobes that interconnect with other areas of the brain. The V1 area is also known as the primary visual cortex (see Figure 2.5) and provides data about object location, colour and spatial information. The V2 area is considered to be the secondary visual cortex (i.e. the ventral network; see Figure 2.3). This is a neural network that connects attention with the assignment of meaning and recognition. The dorsal network connects the V1 and V2 areas and provides guidance for action and object spatial information (see Figure 2.3). The lateral geniculate body, as seen in Figure 2.5, obtains the unprocessed data from the optic nerve and passes this to the visual cortex. Hallucinations can be a symptom of occipital lobe damage (see Box 2.6).

The brain is a complex organ, the workings of which have been compared to a computer. It is through the discipline of computational cognitive science (see Chapter 1) that the mechanisms involved in brain function can be understood through cognitive modelling.

COGNITIVE MODELLING OF THE HUMAN BRAIN

Computational cognitive science applies cognitive modelling as a way of understanding the processes used by the brain to accomplish complex tasks. These complex tasks involve the pillars of cognition:

BOX 2.6   THE HALLUCINATING WOMAN

An 84-year-old woman claimed she was seeing people in her dreams during her waking state; in other words, she was hallucinating. She described seeing bands of three colours on walls. She saw children in old-fashioned clothing, a castle and boxes strewn across streets. When she underwent neurological tests, it was revealed that she had blindness in her right eye and impaired vision in the left. Her score on the Minimental State Examination revealed she was not psychotic. A CT scan revealed damage to two areas of the right occipital lobe caused by a stroke (Paradowski, Kowalczyk, Chojdak-Lukasiewicz, Loster-Niewińska et al. 2013). These sensory phantoms could be due to damage in the neural networks of the occipital lobes (Brzecki, Podemski, Kobel-Buys and Buys 2001).

- attention and perception
- memory and learning
- thinking, decision-making and problem-solving
- language and communication

The objective of cognitive modelling is to provide a scientific account of how such processes work and interact with one another. As mentioned in Chapter 1, there are different types of cognitive models but what they all have in common are the basic principles of cognition. Cognitive models are quite different from neural models despite their interrelatedness. When devising cognitive models, the aim is to bridge the gap between behaviour and its neural underpinnings. According to Rumelhart and McClelland (1986), connectionist models are better at retaining the balance between mathematical models and properties inherent in neural models. Connectionist models resemble the layout and function of interconnecting neurons in the brain. Once a neuron in the brain responds to a stimulus, it becomes activated and sends a message to the next connected neuron to become activated also. Note that it is actually more complicated than this as neurons can become inhibited also. In the same vein as how brain neurons operate, an interconnected network of units or nodes can also have an excitatory or inhibitory action. Moreover, they too have the capacity to weight the sum of all the inputs from other connecting neurons to produce a single response. If the weighted sum goes above the threshold of activity, then there will be a response. As suggested by Sun (2008), connectionist models can have multi-layers (see Figure 2.8).

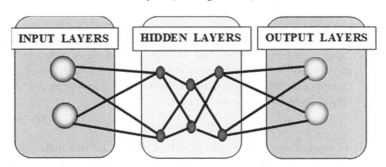

Figure 2.8 Example of a multi-layer connectionist model

For example, when a pattern is presented, the input layer will become activated (just as neurons do in response to a stimulus). Following this the next layer (that is hidden units) are responsible for the spread of activation in an attempt to resemble the pattern, and in so doing, have learned the rule. The final layer provides a response that mimics the pattern originally shown. Connectionist models can be designed to focus on visual processing (as the above example shows), while others on more complex processing integrate more than one type of stimulus. One example of a connectionist model of memory is parallel distributed processing (PDP; McClelland and Rumelhart 1981). According to this, memory is stored via the collective strength of connections between nodes (see above on weighted sum). This implies that the brain is capable of performing a range of memory-related activities in parallel.

The main aim of cognitive neuroscientists is to attain a better understanding of the involvement different areas of the brain have in cognition. Cognitive scientists, alternatively, devise cognitive models based on sound findings from cognitive psychology. One approach in cognitive psychology that has embraced cognitive models is information processing (McLeod, Plunkett and Rolls 1998). Numerous cognitive models based on the information processing approach have been introduced to show information feedforward and feedback systems in perception (see Chapter 3); in memory (see Chapter 4); in thinking and decision-making (see Chapter 5) and in language (see Chapter 6). Models, however, are only as good as the interpretation of the findings from cognitive psychological research. According to Lee, Criss, Devezer, Donkin et al. (2019),

> standard modeling practice is to summarize the ability of a model to capture patterns in the data through an omnibus measure of goodness-of-fit ....A limitation of such an approach is that a single quantity may fail to capture the full richness of information that the data provide for evaluating a model.

(p. 144)

What Lee et al. are implying here, is that models are normally based on one measure of cognitive performance such as reaction times or the number of correctly recalled items. Experiments are devised such that the conditions or variable manipulations under which participants remember information can be changed. The effects such changes have on performance are added to the theoretical knowledge base which is then incorporated into existing models.

While there have been great leaps in the development of connectionism, in particular models of brain structure and function, critics have argued that preservation of our memories and personality onto a 'chip' is a far-fetched notion (see Box 2.7).

BOX 2.7   LIVING INSIDE A 'CHIP'

With professional expertise in computational neuroscience, neural engineering, psychology and information theory, Dr Randal Koene (2014) believes it will be possible in the future to perform mind uploading. Koene outlined how such a feat can be achieved using a Punnett square diagram (see Table 2.1).

Table 2.1 Punnett square of the stages of research before mind uploading can be achieved

Understand how the brain is structured	Understand how the brain functions
✓	✓
Provide connectionist models	Implementation – do we use 'chips'?
✓	?

Koene considers the mind to be a collection of our memories, personality and other unique attributes. With developing technology our mind, he believes, will one day be transferred from the living brain to an 'artificial computational substrate'. And once this can be achieved, the mind becomes a 'substrate-independent mind' (SIM). This SIM, just like a USB (memory stick), can then be used in a structure or hardware that has the software to operate without the need to be rewritten. Koene considers the different states of neural activation in the brain to be the same as computational processes in sophisticated computing machines; only these are able to modify original instructions. By modifying original instructions using skills of reading, writing and erasing, this makes it a dynamic and universal computing machine (an example of this is the Turing machine). Who knows, if Koene is right, then one day in the distant future your mind may exist inside a machine.

SUMMARY

Mapping the structure of the brain is important for understanding how it functions. The architecture of the brain can be considered at two levels; the microanatomy and gross anatomy. While the microanatomy provides information about how the neurons in the brain interconnect and the neural pathways transmit information from one area of the brain to another, the gross structure shows the position of the lobes of the brain. The gross structure also shows how the brain consists of two hemispheres that are bonded via commissures such as the corpus callosum. The microanatomical structures show how intricately connected the two hemispheres are and the lobes of the brain as well as the more hidden structures beneath the cortex. One approach to understanding what the different areas of the brain do is through studying individuals who have brain damage. Cognitive psychologists can ascertain the function of specific areas of the brain by considering the deficits to cognition individuals with damage experience. Of course, it is also possible to ascertain the function of different areas of the brain using modern brain scanning techniques. These methods combined have enabled cognitive psychologists to devise specific tasks that can be used to measure brain function. This has helped computational cognitive scientists to develop models as a means of understanding how structure and function are intricately interconnected. In devising different types of models, they have attempted to equate cognitive performance (behaviour) with the workings of neural networks. Connectionist models are based on an understanding of how the neural connections within the brain operate and thereby interconnect the different areas.

FURTHER READING

Bigos, K.L., Hariri, A. and Weinberger, D. (2015) *Neuroimaging Genetics: Principles and practices*. Oxford: Oxford University Press.

Gazzaniga, M.S., Ivry, R.B. and Mangun, G.R. (2008) *Cognitive Neuroscience: The biology of the mind* (3rd edn). New York: W.W. Norton.

McLeod, P., Plunkett, K. and Rolls, E.T. (1998) *Introduction to Connectionist Modelling of Cognitive Processes*. Oxford: Oxford University Press.

Toates, F. (2011). *Biological Psychology: An integrative approach*. (3rd edn). Harlow: Pearson Education.

ATTENTION AND PERCEPTION

From the time we are born we are constantly trying to make sense of the world. New-born babies appear to be inactive and unable to focus on what is happening around them. To some extent this is true as they find it difficult to focus directly on stimuli. This, in part, is due to an immature sensory system and brain that is still developing. William James described the baby's world as a "blooming, buzzing confusion" (p. 462), implying that the new-born is bombarded with stimuli from its surrounding world. And as yet has not developed the capacity to interpret what this all means. Given time and constant interaction with caregivers and objects, the new-born begins to process stimuli and understand what it all means (albeit at a rudimentary level). The starting point to understanding the world is very much at the basic level of processing information (process of sensation). You may recall this was addressed in Chapter 2 when the structure and function of the human brain, including two of our sensory organs (eyes and ears), was examined. These two sensory organs were selected because there is an abundance of research examining how our visual and auditory systems attend to images and sounds in our immediate environment. Sensory input is clearly processed. But how? What mechanisms do we have to facilitate the processing of important and relevant sensory stimuli? In this chapter the focus is on how we become aware of these stimuli; the role of attention and perception. Attention is the process of selectively focusing on stimuli at the expense of other stimuli. Perception alternatively, is the recognition and interpretation of information derived from sensation and the stimuli we decide to attend to. Hence, perception is the

DOI: 10.4324/9781003014355-3

process of making sense of the information derived from our surroundings. This, in turn, is used to enable further interaction with our environment. Perception uses two types of information: sensory derived and experiential (laid down as memories). Considering our example of the new-born, during their early days of life there will be much reliance on sensory information. They will rely on what they hear, see, smell, taste and feel. They will be born with an innate ability to avoid negative stimuli such as loud noises by turning away from them and to approach positive stimuli by looking at, for example, the caregiver's face. There will be very little experiential information at this stage of life. But with a repetitive daily schedule, the new-born will begin to associate specific stimuli together such as the caregiver's face and lactation. This association between stimuli becomes learned and eventually a memory is formed of the link between the two events. In order to develop memories, the new-born needs to attend to specific stimuli or be selective. They will also need to apply previous knowledge derived from their experiences with the caregiver so that they can make inferences about what to expect (e.g. a cuddle versus ignore). The new-born's brain will then need to be able to organise their sensations into mental representations of their world. These three processes are important for perception.

In order to understand how perception operates it makes sense to consider first how we attend to stimuli in our environment. Models describing how we process sensory information have a long history extending back to the works of American psychologist William James. James is arguably the first to establish a laboratory and describe what psychology should be about in his book, *Principles of Psychology* in 1890. Of relevance here, James introduced the idea that we have a 'stream of consciousness', such that our thoughts and reactions to events are experienced as a continuous flow (see Chapter 7). He speculated on how the brain enables us to process information to maintain this continuous flow. In the case of new-borns, they would initially be confused by the world around them. As they become better able to focus on stimuli and form memories, however, their waking world begins to make more sense and they begin to experience life as a continuous flow — a stream of consciousness that James so eloquently described.

According to James the processing of information is reliant on two types of attention – active and passive. In the case of active attention, we selectively process information occurring in our immediate environment that we are aware of. This could be searching for a friend in a crowd where attention is directed specifically towards a female with long hair. In this case attention is driven by the individual's motivation and intention to spot a friend in the crowd. A new-born might focus on the sound of the caregiver's voice and associate this with being soothed and cuddled. Passive attention conversely is the processing of information that is not driven by the individual but rather is a response to events. For example, a flash of light is likely to draw an individual's attention towards its source. The reaction is often spontaneous and autonomous. James' distinction between active and passive attention remains very much at the core of how cognitive psychologists currently understand and research attention. James also considered the process of automaticity. This is best highlighted by the example of walking. Once walking has been mastered the execution of a series of actions enabling us to walk no longer need to be consciously vocalised or referred to. The act has become automated. Infants learning to walk crawl before eventually struggling to stand up and take their first steps. They appear awkward while continuing to learn how to keep their balance and put one foot in front of the other. For infants the action of walking is far from automated. Another example is when we learn to drive. When under the supervision of the driving instructor, the actions of clutch and accelerator control in gear changing are clumsy. With experience, however, these actions become so engrained that we no longer need to think about performing them – they have become automated. We can even drive and talk except when approaching a congested junction, when suddenly talking becomes difficult. The cognitive processing necessary for conversing has become compromised by the need to focus on the driving conditions. There are therefore conditions where our attention can be divided across different tasks (especially when one task is automated) but not when both tasks require equal amounts of concentration. In 1890 James wrote about focused and divided attention which has spurred theoretical explanations for how attention operates and ultimately influences perception (see later).

As we discussed in Chapter 2, sensory organs (such as the eyes and ears) have receptor cells which respond to specific types of stimuli – these can be so specific that they respond to a horizontal or vertical line. Such information is passed on to higher ordered cells in the brain ready to be interpreted. This then becomes the beginning of the process of perception. External information from our immediate environment is therefore transformed to a format that the brain can understand and to which we can then provide the context of meaning. This context of meaning is based on learning and memories from previous similar encounters with our environment. Returning to the example of our new-born, there will be many stimuli processed in this way and connections made between these stimuli then become stored as memories. The person who approaches the crib, speaks gently and then caresses and feeds the infant will begin as a series of stimuli but will rapidly become associated and recognised as the caregiver. Clearly, the role attention plays in enabling stimuli to be processed and interpreted by the brain is important. Cognitive psychologists have provided models of how this might be achieved which we will consider next.

ATTENTION

MODELS OF AUDITORY ATTENTION

One of the first studies of attention that students are often introduced to is that of Colin Cherry in 1953. He noticed that when there are many groups of people in conversation, the focus of attention is with what is being discussed by those in the same group. What is being discussed by people in other groups remains generally inaudible. Cherry found there are, however, circumstances where what is being discussed by other groups can become heard. This appeared to occur when the topic of conversation was pertinent to the individual such as their name or the fact that they too experience Seasonal Affective Disorder (SAD). This phenomenon became known as the Cocktail Party Effect. Cherry investigated this phenomenon through a series of experiments using the method of 'dichotic listening'. Dichotic listening tasks are devised as follows:

- Participants wear headphones where they hear two spoken messages

- One message is presented to the left ear and the other to the right ear
- The two spoken messages are different
- Participants are instructed to repeat the words of the message to say the right ear as they hear it out loud (this is called shadowing)
- On completion of the task they are asked questions about the message to the left ear (the unattended message)
- Questions could be simple such as the sex of the voice (i.e. a physical attribute) or a complex question about what was said (i.e. meaning of the language spoken)

The findings indicate that very little about the unattended message, barring simple physical attributes, is discerned. These findings led to a series of proposed filter models showing what happens to stimuli that are attended to and those that are not. All stimuli compete to pass through a 'bottleneck'. This bottleneck allows only so many stimuli to be fully processed, and this depends on the level of attention it receives. There is debate, however, regarding whether the bottleneck occurs early or late on during processing. To understand how filter models work refer to Figure 3.1 (models by Broadbent (1958); Treisman (1964) and Deutsch and Deutsch (1963)).

As we can see from Broadbent's single filter model, many auditory signals enter the sensory buffer (a holding site) but only a few will be processed further. Once in the selective filter, only a couple (in the case of Figure 3.1) continue their journey into our attention. These will be examined further at a higher ordered level of processing in the brain. Broadbent's model is an example of an early bottleneck. In the case of Treisman's attenuator model, signal selection occurs later in the system. She considered a model that is far more flexible than that proposed by Broadbent. For Treisman all auditory signals are processed superficially for physical attributes. The signal continues to the semantic filter where they are either processed fully or attenuated. Depending on the importance of these signals and our expectations, they continue into our attention or remain in an attenuated form. Further processing of these stimuli also depends on our expectations of what is important, and what we should be attending to. Directing our attention in this way is a

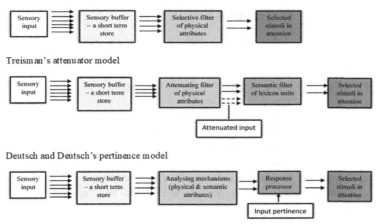

Figure 3.1 Filter models and selected stimuli

top-down processing strategy. In Treisman's study levels of top-down processing had occurred when some individuals recalled words from the unattended message whilst shadowing the message in the right ear. Treisman claimed this to be a consequence of these words fitting in with the context of the shadowed message. Deutsch and Deutsch argued for a late bottleneck. This means that all stimuli are fully processed but only those most important to the current situation are likely to influence and direct an individual's behaviour. Today there is general consensus that the attended message is managed largely by top-down processing (see Box 3.1).

Audition is just one sensory input researched by cognitive psychologists – we also have others including vision. We might ask whether visual stimuli are subjected to the same selection processes. In vision are there also bottom-up and top-down processes occurring simultaneously?

VISUAL ATTENTION

Corbetta and Shulman (2002) identified two attention systems; one operating on the basis of top-down or goal-directed attention and the other resembling a bottom-up or stimulus-driven attention system.

BOX 3.1   TOP-DOWN PROCESSING FOR THE ATTENDED MESSAGE?

Based on dichotic listening experiments, filter models suggest that auditory information is picked up by our ears and briefly stored in a sensory buffer. This information is passed through the bottleneck filter but only if it is attended to. This, it has been argued, occurs when we use top-down processing. Note that a top-down processing strategy means we direct our focus and use knowledge from our previous experiences. And it is during dichotic listening tasks that the top-down strategy is used to process the attended message. This is largely due to the instructions to shadow the message in the right ear. In 2009 McDermott suggested that top-down processing is involved in understanding speech (such as how words are separated in a sentence). This, in part, comes from our experience of hearing language and acquiring knowledge and expectations of how words in sentences are ordered. This makes it easier to separate messages more clearly and even to 'pick' bits out from the unattended message. But do we also rely on the opposite strategy of **bottom-up processing**? In the case of bottom-up processing, the auditory stimulus which has the most dominant presence is processed fully at the expense of other potential stimuli. In this case knowledge, motives and expectations do not determine whether the auditory stimulus is processed further or not. This makes perfect sense when we consider our new-born who is relying on sensory input rather than knowledge to understand what is happening around them (given they haven't been in the world very long!). Which stimulus is likely to be most dominant – the sound of mum's voice or the dog barking? It's most likely that mum's voice will pass through the bottleneck.

Top-down processing is adopted when a cue showing the location of a target is shown. Bottom-up attention is stimulus-driven and kicks into action when an unexpected and pertinent stimulus occurs. This potentially life-saving mechanism is designed to redirect top-down controlled visual attention. The way in which top-down and bottom-up attention works is best illustrated by an example. Suppose you are watching your favourite television programme and suddenly a flash of flames and smoke filters from under the lounge door. Immediately the bottom–up attention system redirects your focus from the television to the fire and smoke. In this case bottom–up processing disrupts top–down processing, potentially saving your life. These two processing systems operate interactively (Corbetta, Patel and Shulman 2008). In the case of mundane stimuli, then, distractor information such as a car passing the house (bottom–up processing) is stopped from interrupting what we are focusing on, in this case the television (top–down processing). Hence, bottom–up processing can stop or override top–down processing when it is highly pertinent to do so. Having both systems helps us to focus and direct attention away towards a potentially threatening situation.

Devising experiments to analyse how visual attention works is more challenging than it is for auditory attention. Egly, Driver and Rafal in 1994, however, developed a successful method (see Box 3.2).

Theories of visual attention

In 1980 Posner argued that visual attention is like a single spotlight casting a ray. Others such as Eriksen and St James (1986) instead argued for a zoom lens analogy. Just as a camera can adjust the focus of a visual field so too can our eyes. In 2000, however, Awh and Pashler introduced the spotlights theory. Unlike Posner, Awh and Pashler's spotlights theory argues that our attention can be split so that many separate and non–adjacent areas in our visual field can be covered. Not everyone agrees with this split attention theory. One criticism is to ask what happens to the areas of space where there is no focused attention? For example, what happens to the middle space when there is only extreme left and right focus? Jans, Peters and de Weerd (2010) argued that such a split would interfere with decisions about appropriate action. What if the two visual fields are contradictory or require differences of action? Conversely, Cave, Bush and Taylor (2010) argued that this would not cause interference but instead provide flexibility to increase the likelihood of the best response. Various research findings support all three approaches. The consensus, however, is that the way visual attention is used will depend on the demands of the situation and the goals of

BOX 3.2   VISUAL ATTENTION METHODOLOGY

Egly et al. were interested in whether we are more likely to focus our attention on objects or 'pockets of space' within our visual field. In their study participants were instructed to detect a visual target as quickly as possible. They were presented with a cue (prior to the target) showing where the target will most likely be. This cue either showed the same location (i.e. valid) or a different location (i.e. invalid) to the target's location. Cues could also be of the same object form or different to that of the target. Their findings suggested that the response rate for target detection was quicker when the valid cues were presented beforehand. Only when the invalid cue was of the same object form as the target, were response rates faster than that for valid cues. They concluded that attention was, in part, object-based. Hollingworth, Maxcey-Richard and Vecera (2012) introduced a similar task. But this time they wanted to explore whether space-based attention is also present. Invalid cues (that were either the same object or different to the target) varied in their distance from the target's location. They found:

- Detection time was faster when the invalid cue was the same as the target object than when it was different
- Detection time increased when the same object invalid cue was furthest away from where the target was located
- Hence, detection time was the slowest when the invalid cue was furthest away from the target's location but gradually increased in speed as the cue's distance became closer to where the target would be
- Implication is that both object-based and space-based attention work in tandem

Researchers in this field have also identified feature-based attention. This occurs when we look for relevant features belonging to a friend for example – features such as long blonde hair. In this case colour and hair length become focused features against a backdrop of many other hair colours and styles.

All three types of visual attention are shown to interact to improve our overall visual experience (Kravitz and Behrmann 2011).

the individual. Hence all three approaches will be used at some point or another as required.

When we consider the spotlight and zoom lens approaches, the implication is that selective attention is drawn towards areas or space – often referred to as space-based attention. On examining what we selectively attend to, however, studies reveal that we generally focus on objects rather than space (see later in chapter). Object-based attention fits well with our pattern of visual-based behaviour, as we often search for objects such as a specific building or a post-box. We can nevertheless focus on both space and objects which the spotlight, zoom lens and split spotlights approaches account for effectively. In the case of object-based attention, Hou and Liu (2012) found that top-down processes are involved. This is not surprising given we often interact with our surroundings by focusing on objects (e.g. when we navigate through a town, we look for signposts or a bus stop). For some individuals, however, being able to focus on objects fully is problematic. These individuals are likely to have visual attention disorders. Individuals with visual attention disorders have problems with top-down and bottom-up processing. Neuroimaging shows that top-down and bottom-up processing have separate networks operating within the parietal lobes of the brain (Talsma, Coe, Munoz and Theeuwes 2010). How top-down and bottom-up processing work has been studied by cognitive neurologists (see Box 3.3). Although all forms of sensory information help us to navigate our surroundings, we live in a very visual world. We are constantly bombarded with visual images of people and objects and have to distinguish relevant from irrelevant visual stimuli. Visual search is a constant process but how is it performed?

Visual search

There are three main accounts of how visual search occurs.

1. FEATURE INTEGRATION THEORY

Treisman and Gelade (1980) argued the visual system performs a quick breakdown of an object into its component features pre-attentively. The recombination of these features, however, relies

BOX 3.3   VISUAL ATTENTION DISORDERS

There are two recognised visual attention problems studied by cognitive psychologists: spatial neglect and extinction. The term spatial neglect refers to a lack of awareness of stimuli. It follows brain damage leading to a deficit in awareness of stimuli presented to the opposite side to where the damage occurred (known as the contralateral side). In most people with visual attention disorders the damage is to the right hemisphere of the brain leading to neglect in the left visual field. This means that if the individual is shown a stimulus such as a toy to their left visual field, they will not see it. The example of a toy failing to be seen by an individual demonstrates what is called subject-centred or egocentric neglect. In contrast, object-centred or allocentric neglect shows itself as a problem of not seeing the left side of the object – hence in our example only the right side of the toy is seen. When asked to draw an object, individuals with this problem will only draw the right side of it. This becomes a problem when there are multiple objects in both the right and left visual fields (Gainotti and Ciaaffa 2013). Interestingly, evidence of an overlap of the brain areas associated with both types of neglect has been found (Rorden, Hjaltason, Fillmore, Fridrikasson et al. 2012). Corbetta and Shulman (2011) argued that it is the ventral attention network controlling bottom-up processing that is damaged. This has a knock-on effect on top-down processing (the dorsal attention network; see Chapter 2). This raises the question of how this occurs. Corbetta and Shulman claim that the two systems interact such that an impaired ventral attention network influences the functioning of the dorsal attention network. The result of this is an inability to stay focused.

In the case of extinction, individuals demonstrate a specific form of neglect. It operates as follows:

● when two stimuli are presented simultaneously to the left and right visual fields then the stimulus in the visual field associated with the damaged hemisphere is ignored and only the remaining stimulus is reported as seen

An example of this is a patient presented with a plateful of food who eats only half of the meal in the unaffected visual field (i.e. either the left or the right). The other half of the food is left uneaten. In such cases rotating the plate by 180 degrees, generally leads to completion of the meal. Extinction is problematic. This is because of the way we visually interact with our environment. We constantly see a multitude of objects and spaces between objects in both visual fields. De Haan, Karnath and Driver (2012) claim that individuals with extinction have impaired attention capacity such that they are only able to detect one target stimulus. And this is generally the stimulus presented to the right visual field.

on focused attention. This process is important and aids in the correct interpretation of the recombination of features – a long-haired blonde friend and not a banana!

2. TEXTURE TILING MODEL

Rosenholtz, Huang and Ehinger (2012) claimed that when we focus on a visual scene the central details are processed clearly but the more peripheral aspects are lost. Hence there is a texture variation across the visual scene. This means that central details are clear while peripheral details are less defined. They argue for gradations of texture – such that acuity decreases the further away it is from the point of focus.

3. DUAL-PATH MODEL

Wolfe, Võ, Evans and Greene (2011) suggested there are two pathways involved in visual search: selective and non-selective. In the case of the selective pathway objects are found individually for recognition. For the non-selected pathway, the gist of a scene is processed to aid the selective pathway. The non-selected pathway interacts strongly with our general knowledge of our surroundings such as the design of a train platform. In support of this Ehinger, Hidalgo-Sotelo, Torraiba and Oliva (2009) gave participants different pictures to find either people or outdoor objects such as pavements. Eye fixations were recorded to measure which areas in the pictures individuals focused on to find the target. Top-down processing was used, and eye fixations shifted to areas where they believed a person or pavement was most likely to be.

Divided attention

William James (1890) made the observation that we can perform two tasks at the same time provided one of the tasks was automated (limited focused attention required). James was describing divided attention. Being able to divide our attention across many tasks enables us to process various kinds of information at the same time. So, what is the evidence for divided attention? Treisman and Davies (1973) found deficits when performing tasks that competed for the same processing capacity. This was apparent when the same sense modality (auditory or visual) was required. They found that performance was compromised when participants were instructed to monitor two stimuli from the same sense modality (visual or auditory). Hence, these stimuli were interfering with one another. If, however, the dual-tasks rely on different sense modalities, different processing components and resources are used. Hence, both tasks can be successfully performed (Wickens 1984, 2008). Taylor (2018) explored the effects of divided attention on the recognition of face-name pairs (full-frontal face photos with the name underneath). She found that when attempting to process both names and faces simultaneously, performance for the recognition of names was significantly compromised. This suggests the processing of names is effortful while, in contrast, the processing of faces is automatic.

Automatic processing

Another of William James' (1890) observations is that we can divide our attention and perform more than one task at the same time provided one of the tasks has become automated. The use of controlled and automatic processes was introduced by Shiffrin and Schneider in 1977. They argued that controlled processes (or effortful processing) rely on attention and are dependent on limited capacity. In contrast, automatic processes did not rely on attention or have capacity limitations. The notion of controlled versus automatic processes, however, was criticised by Moors and de Houwer (2006). They argued that automaticity should:

- have no conscious awareness of ongoing processing
- not require attentional resources to be an efficient system
- be a rapid process
- be independent of any goals
- not require the above factors to occur simultaneously – it is not an 'all or nothing' process

Moreover, Hasher and Zacks (1979) have suggested that there is some overlap between automaticity and involuntary processing.

Our ability to attend to stimuli in our environment is very much at the forefront of being able to interpret what is occurring around us. That is our ability to perceive.

PERCEPTION

As mentioned earlier in this chapter, perception uses information derived from our sensory systems and from memories of our experiences. Perception is a complex process relying on a multitude of **cognitive algorithms** designed to help us understand our world. Basic processing of sensory information and the specialised areas of the brain dealing with such information were discussed in Chapter 2. We will first consider how we perceive colour, size and depth as they are so fundamental to understanding our world.

PERCEPTION OF SIZE, COLOUR AND DEPTH

In Chapter 2, we examined the structure of the eye and the ear. How the images on the retina of the eye are focused for instance appear very different from what we actually 'see'. The image on the retina is upside down but that is not how we perceive the world. Even a new-born does not perceive the world upside down. The brain interprets the images as they appear in reality and assorts them such that we have continuity – a bit like watching a film. So how does the brain do this? How does the brain know when one object is further away than another? Also, how does the brain know that the shape of a door is the same regardless of its angle? Or even that an object's colour remains consistent regardless of differences in luminosity? The brain makes use of perceptual constancies for aspects of objects such as size, shape, lightness and colour. A constancy is defined as, "the tendency to perceive objects or their qualities in the same or similar ways, despite differences in their retinal images" (Cheyne and Davies 1999, p. 579).

Size constancy is important as it helps us to determine when some objects are further away than other objects. An image of an object is cast on the retina but as the object moves further away from us, the retinal image decreases. Nevertheless, the size of the distant object remains correct. A cow in the distance will look smaller but we still can gauge its true size. Under conditions where it is difficult to recognise an object or judge its distance, however, size constancy breaks down. Haber and Levin (2001) investigated whether object familiarity or variations in viewing distances play an important role in correct judgements of size. In their study there were three categories of objects all viewed from close or distant viewing points: familiar but invariant in size (e.g. cricket bat), familiar but size variant (e.g. television) and unfamiliar (e.g. shapes). They found that participants were better at judging size when the objects were familiar. Nevertheless, participants made fairly accurate judgements of size for the unfamiliar objects also. The viewing distance did not appear to affect size judgements. Interestingly, van der Hoort, Guterstam and Ehrsson (2011) showed a body size effect where we tend to perceive the size of objects relative to our own body size. In van der Hoort et al.'s study, participants wore attached CCTV cameras and viewed their surroundings from the perspective of a doll which was either small or large. This affected how they perceived the size of objects. When the doll was small objects were seen as further away and larger. Not so when the doll was large. An interesting example of how we can fool our size constancy perception is the Ames room (Ames 1952; see Figure 3.2). This room has an unusual shape such that one wall is out of synch with the other walls and the floor slopes. This has a robust effect on the perception of size of a person inside the room. When participants looked through a peephole, the illusion is set. The person inside when walking across the room will appear tall scaling down to small. The perception of size in this case appears to be influenced by the perceived distance.

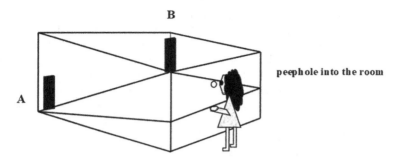

Figure 3.2 A representation of the illusion of two objects of different heights in the Ames Room by looking through a peephole

Colour constancy helps us to perceive the colour of an object as invariant despite changes of luminosity. Objects show changes of colour as the light projected on them alters throughout the day. And yet we do not perceive colour changes to these objects. We may see reflections of work surfaces on an object such as a yellow mug, but the yellow colour of the mug is retained. Interestingly, Shepherd (2020) points out how colour constancy can be imperfect. She provides the example of #TheDress in 2015 which became a viral sensation. Some people perceived the colour of the dress as blue and black while others saw it as white and gold. Shepherd concluded that lighting and our expectations contributed towards the divergent colour perceptions.

The shape of objects remains constant despite changes of angle. For instance, the angle of an open door appears different to when it is closed but shape constancy enables us to perceive it as a constant shape – a long oblong. There is a strong element of learning involved with how we perceive objects. Objects become familiar through repetitive interactions with them. We learn that an orange is of the colour orange and an edible banana is yellow. An infant has yet to learn about what the size, shape and colour of objects should be, but through interacting with their environment, the learning curve is rapid. Moreover, this learning coupled with constancy, provides us with a greater understanding of how objects interact with one another.

The ability to perceive a two-dimensional (2-D) image cast on the retina as a three-dimensional (3-D) entity is achieved by different types of sensory information. This ability can be important when judging heights. There are three types of cues which help us to determine whether we are looking at something that could potentially be of a dangerous height or depth – such as an extreme drop from a cliff or the 'Buttertubs' seen in Yorkshire. These cues have been categorised as monocular (based on viewings from one eye), binocular (based on simultaneous viewings from both eyes) and oculomotor (based on muscular contractions around the eyes providing a muscle sense called kinaesthesia). Monocular cues are often used by artists to achieve the illusion of a 3-D representation on a flat 2-D surface such as a canvas. There are many monocular cues which help us put objects into perspective but also to determine the depth of what we see. We are surrounded by at least one of these monocular cues daily. Parallel lines that are tall indicate closeness, but the shorter they become the more we perceive them as being further away. For example, driving on a straight flat road, the telegraph poles to the side appear tall but the more distant ones seem much shorter – this cue is called linear perspective. Texture of a visual scene also provides information about distance. The closer an object the more detail of texture there is such that a cobbled path will have larger and more regular stone patterning the closer it is but as it increases in distance the stones appear smaller and closer together. There is a gradual texture gradient which provides the look of a cobbled path receding into the distance. Shading provides objects with a 3-D outlook by making them look solid and projecting out from their contextual backdrop. Another cue which gives the illusion of distance is when objects overlap one on top of the other. This partially obscures the object underneath which makes it appear as further away. This is known as interposition (see Figure 3.3).

Motion parallax also provides information about distance and depth. This refers to how an image of a moving object traverses across the retina. It is interesting that nearer objects appear to move in the opposite direction to one's head such that they move further and more quickly. Distant objects, however, move in the same direction as one's head but more slowly. This is best demonstrated when looking out of the window from a travelling train. The objects close to the track pass by quickly unlike the hills in the distance which move slowly. Looming also provides information

Figure 3.3 Demonstration of how shapes can appear more distant due to interposition

about depth. Looming occurs when an object moves towards us thereby expanding the retinal image (the reverse occurs when an object moves away from us). Bridge (2020) raises an important question of why the world remains still as our eyes move around. She addresses this question by explaining how the brain is able to calculate whether we are moving, or our environment is moving, by using the retinal images and information about the position of our eyes. Lastly, the familiarity of an object provides us with size dimensions thus helping us to judge depth in the absence of other cues.

Binocular cues, sometimes referred to as stereoscopic vision, occur when both eyes cast an independent retinal image. Due to the structure of the eye and position there are slight differences in the two retinal images – known as binocular disparity. Thus, when both eyes focus on the same object there is a slightly different image on the left and right retina which are then compared and integrated. As a result of this automatic process of integration, known as stereopsis, we are able to perceive depth. Both oculomotor and binocular cues help us to make judgements of distance based on being able to perceive depth. Oculomotor cues help to perceive depth by sensing the muscle contractions occurring around the eyes when we focus on a distant or near object. Two processes arise from oculomotor cues: vergence and accommodation. In the case of viewing close objects our eyes converge more than for distant ones and this is controlled via the muscular contractions surrounding our eyes. This process is called vergence. Accommodation, alternatively, operates by thickening the eye lens when focusing on a close object. This heightens optical clarity but generally of one object at a time. We integrate information from monocular, binocular and oculomotor cues to ascertain both distance and depth. Nardini (2020) found that the way in which children integrate all these cues is different from adults. In fact, Nardini's data suggest that this does not occur until about 10–12 years of age. Only then does the precision of perceptual judgements improve. Neuroimaging studies confirm how visual reshaping continues into late childhood.

Occasionally, however, we are tricked by what our eyes are telling us about the depth of an object. This usually occurs when a 2-D image is made into a 3-D representation by using contradictory monocular cues. This is one way in which visual illusions work. Visual illusions are very robust and difficult to ignore (see Figure 3.4).

In the case of the Necker cube the brain finds it difficult to not flicker from one interpretation to another. The shaded square either shifts to the background or to the foreground in an effort to perceptually resolve the ambiguous figure. The Poggendorf illusion provides a context for line misalignment. The Müller-Lyer illusion makes the two vertical lines appear of different size when in fact they are exactly the same length. The inward and outward directions of the arrowheads provide cues of distance. This can be seen when comparisons between vertical lines of the same length of an interior corner of a room and the exterior corner of a building are viewed. The same illusion is created. The brain perceives the different regions of the Penrose figure as 3-D. Due to its paradoxical nature the whole figure appears twisted and contorted. It does not obey the algorithms of a truly 3-D object. There have been different theories explaining how our brain is fooled by visual illusions, such as 'Gestalt theory'

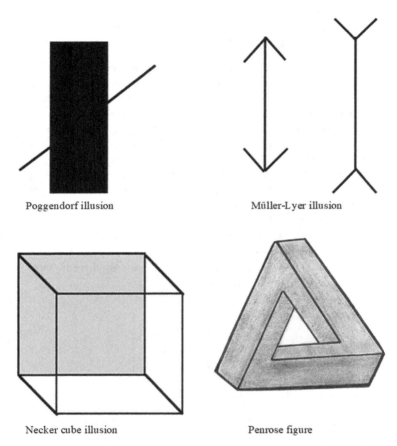

Poggendorf illusion

Müller-Lyer illusion

Necker cube illusion

Penrose figure

Figure 3.4 Examples of visual illusions

which highlights how the organisation of perception is robust in accounting for visual illusions (see Box 3.4). The perceptions of size, colour and depth help us to understand the attributes of objects, in particular how they move (see later).

OBJECT PERCEPTION

When we distinguish objects from each other we rely on being able to recognise patterns. In other words, we engage in pattern

BOX 3.4   GESTALT THEORY OF PERCEPTUAL ORGANISATION

The Gestalt school of thought was developed in Germany under the auspices of Wertheimer (1880–1943), Koffka (1886–1941) and Kohler (1887–1964). The underlying premise of their work was that we have innate brain processes used to explain the relationship between our experiences and the world. They focused primarily on perceptual processes and developed a series of basic laws of perception. The Gestaltists emphasised the point that we perceive objects as 'wholes' rather than a breakdown of their component parts. They introduced the overarching law of Prägnanz which states that the simplest perceptual organisation will occur. There are other laws subsumed under the law of Prägnanz accounting for the grouping of stimuli as a way of trying to interpret them. The law of proximity describes the need for perceiving elements of a stimulus together, given their closeness. Hence in the case of Figure 3.5, there are three pairs of lines and one odd line.

Figure 3.5 Parallel lines of proximity

The law of closure is the inclination to see a complete object.

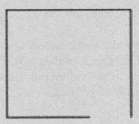

Figure 3.6 An almost complete 'rectangle'

The law of similarity groups similar stimuli together.

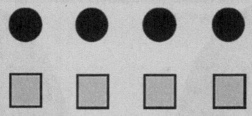

Figure 3.7 Similar objects are grouped together

The law of good continuation enables us to see a clear and continuous pattern.

Figure 3.8 Two separate but continuous patterns

Figure-ground segregation, Gestaltists argue, is an important aspect of how we perceive objects. Our brain perceives an object in the context of the background in which it resides. In the famous ambiguous drawing, a depiction of two non-featured side profiles of human faces amidst a neutral background is often perceived (the Rubin vase). The dominant image, however, can flitter between the two faces and the space between them of a vase (see Figure 3.9). It works even when it is not perfectly symmetrical.

The perceived figures have form and are in the foreground, in contrast to the space between them which is in the background. According to Wagemans, Elder, Kubovy, Palmer et al. (2012), areas of figures which curve outwards and are symmetrical tend to be perceived in the foreground as the dominant features. Researchers have tested Gestalt laws and concluded that these hold up very well in the light of how we perceive objects (Elder and Goldberg 2002). For Gestaltists, however, figure-ground segregation is an innate ability independent of any learning. When considering the work of the Gestaltists, there is much description but little explanation of how these principles might operate. Kersten, Mamassion and Yuille (2004) have attempted to address this by making use of the Bayesian approach. In fact, many experts today consider the

Figure 3.9 The Rubin vase optical illusion

Bayesian approach to be a good explanation for the Gestalt
principles of visual perception. Kersten et al. suggest that we, as
observers, consider statistical regularities in our environment.
Hence, in relation to proximity or similarity, our interactions with
our environment enable us to learn about the relationship of the
visual elements of objects. This means we learn about what belongs
to an object or patterns we see. Moreover, our knowledge of this is
used to distinguish figures from backgrounds (e.g. figure-ground
segregation).

recognition. Pattern recognition occurs constantly on a daily basis. In tasks such as reading, the letters printed are identified by specialised visual cells – some cells are designed to identify vertical lines whereas others identify curves. These are then integrated to form a letter of the alphabet. How this is interpreted depends on previous experience of language and the operation of the lexicon (see Chapter 6).

As mentioned in Chapter 2, feature detectors respond to specific elements of a stimulus such as a horizontal line. These elements are eventually integrated with the other elements of the stimulus concerned which the brain then deciphers for meaning. This represents a bottom–up processing strategy (see earlier). Much of our understanding of feature detection models comes from the neurophysiological research of Hűbel and Wiesel (1959). In 1959 they studied visual perception in cats. Using simple stimuli presented to the cat's visual system, electrodes recorded activity of cortical cells responding to specific types of patterns such as lines or edges. Hűbel and Wiesel concluded that individual cells extract unambiguous data from the features of the objects seen. All this information is then constructed by the visual system to form perceptions of objects. Our visual system operates similarly. It is hierarchically organised such that there are levels of feature detectors (see Figure 2.5). This means the output from one level is passed on to the next level as input. This continues through a number of levels of processing to eventually build up a complete picture by integrating the features from each level. This is how it is believed that, beginning with a series of individual cells firing, we finally end up being able to recognise our own grandmother.

In contrast to bottom–up processing as described by Hűbel and Wiesel, template matching is an example of top–down processing (Selfridge and Neisser 1960). In this case shapes or patterns detected by the visual system are compared holistically with existing templates stored in memory. These templates are acquired as a consequence of previous interactions with our environment. If there is a sufficient overlap with an existing template, then the stimulus is considered to belong to the class of objects the template represents (see Box 3.5 for further theories of object recognition).

Cognitive psychologists acknowledge that both top–down and bottom–up processing often operate in tandem or that one occurs

BOX 3.5   THEORIES OF OBJECT RECOGNITION

The new-born's visual system is still immature but begins to develop as increasingly it interacts with objects; hence, "the brain has to 'learn to see' during infancy and childhood" (Nardini 2020, p. 42). Visual sharpness and acuity of objects improves. The recognition of an object is 'coarse' to begin with but will eventually progress from coarse to fine as the missing finer details are added (Hegdé 2008). There are cells in the visual cortex responding to low or high spatial frequencies which capture coarse and fine detail respectively. Hegdé argued that coarse processing is fast-tracked by a specific brain pathway (magnocellular); hence the images appear as blurred. This is followed by a slower brain pathway (parvocellular) which conveys the finer detail of stimuli. In a study by Musel, Chauvin, Guyader, Chokron et al. (2012), participants were shown images (for 150 ms) which progressively changed from coarse (i.e. low spatial frequency) to fine detail (i.e. high spatial frequency) and vice versa. Decisions about the type of images shown, such as indoor or outdoor scenes, were measured using reaction times. Reaction times favoured the coarse-to-fine rather than the fine-to-coarse direction of processing. This meant that low followed by high spatial frequency was the norm. In line with Navon's (1977) research, the findings suggest that global processing relies on low spatial frequency, local processing on high spatial frequency (Flevaris, Martinez and Hillyard 2014). Low and high spatial frequencies provide us with an approach that is in keeping with how visual cortical cells and brain pathways operate. Theoretical approaches either emphasise a global (top-down) or local (bottom-up) slant. For example, Marr's (1982) computational model describes a series of processing stages: primal sketch (providing a 2-D description of input such as contours and blobs); 2 ½ -D sketch (providing descriptions of depth and orientation); 3-D model representation (providing fuller information of objects independent of viewpoint). Biederman (1987) modified Marr's model in his recognition-by-components theory. He referred to the components of objects, such as their shapes, as 'geons' and identified as many as 36. Of importance is the ability to distinguish objects from surfaces. For example, the edges of an object help to form a basic line-drawing representation separate from any background. Also, concave shapes provide information of an object's contour. The processing of object edges is independent of any viewing point. This implies edges have invariant properties so that they remain constant despite changes of orientation. Biederman claims there are five invariant properties concerning edges such as curvature (set points on a curve) and symmetry (opposing asymmetry). And it is these invariant properties driving how geons are constructed. For instance, a cylinder is considered a geon as is a triangle or square (see Figure 3.10).

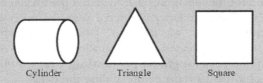

Cylinder   Triangle   Square

Figure 3.10 Examples of 'geons'

Once the geons of an object are established comparisons are made in memory to find a match (analogous to template matching). Biederman's theory, nevertheless, is very much a bottom-up processing approach, and has some neurological support. The neurological support shows that information is progressively constructed as it passes through the hierarchy of visual neurons; hence operating on a feedforward basis. There are, however, neurons operating in a different way such as backward processing (Gilbert and Li 2013). This supports top-down processing. Evidence for the influence of top-down processing in the recognition of objects comes from the use of ambiguous pictures. When one of two image interpretations are shown prior to the ambiguous picture, participants are influenced by the interpretation they see beforehand. In other words, they have been primed to see the same image in the ambiguous picture. Hence, "during our attempts to interpret the world around us, perception relies on existing knowledge as much as it does on incoming information" (Yardley, Perlovsky and Bar 2012, p.1).

more dominantly depending on the demands of the situation. Kinchla and Wolfe (1979) claimed our visual system does not necessarily operate on a bottom–up or top–down basis but on a 'middle–out' basis. Hence, our visual system operates by using the information it has available at the time such as the size of a stimulus or its distance. Their conclusions are based largely on a study by Navon (1977). His method considered how 'global' and 'local' processing operate in pattern recognition. By presenting a large letter such as 'S' or 'H' which comprises smaller letters such as 'S' or 'H', Navon was able to determine when global or **local processing** occurred using reaction times (see Figure 3.11). For some trials, participants had to decide whether the large letter was an 'S' or 'H'. And for the remaining trials whether the smaller letters were 'Ss' or 'Hs'. The large letter interfered with the processing of the smaller letters when it was different. The processing speed of the large letter was unaffected by the smaller letters. These findings suggest a preference for **global processing**, which enables general scanning of visual patterns before adding the detail.

FACE PERCEPTION

New-borns will instinctively scrutinise face-like stimuli (Shah 2020). Shah, Gaule, Bird and Cook (2013) even showed this to be the case with adults on the autism spectrum. This suggests that their instinctive responding to face-like stimuli remains intact despite showing deficits in other areas. An infant's ability to perceive faces (albeit in a primitive form until the visual system develops further) is paramount to survival. Being able to recognise the caregiver's face, in particular, and associate this with love and care helps it to thrive. Face perception appears to be an innate ability that is unaffected by divided attention and separates it from perceiving objects (see Box 3.6).

Evidence suggests that faces are processed holistically rather than on a feature-by-feature basis. Hence a top-down rather than a bottom-up processing strategy. Holistic processing enables facial features, and the inter-spacing between features, to remain integrated. Holistic processing is fast and allows features to be processed in parallel rather than serially. Bruyer (2011) demonstrated holistic processing in faces using the face inversion effect where faces were presented upside down, inverted or upright; faces are difficult to recognise under upside down and inverted presentations. This is not the case for non-facial stimuli, which suggests there is something special about the way faces are processed.

One well-developed theory concerning how we process faces is that of Bruce and Young (1986). They introduced a model

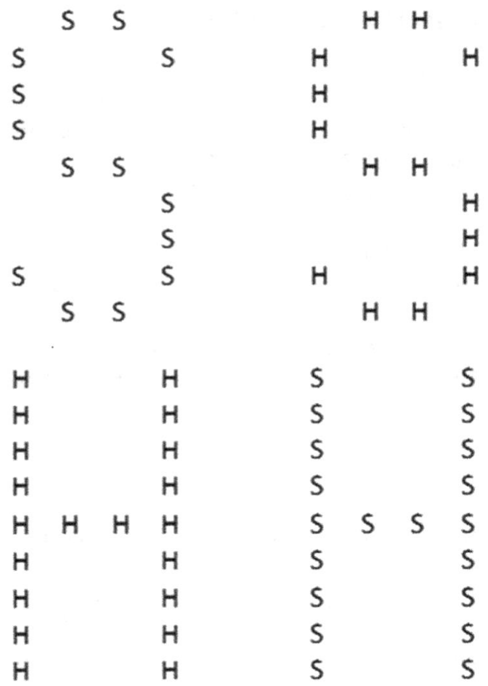

```
    S  S                    H  H
 S        S           H           H
 S                    H
 S                    H
    S  S                    H  H
          S                       H
          S                       H
 S        S           H           H
    S  S                    H  H

 H        H           S           S
 H        H           S           S
 H        H           S           S
 H        H           S           S
 H  H  H  H           S  S  S  S
 H        H           S           S
 H        H           S           S
 H        H           S           S
 H        H           S           S
```

Figure 3.11 The global (large) 'S' and 'H'; the local (smaller) 'Ss' and 'Hs'

consisting of a number of components each with a defined function (see Figure 3.12). In the case of 'structural codes', a literal pictorial representation of the face is produced. This means that if a full-frontal view of the face is presented then the pictorial representation will be the same; if on the other hand a ¾ profile is viewed then this will be depicted as such. Familiar faces will have more structural codes depicting different angles of the face unlike unfamiliar faces where there is one pictorial representation. Information from the structural codes is passed on to 'face recognition units' for processing. This information is then compared with facial data stored in memory (as part of our 'cognitive system'). Information regarding 'person identification' and 'name generation' is

BOX 3.6   BRAIN AND FACIAL PROCESSING

fMRI has provided evidence for facial processing occurring in a separate area of the brain - the fusiform gyrus located in the occipitotemporal lobes (Tsao and Livingstone 2008). Jonas, Jacques, Liu-Shuang, Brissart et al. (2016) found a right hemisphere dominance for face recognition (see Chapter 8). Interestingly, man's best friend, the dog, has been considered by many dog owners to be good at reading our faces. This may well be the case, but recent fMRI scans have found no areas in the dog's brain for encoding human faces. Instead, dogs have brain specialisation for conspecific-preference (Bunford, Hernández-Pérez, Farkas, Cuaya et al. 2020). In other words, they are geared towards identifying other dogs.

processed further down the chain which ultimately is interpreted by our cognitive system.

Bruce and Young's model is actually a little more complex than that depicted in Figure 3.12. There are, for example, separate routes for the analysis of facial expression and facial speech analysis. This suggests that in reality when trying to recognise faces we also draw upon expression and speech. In addition to recognising objects and faces, we also recognise these in relation to how we perceive movement, our next topic.

PERCEPTION OF MOTION AND ACTION

James Gibson (1966) introduced the ecological theory of perception which is known also as direct perception. He referred to his theory as ecological because it explained perception in the real world. Gibson argued that perception is about 'picking up' information from arrays of light belonging to objects we see in our visual field. As this occurs in a direct way, Gibson believed sensation to be more informative than perception. His approach belongs to the bottom–up genre. He added that objects are directly perceivable because of their functional properties (or their 'affordances'). For example, a bed 'affords' lying down while a steering

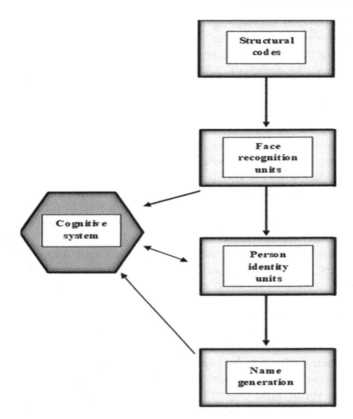

Figure 3.12 Face recognition model
Source: Adapted from Bruce and Young (1986)

wheel 'affords' turning to direct a car. Hence, these affordances provide us with opportunities for action.

Our memory system also plays an important role in deciphering sensory information from the optic arrays picked up by retinal cells. Similar or repetitive events become stored as memories. It is these memories which enable us to respond to future events. Memories of appropriate action to take when a car heads towards us, for instance, is potentially life-saving. Gibson argued that we perceive the movement of objects by their covering and uncovering of parts of the background. This enables us to track an object's trajectory. According to Gibson, the invariance of this process enables us to perceive motion and distance. In terms of what prompts us to act appropriately, Gibson further claimed that object affordances trigger motor action. This means that when we see a rake, specific areas of the brain are activated to prepare motor action consistent with raking a lawn. What happens, however, when we are presented with 'graspable' and 'non-graspable' objects? Wilf, Holmes, Schwartz and Makin (2013) looked at the effect of affordance 'graspability' on motor action. Participants had to move their arm in a way that reflected the appropriate 'reach-like movement'. They found faster reaction times for 'graspable' objects and concluded that affordance does play a role in motor activation. Given that humans are social beings, the ability to perceive other people's movements is an important skill. An interesting study had observers view the movement of lights attached to the joints of a person dressed in black in the confines of a darkened room (Johansson 1973). The accuracy of perceived movement was achieved with only six lights placed on various points on the body ('point-lights'). The level of competency in motion detection was further explored by Runeson and Frykholm (1983). In their study people (with the same light placement set-up) performed actions consistent with how they would naturally do them versus how they think the opposite gender would. The correct gender identification occurred at 85 per cent but reducing to 75 per cent when deception of gender was used. This suggests that, not only are we good at detecting human motion, but we are also able to identify gender based on this motion. Even new-borns appear to have an innate ability to detect motion relating to living creatures, especially humans (Pinto 2006). This makes perfect sense given how reliant new-borns and infants are on human contact and care. This raises the question of whether, in addition to the detection of faces, human motion also receives specialised processing. Evidence suggests that when provided with limited sensory information (i.e. bottom-up processing), top-down processing plays an important role in perceiving human motion. We might ask is this, therefore, reflected in the way the brain functions (see Box 3.7)?

BOX 3.7   BRAIN AND HUMAN MOTION DETECTION

Our ability to detect human motion exceeds the success rates for the detection of other animal movement (Shiffrar and Thomas 2013). There are designated areas of the brain that appear most active when detecting human motion. Areas such as the superior temporal sulcus and the inferior frontal gyrus are involved in the recognition of human actions and the interpretation of the underlying goals of these actions respectively. There is evidence from neurocognitive brain imagery that the super temporal sulcus plays a more important role in detecting human motion than any other type of non-biological motion (Gilaie-Dotan, Kanai, Bahrami, Rees et al. 2013). So why is biological, especially human, motion special? Some argue this is because we can both perceive and create motion. There is some support for this when individuals with damage to parts of the motor cortex have problems associated with interpreting a person's movement. Others argue that with increased experience of human movement our visual system becomes more sensitised to it. Again, there is some support for this. Jacobs, Pinto and Shiffrar (2004) found that practice makes perfect. Participants observed different walkers who wore dark clothes and had point-lights attached to their joints. Of the walkers they had previously seen, their identification rate was higher than it was for non-familiar walkers. Atkinson, Dittrich, Gemmel and Young (2004) found evidence to support the view that human motion provides us with emotional and social data; useful in guiding our responses to others. They showed how body movements and posture (using point-lights) provide information regarding the human emotional state. Actors, whose faces were covered, expressed emotions of fear, anger, sadness, disgust and happiness using body movement. A detection rate of 80 per cent for emotions such as fear, sadness and happiness was explained by exaggerated movement. When we observe what others do, we can imitate or mirror their actions (to some extent). Interestingly, this ability arises from sensorimotor neurons in the brain known as 'mirror neurons' (see Chapter 8). Areas of the brain such as the inferior frontal gyrus and inferior parietal lobe are associated with mirror neuron activation. These areas are also involved in the perception of motion and in the production of actions. It has been suggested that mirror neurons enable us to understand the intention behind the action, which improves significantly when the context of the action is also present. Understanding actions involves a combination of mirror neurons and cognitive processing in the prefrontal cortex (Lingnau and Petris 2013).

SUMMARY

Our focus has been on how we attend to and process sensory information in our environment. Attention is key to how we perceive the world, in that sensory information is guided by what we see, hear, smell, taste or touch. The models of attention have been inspired by Cherry's Cocktail Party Effect, where we can tune in to other conversations when we hear our name or hear something pertinent to us. Most models of attention use the notion of a bottleneck but differ in where it is located; some have no bottleneck. When task demands are simple or one action is automated, we can perform both successfully at the same time. Hence, we can divide our attention. This is lost once the demands of one task requires our full attention, such as approaching a complicated road junction. In this situation, our ability to have a conversation is compromised. Attention helps us to process relevant sensory stimuli and enables these to be processed fully for interpretation. This bottom-up processing is useful especially when learning new information for the first time. As our knowledge-base of events increases, we have a memory store in which to draw upon; thereby adopting a top-down processing strategy. When our brain provides meaning to stimuli, this is known as perception. We understand our environment by sensing and perceiving objects and how they interact. Gibson claimed we understand objects by their 'affordances', hence direct perception. We use monocular and binocular cues to calculate depth and distance and rely on shape, size and colour constancies to provide information about objects. Our brain has specialised areas for processing human faces and motion, which makes sense given our reliance on human social interaction.

FURTHER READING

Bruce, V. and Tadmor, Y. (2015) Direct perception: Beyond Gibson's (1950) direct perception. In M.W. Eysenck and D. Groome (eds) *Cognitive Psychology: Revisiting the classic studies*. London: Sage.

Bruce, V. and Young, A. (2012) *Face Perception*. Hove: Psychology Press.

Wade, N.J. and Swanston, M.T. (2013) *Visual Perception: An introduction* (3rd edn). Hove: Psychology Press.

Wu, W. (2014) *Attention*. Hove: Psychology Press.

MEMORY AND LEARNING

Throughout our development we are constantly learning new skills and perfecting the skills we have already acquired. In order to achieve this, as we have previously seen in Chapter 2, the architecture of the human brain and its neural connections is structured to enable learning. In infancy the number of synaptic connections far exceed the number we have as adults. This excess of synapses becomes 'pruned' during infancy as part of a process of maintaining only the pertinent connections. According to Creutzfeldt (1977) the structure of our brain is filled with many meaningless, useless and ineffective synaptic connections. By pruning the synaptic landscape of the brain, we create a neural system that is stable and effective. So how is this achieved? It is achieved by interacting with our environment through learning. Learning enables the developing new-born to engage with the environment by performing actions – albeit very limited actions to begin with. These actions will eventually become refined as they are repeated. Such repetition of actions help reinforce stable synaptic connections, which themselves become modified as more effective ways of performing actions are mastered. The acquisition of new skills through learning, however, relies on an individual's ability to remember how they were acquired. This is where the interface between learning and memory is crucial for human development. Cases of individuals, documented by cognitive neuropsychologists, who fail to store information in memory (whether in the short or long term) experience detrimental life consequences. When there are problems in remembering recently performed actions, individuals find it difficult to learn new skills or retain new information. Alternatively, for those who find it difficult to retrieve distant

DOI: 10.4324/9781003014355-4

memories, their ability to perform past skills can be severely compromised. The interface between learning and memory is a dynamic one, where remembering a newly acquired skill can be improved as more skills and new information are assimilated from further learning. Memory can also be fine-tuned through effective learning strategies. The more effective the learning strategy, the more information can be retained effectively in memory.

MEMORY

According to Klahr and MacWhinney (1998) memory is an aspect of information processing because information flows through a series of stages. This flow of information is demonstrated using models. These models are a metaphor for how memory might be structured, and how the flow of information is directed. There are many models which have focused on how memory is structured, and the information processed by different structural components. It is Atkinson and Shiffrin's 1968 multi-store model, however, that is the most well-known. We will begin with the multi-store model and then progress to other models that have been added to this basic structure.

STRUCTURE OF MEMORY

Multi-store model

Atkinson and Shiffrin outlined a model of memory comprising three basic sequential components: sensory store (SS), short-term memory (STM) and long-term memory (LTM) (see Figure 4.1).

The sensory store is considered to be modality specific which means that there is a separate sensory store for both visual and auditory stimuli. Hence, when visual stimuli are presented, SS will very briefly hold a representation of the image seen. In the case of auditory stimuli there is an identical sound-byte. Early researchers such as Sperling (1960), estimated that visual images, for example, remain in SS for 500 milliseconds. Other cognitive psychologists, however, argue that such stimuli are held for longer. This is a reasonable assumption when we consider what we need to do in order to read a passage of prose. Accomplished readers are able to process individual letters and words very quickly in order to maintain the continuity of the act of reading

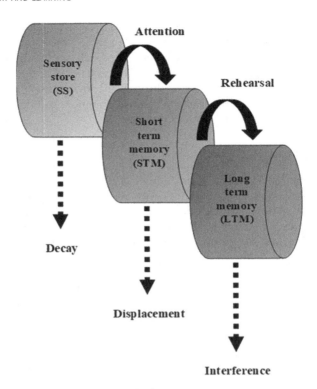

Figure 4.1 The multi-store model of memory
Source: Adapted from Atkinson and Shiffrin (1968)

(see Chapter 6). Moreover, when words are learnt and familiar to us, we are able to perform even more quickly, often by glimpsing over the words. Even with prior knowledge of words and their predictive grammatical order, we still need to hold words in SS long enough for them to be processed. Information held long enough in SS can be transferred to STM provided we attend to it. STM has a limited capacity and is not the most efficient way of remembering something. It is because of this limited capacity that for items in STM to be maintained, they receive rehearsal. According to Atkinson and Shiffrin, LTM has unlimited storage capacity and can retain memories for a lifetime – it therefore makes sense to transfer information to be retained from STM to LTM (see Box 4.1).

BOX 4.1   THE ROLE OF REHEARSAL IN INFORMATION TRANSFERENCE

There are two types of rehearsal known as maintenance (or Type I) and elaborative (or Type II). Maintenance rehearsal is used to keep information long enough in STM to be acted upon. Maintenance rehearsal occurs through repeating information over and over again, such as remembering a new telephone number just long enough to dial it. If the number is engaged and you need to redial, then this number has to be looked up once more and repeated yet again. In other words, the number has not been learned but merely held in STM long enough for the action of dialling. Another example of this, occurs when we receive a series of convoluted directions to a holiday cottage. It is important in this case that these directions are maintained in STM by rehearsing the information repeatedly out loud or to ourselves. If this rehearsal process is interrupted, however, it is very likely that only a few fragments of the directions will be retained. Furthermore, if new relevant information is introduced to the mix, the previous information in STM could become redundant and displaced. Research by Miller (1956) suggested the number of items that can comfortably be rehearsed simultaneously for maintenance in STM is the 'magic' figure of 7 ± 2. Given the conditions of rehearsal and individual differences in ability to rehearse items, individuals typically vary between five and nine. Remembering more numbers can be achieved by what Miller (1956) referred to as 'chunking'. Instead of rehearsing each number individually, numbers can be combined so that in the case of ten numbers, this can become five numbers (i.e. 56, 90, 21, 13 and 97). This reduces the capacity needed and the rehearsal required. Earlier, Ebbinghaus (1879–80), considered how information can be transferred from STM to LTM using repetition. He memorised many lists of three consonant-vowel-consonant nonsense syllables (i.e. ZEQ) using repetition until he could recall the lists correctly. Interestingly, mere maintenance repetition led to LTM of these nonsense syllables. Another phenomenon regarding STM is the serial position curve (Glanzer and Cunitz 1966; see Figure 4.2). Items at the beginning (primacy effect) and end (recency effect) are remembered more effectively than are items in the middle of a sequence. Primacy numbers receive more rehearsal (transferred to LTM) and recency numbers remain active in STM during recall.

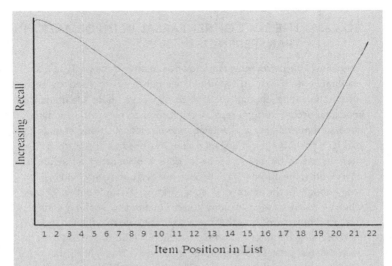

Figure 4.2 Serial position curve

Source: Adapted from Glanzer and Cunitz (1966)

It is a different situation when we want to remember the information on a long-term basis. In this case maintenance rehearsal is replaced by elaborative rehearsal. Here, the information is rehearsed to a profound level of analysis (such as for meaning). By using elaborative rehearsal, it is possible to establish a memory trace that can be stored in LTM (this will be discussed further in relation to Craik and Lockhart's 'levels of processing model'). Hence, it is in STM that stimuli receive processing either to maintain the information long enough to achieve its purpose or to transfer it to LTM.

The retrieval of LTM memories, however, can also be compromised through interference caused by new similar memory traces. Such new memory traces can mistakenly be retrieved at the expense of older ones. This can cause problems concerning the accuracy of when an event first occurred. For example, in many cases of sexual abuse victims sometimes confuse the timeline of when one event occurred over another. This primarily occurs due to non-distinct memories of many separate but similar events that have occurred repeatedly. Support for the multi-store structure comes from research on brain injury. In the case of some brain injuries, the sufferer loses the ability to retain long-term memories but is still able to make use of STM. In other cases, we observe the opposite. Nevertheless, despite empirical support for the multi-store model, cognitive psychologists agree that the structure is over-simplified. Consequently, over the years there have been modifications to the multi-store model: first, to STM by introducing the notion of working memory. The working memory model is complex and consists of many components. Second, additional components have been introduced to the concept of LTM.

Working memory model

The notion of a working memory was introduced by Baddeley and Hitch in 1974 and consisted of three components: central executive, phonological loop and a visuospatial sketchpad. Working memory (WM) was generally considered to be a form of STM but Baddeley and Hitch argued that it is more than this. They provided examples where WM is involved in the execution of complex tasks – hence, the label 'working memory'. WM is also involved in tasks that are not considered to be strictly memory-oriented tasks. For example, in the execution of reading, we store many words comprising a sentence in WM but in order to understand the context of these words, we draw upon other existing knowledge (see Chapter 6). Likewise, when solving a complicated numerical problem, information is held in WM while existing knowledge of formulae and rules are simultaneously applied. In 2000 Baddeley added the episodic buffer (see Figure 4.3).

As Figure 4.3 shows, the four components of WM interact not only with each other but also with LTM. This interaction with LTM demonstrates how learned and known knowledge is drawn from LTM storage to help solve the problem at hand. When reading we draw on both our knowledge of words and grammar and their physical appearance from LTM via the phonological loop and visuospatial sketchpad respectively. These two structures allow us to hear what we are reading and identify what it is

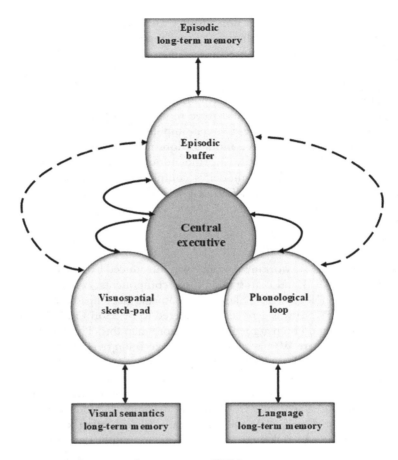

Figure 4.3 The structural components of WM
Source: Adapted from Baddeley and Hitch (1974); Baddeley (2000)

we see written on the page. When we read a sentence aloud, it is the phonological loop that enables us to hold all the words in active memory until the sentence is completed and its meaning understood. The same principle applies to the identification of 'squiggles' representing the words vocalised. Clearly both the visuospatial sketchpad and phonological loop play an important role in reading.

A. CENTRAL EXECUTIVE

The central executive is synonymous with an attentional system. Despite being involved in all complex cognitive activity, however, it is not a depository of information. Instead its role is one of organising and coordinating cognition so that we can achieve our goals. In order to organise and coordinate effectively, Baddeley (1996) identified four executive processes undertaken by the central executive:

1   The ability to focus attention or concentrate on specific events
2   The ability to divide our attention between two events
3   The ability to switch attention across tasks
4   The ability to interact with information stored in LTM

Brain scanning studies provide support for the existence of a central executive. Mottaghy (2006) conducted a review of the studies that had adopted transcranial magnetic stimulation (rTMS; see Chapter 1) as a way of disrupting the function of the prefrontal cortex. Many iconic executive processes were impaired by this procedure which led to the conclusion that the prefrontal cortex is a likely location in the brain for central executive control. What has become known as dysexecutive syndrome, however, demonstrates that there are other areas of the brain involved in executive processing (see Box 4.2).

B. PHONOLOGICAL LOOP

Baddeley and Hitch referred to the phonological loop as being a 'slave' system to the central executive. This is due to the control executed by the central executive which guides our cognition through the manipulation of the WM components. The phonological loop is involved in processing speech–based information that is cycled in a loop for brief storage (see Figure 4.4). This can be seen when we try to remember a novel phone number which we then repeat sub-vocally over and over again until we no longer need to remember it (see Box 4.1). There are two components to the phonological loop: a phonological store and an articulatory process enabling the rehearsal of items.

BOX 4.2   WHAT IS DYSEXECUTIVE SYNDROME?

As we have seen, executive processing involves our ability to direct our attention to relevant and important events in our immediate environment. In Chapter 3, how attention operates and feeds into our perception of the world was discussed in relation to the processing of contents currently active in the brain; the dorsal and ventral attention networks in the case of visual information for instance (see Chapter 2). Directing attention and being able to control this direction is governed by the central executive. Executive processing, however, is complicated and elicits other cognitive processes such as memory, thinking (decision-making) and language. These processes all interact dynamically through the central executive. A good analogy of how the central executive orchestrates cognitive processing is how a thermostat regulates the temperature of a room by switching the heating on and off in response to feedback fluctuations of above (hot) or below (cold) the set-point gauge. Just as the thermostat monitors and regulates, so does the central executive. It constantly monitors and adjusts the direction of cognitive processing in response to demands. Therefore, when the central executive fails to perform effectively, the result is a dysexecutive syndrome (Baddeley 1996). Shimamura (2001) describes dysexecutive syndromes as, "problems controlling their attention, memory, emotion and actions...Deficits in controlling mental processes...including those that involve paying attention, searching for memories, making plans, controlling emotions and initiating actions" (p. 3911). In 1998, Baldo and Shimamura showed that patients who had frontal lobe damage found it difficult to direct their memory searches such as retrieving as many animal names beginning with the letter 'A' as they can. They typically found that these individuals retrieved only around five and six words within a minute with many repetitions. Shimamura (2001) describes dysexecutive syndrome akin to a library without a librarian. In the same vein as a thermostat, Stuss (2011) identified the importance of integrating and coordinating information as an executive process: "[it includes] recognising the differences between what one knows [and] what one believes" (p.761). This type of executive function uses metacognition (see Chapter 7).

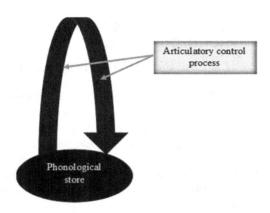

Figure 4.4 A representation of the phonological loop

If there are two tasks performed simultaneously that require access to the same component of working memory such as the phonological loop, then the success of the tasks will be compromised. If, however, one task involved the phonological loop and the other the visuospatial sketchpad, then both can be performed without interfering with each other. It is possible to compromise the performance of the phonological loop whilst listening to a poem by asking the participant to rapidly repeat a word such as 'rhubarb'. Performance is compromised because there is articulatory suppression of the phonological loop. The word 'rhubarb' displaces the words of the poem as it cycles the phonological loop. It therefore becomes very difficult for the participant to keep track of the poem; in a similar vein to what happens to the unattended message in dichotic listening tasks (see Chapter 3).

The phonological store component is responsible for speech perception – in other words understanding what is being said. The articulatory control process enables what is being rehearsed (in the phonological loop) to interact with the phonological store. This makes perfect sense as we need to be able to understand what is being said to us as it is being said. Moreover, being able to monitor what is being said helps us to respond verbally to the speaker. The rehearsal of information in the phonological loop is influenced by two phenomena: word-length effect and phonological similarity effect (see Box 4.3).

BOX 4.3   WHAT INFLUENCES REHEARSAL IN THE PHONOLOGICAL LOOP?

The amount of rehearsal occurring in the phonological loop can be affected by word-length and how similar the words sound (or phonological similarity). Baddeley, Thomson and Buchanan (1975) found evidence that the amount of rehearsal is influenced by the length of the word. Shorter words can be repeated more easily and more often than longer words (Baddeley 2012). Furthermore, the immediate recall of words that are similar in length and rhyme, is reduced in comparison with words that are phonologically different (Larsen, Baddeley and Andrade 2000). Schweppe, Grice and Rummer (2011), however, explained this as resulting from how similar the words sounded (i.e. acoustic similarity) and not the similarity in how these words are articulated (i.e. the movements involved in making the word sounds; articulatory similarity).

C. VISUOSPATIAL SKETCHPAD

Just as the phonological loop is a slave to the central executive so is the visuospatial sketchpad. The visuo–spatial sketchpad stores information about a visual stimulus such as its shape and colour. This enables us to visualise images in our mind and to manipulate them. This can be demonstrated in a game of Tetris where shapes are rotated, in one's mind, to fit together to build a solid block. Another example is when assembling IKEA furniture by following the diagrams; here we have to imagine the parts being rotated to get them to match. Another function of the visuospatial sketchpad is its role in helping us navigate through our surroundings. Logie (1995) outlined two components: visual cache and inner scribe (see Figure 4.5). It is the visual cache, he argues, that stores details about the visual stimulus whereas the inner scribe is concerned with spatial and movement properties. The inner scribe rehearses information contained in the visual cache which is then transferred to the central executive.

D. EPISODIC BUFFER

This component was introduced by Baddeley (2000) as a means of integrating stimuli from the phonological loop and the visuospatial sketchpad. The episodic buffer not only provides storage for these

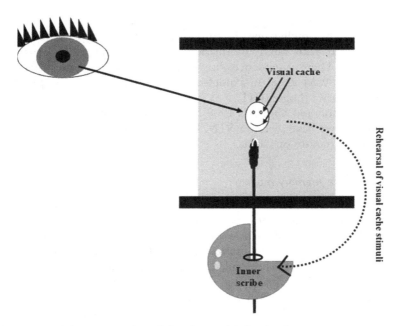

Figure 4.5 A representation of the visuospatial sketchpad

stimuli, but, more importantly, holds 'chunks' of information about episodes or events. Baddeley (2012) describes chunks as referring to entities of integrated information (as many as four) in the episodic buffer. Moreover, the episodic buffer interfaces with other sources of information such as perception and that stored in LTM (see later). This enables us to effectively process and recall long complicated sentences. Baddeley and Wilson (2002) claimed that this is possible because the episodic buffer has the capacity to store such information. Studies generally suggest this ability to hold extensive prose is due to the capacity of the episodic buffer (Allen, Hitch, Mate and Baddeley 2012). The role of the episodic buffer is best explained by Baddeley 2012: "The episodic buffer [is] an essentially passive structure on which bindings [integration of information] achieved elsewhere can be displayed" (p. 17).

The WM model has played an important role in explaining how we can understand and respond so readily during conversation but has also explained the workings of executive processing with brain-damaged individuals. Interestingly, WM capacity has been associated with intelligence. In particular, fluid intelligence which is associated with rapid information processing and its temporary storage. There is evidence showing that individuals with a high-capacity WM excel in complex tasks unlike their low-capacity counterparts (Logie 2011).

Atkinson and Shiffrin's 1968 model has been structurally modified, as we have seen, for STM but there have also been additions to the structure of LTM.

Long-term memory models

Long-term memory is divided into declarative (explicit) and non-declarative (implicit) memory. Declarative memories can be consciously recollected such as events that have occurred and factual information. These memories are therefore explicit in that the learning of them can be recalled. Non-declarative memories are those acquired without being able to stipulate a timeframe of when or recollect how. Non-declarative memories are interesting because they imply that we can learn how to do things without having any conscious recollection. Hence, it is because we have difficulty declaring such memories that they are implicit. Declarative and non-declarative memory are divided further (see Figure 4.6).

It was Tulving (1972) who recognised three different types of LTM: episodic, semantic and procedural. Episodic memory encapsulates memories that can be clustered under individually time-framed events or personal experiences (see Box 4.4).

Hence, the event of having breakfast is more than the recollection of eating a boiled egg at a specific time; it can include the Earl Grey tea drunk from a china cup for instance. Going to the dentist can include not just sitting in the dentist chair but also in the waiting room. Semantic memory is described as a store of world knowledge where information is held as a series of facts. Semantic memory contains factual information that we have learned over the years which is stored in an organised way. How factual information is stored and organised can have a significant influence on the speed of retrieval or the increased probability of forgetfulness. Our world knowledge stored as facts in semantic memory is considered to be hierarchical, which is why a cat can

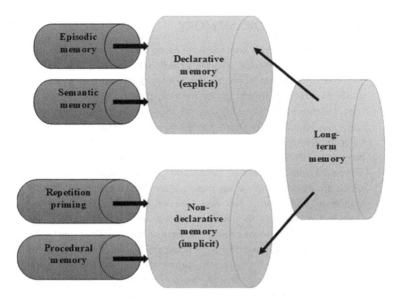

Figure 4.6 A representation of the structure of LTM

be classified as a member of the feline family, as a mammal, an animal and an organism. Hence, facts can be stored under a superordinate category such as animal, a basic-level category such as cat and subordinate category such as Persian blue cat (see Box 4.5). It depends on what we want to retrieve, but basic-level categories tend to provide information that helps inform us about the category and provides some level of distinctiveness. If, however, we want to know something very specific about the category in question then looking towards the subordinate level of detail would be most effective (Rosch, Mervis, Gray, Johnson et al. 1976).

Although episodic and semantic memory are compartmentalised, the two clearly interact. When having breakfast, we have factual information at our fingertips, for we understand the concept of breakfast and what it entails which comes from world knowledge in semantic memory. At the same time, we remember breakfast as an event and a personal experience derived from episodic memory. Does this mean that the two memory systems are not exclusive?

BOX 4.4   EPISODIC MEMORY

Recognition and recall are measures used to test how well we can form episodic memories. We are generally better at remembering pictorial information such as old photographs from high-school yearbooks used as in a study by Bahrick, Bahrick and Wittlinger in 1975. In their study, not only was the recognition of faces and their names as high as 90 per cent, but the longevity of this lasted almost 50 years. Recognition has been explored using the remember/know procedure. This is a simple procedure where participants are presented with a series of items and are later asked to indicate which are 'new' or 'old' when shown again. When providing an 'old' response, participants can elaborate on this by responding 're-member' or 'know'. In the case of 'remember' participants are claiming recollection of seeing the item in the previous presenta-tion. When they respond 'know' they are claiming not to be aware of having seen the item previously; hence, they are familiar with the item from some other source. It has been argued that the difference between the two responses rests on the fact that stronger traces equate with recollection and weaker traces with familiarity. The remember/know procedure has also been used for recall. Participants respond in the same way; 'old' or 'new' and for 'old' a further division of 'remember' or 'know'. In this case, however, with each word presented there was a question asked about it such as 'is it living or non-living?' Most of the words recalled were listed as 'remember'. For each of these words participants correctly answered the question asked. This was not the case for words listed as 'know'. In the case of recognition and recall, the amount of contextualised information processed increases for recalled words listed as 'remember'.

The short answer is that they are two exclusive memory systems (see Box 4.6).

Finally, according to Tulving, procedural memory involves the gradual learning of a skill such as pedalling a bicycle. Such a skill is acquired over time without awareness of what had been learned with each successive trial. It is called procedural because the learner knows how to perform the actions of the skill acquired. Since

BOX 4.5   SEMANTIC MEMORY

We are able to form concepts about our world, often as mental representations. It has been argued that these representations can be abstract in that they do not resemble our sensory information and yet when people are asked to form a representation of any concept provided, they develop a similar one. For example, in the concept of 'loss of freedom', we might represent this as a man dressed in a stripy outfit with a chain and ball attached to his ankle. The concept 'loss of freedom' in itself is quite abstract and difficult to represent directly. Barsalou (2009) argues that the type of representation activated depends on the current goals of the individual. This means that a broken leg of a chair is likely to come to mind if the goal is to be able to sit on the chair. If, however, the goal is to furnish a newly decorated dining room, then the colour and style of the chair might be activated instead. If specific words such as 'grapefruit' or 'half a grapefruit' are given to participants, then the properties they mention are different; outer properties such as the rind for grapefruit versus inner properties like segments for half a grapefruit. This, Barsalou argues, is due to the differences of perceptual input that these words evoke. Semantic memories are not only represented conceptually but can be encapsulated in structures known as schemes. These schemes contain an abundance of information about our knowledge of the world and how it operates. Hence, university students will have a scheme for how lectures work and what lecturers do. Moreover, these schemes will contain scripts outlining a sequence of events. For example, when students arrive in the lecture theatre, they find a place to sit, listen to the lecturer, make notes and ask questions once the lecturer has invited them to do so. Schemes and scripts have been used to explain why eyewitnesses can make errors in their accounts of a crime. Milne and Bull (2003) considered the significance of misleading script-consistent and misleading script-inconsistent suggestive questions put to children who were inter- viewed about a crime. Script-consistent misleading questions contained information that could feasibly have occurred in the crime event recalled by the child. For instance, in scripts of sexual abuse, it is typical for certain behaviours to occur such as getting the child to perform a sexual act. If the question alludes to such actions consistent with the expectations of the sex abuse script, then child witnesses were more likely to agree with the inherent suggestibility in the question even though it hadn't occurred. Alternatively, there was less suggestibility when the question posed misleading script-inconsistent content. In support of their hypothesis, Milne and Bull demonstrated that these children were more resistant to script-inconsistent misleading questions. Schemes and scripts can facilitate memory recall of events but equally they can merge information and the specific details become lost.

Tulving outlined these three facets of LTM, these have been divided according to declarative and non-declarative, such that both procedural and repetition priming are considered as non-declarative memory. Repetition priming involves the presentation of a stimulus that has been shown before or as a similar stimulus. A picture of a house, for example, can have a priming effect on a later picture of a house such that further processing occurs. Repetition priming is an important learning mechanism (see later in the learning section of this chapter).

Thus far our focus has been on the structure of memory which has been primarily based on experimental research in laboratory settings. There has, however, been a movement in the last 40 years towards studying everyday memory. The focus has shifted away from testing the memory of participants for irrelevant stimuli they have just learnt to the study of autobiographical memories.

EVERYDAY MEMORY

According to Neisser (1996), "Remembering is a form of purposeful action" (p. 204). This implies that when we remember information we do so for good reason. We need to be motivated and for the information to fit in with our personal goals. Other factors such as the situations we encounter can influence how motivated we are to engage with information. For example, when giving a PowerPoint presentation to potential business partners, knowing the information and being able to respond to questions will help to 'seal the deal'. This everyday recalling of information is a far cry

BOX 4.6   AMNESIA SPLITS EPISODIC AND SEMANTIC MEMORY

Findings from individuals with different types of **amnesia** have demonstrated that episodic and semantic memories are separate, despite there being a relationship between them. There are two ways of considering amnesia: anterograde (after the onset of amnesia) and retrograde (before the onset of amnesia). In the case of anterograde amnesia, a study of 147 individuals with amnesia caused by damage to the hippocampus exhibited impairment in the formation of new episodic memories while new semantic memories were formed (Spiers, Maguire and Burgess 2001). Bindschaedler, Peter-Favre, Maeder, Hirsbrunner et al. (2011) described deficits to episodic memory but preserved semantic memory in a boy with severe hippocampal damage. In the case of retrograde amnesia, Tulving (2002) found that episodic memories are impaired but semantic ones preserved. More distant episodic memories, however, are remembered more clearly than those closest to the onset of amnesia. Consolidation theory explains this through the extensive processing of older episodic memories received which are then stored away from the hippocampus. Another explanation is that older episodic memories evolve into semantic memories. And finally, some researchers advocate that episodic memories are learnt on one occasion unlike their semantic counterparts.

from the laboratory-based memory research requiring the immediate recall of numbers and words. This is why researchers such as Neisser and Hyman (1982), advocated an ecologically valid way of understanding memory; that is to study memory in as natural a format as possible. If the experiment is conducted in a naturalistic way such that the tasks and stimuli used reflect what we remember on a daily basis, then the findings can be generalised to the wider population. Based on an ecologically valid approach to understanding memory, it makes perfect sense to study autobiographical memory – our own personal memories comprising our own life story.

AUTOBIOGRAPHICAL MEMORY

Parallels between autobiographical and episodic memory are often drawn, and indeed our personal autobiographical memories do tend to have timeframes attached to when specific events occurred. Moreover, in order to make sense of experiences, autobiographical memory needs to interface with semantic memory. Neural network activation (see Chapter 2) engages the frontal, temporal and parietal lobes of the brain which operate together in the retrieval of information that overlaps with autobiographical, episodic and semantic memory (Burianova, McIntosh and Grady 2010). In order to understand the way autobiographical memory might be structured and how our life story can be encapsulated in the memories we form, Conway and Pleydell-Pearce (2000) developed the self-memory system model (see Box 4.7). This model provides a good account of the organisation and timeline of our life story.

Flashbulb memories

Some autobiographical memories are recalled in great clarity and are immortalised in a set timeframe. These have been labelled as flashbulb memories (Brown and Kulik 1977). One method of assessing flashbulb memories, is to ask participants what they were doing (and to embellish this further) when '9/11 occurred' or 'George Floyd lay on the ground' or 'the announcement of the Covid-19 pandemic'. Brown and Kulik argued that surprising events trigger a robust imprint on the memory system that often contain information about the source, location, event details, emotional state of self/others at the time and the impact made. Given the clarity and richness of detail retrieved, such flashbulb memories are not always accurate (Pezdek 2003). Accuracy, however, can be assumed if the content of the flashbulb memory is consistent across time. Unfortunately, researchers have found that the level of consistency is no different from other autobiographical memories (Talarico and Rubin 2003, 2019) and there is no clear division between flashbulb and other autobiographical memories (Brewin 2014).

Lifetime memories

An interesting aspect of autobiographical memory is how difficult we find it to remember events during our first two to three years of life. This is often labelled as 'childhood amnesia' (see Figure 4.8). Why can't we remember events during this age? One theory is that in the early years of life, infants have no self-concept: as demonstrated by the 'rouge on the nose test'. Infants of different age

---

BOX 4.7   STRUCTURE OF AUTOBIOGRAPHICAL MEMORIES

There are two main components of the self-memory system model (Conway and Pleydell-Pearce 2000): an autobiographical memory knowledge base and a working self. The autobiographical memory knowledge base contains three levels of personal information:

1   Lifetime periods – these are periods in a person's life which are demarcated by major situations (e.g. length of time living at home with the parents)
2   General events – these can be frequent or single events (e.g. attending classes or meeting the Queen respectively)
3   Event specific knowledge – this can pertain to pictorial, emotional or semantic information about general events over a lifetime that are temporally (time-based) sequenced

The working self can be concerned with past, present and future selves. Different autobiographical memories will be activated depending on previous, current or future goals and plans and, as such, act as a record of one's life. Therefore, retrieved autobiographical memories can be positive (focusing on successes) or negative (focusing on failures). In Figure 4.7 we can see how the autobiographical memories retrieved are organised, such that there is a theme (i.e. work), a lifetime period (i.e. working for the police), general events (i.e. events relating to working for the police) and event specific knowledge (i.e. specific events relating to events occurring while working for the police).

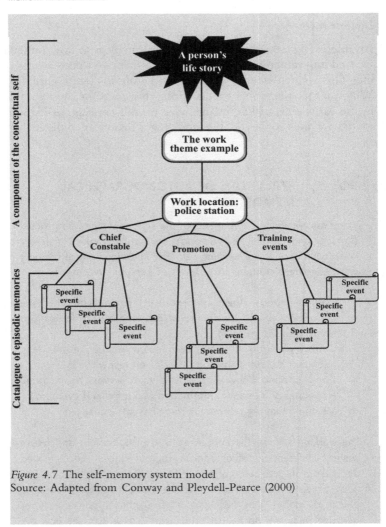

Figure 4.7 The self-memory system model
Source: Adapted from Conway and Pleydell-Pearce (2000)

groups are placed in front of a mirror and a dab of rouge is placed on their nose. When there is no understanding that the image in the mirror is theirs and that they have rouge on their nose, it is concluded they have yet to develop a self-concept. Once self-concept is attained, however, infants laugh at their reflection and

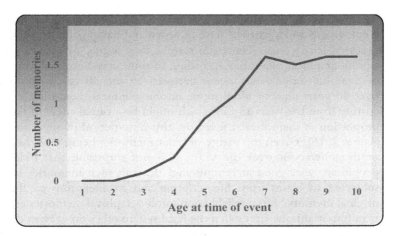

Figure 4.8 Curve of autobiographical memories in early childhood
Source: Adapted from data by Rubin and Schulkind (1997)

try to touch their nose to remove the rouge (Lewis and Brooks-Gunn 1979). Hence, if there is no understanding of the self, then events surrounding the infant will have little personal significance and are unlikely to be remembered (Jack and Hayne 2010). Furthermore, Jack and Hayne describe the development of aspects of cognition, such as self-recognition and language, as precursors to the formation of autobiographical memories. Ma, Li, Li and Zhou (2020) added to this by describing how young children's immature episodic memory will compromise their ability to output memories. In a similar vein, Alberini and Travaglia (2017) conclude that an infant's brain is still developing such that newly experienced events fail to become consolidated into LTM.

When retrieving autobiographical memories throughout the lifespan, differences in how many are retrieved at different ages have been referred to as a reminiscence bump. In terms of the reminiscence bump, the largest number of memories recalled is found to be from the age cross-section of 10–30 years. This reminiscence bump is a cross-cultural phenomenon (Conway, Wang, Hanyu and Haque 2005) and has been explained by the existence of a 'life script'. According to Rubin and Berntsen (2003) a life script provides individuals with a guide to what events we should expect throughout our lifetime. These events include typical occurrences in our lives such as having an education, finding employment and a partner, settling down and having children and death of loved ones. These life scripts, they argue, organise our autobiographical memories according to time snapshots, and most of these life script events occur between 15 and 30 years. Adults over 40 years tend to recall more autobiographical memories occurring from the years 15−30 which might be a causal effect of the proportion of memories arising from this time-period (Koppel and Rubin 2016). Given the nature of older memories being rehearsed or thought about over the years, it is not surprising that older people are very good at reminiscing! But can such memories be subjected to biases from life scripting and to alterations to the original memory? How reliable our autobiographical memories are is an important question when the legal system relies on eyewitness memories to solve criminal cases.

Eyewitness memories

Eyewitness memories have come under intense scrutiny. Given that eyewitness accounts are often used to provide police with information about the 'what', 'when' and 'who' of a crime, the level of accuracy is paramount in order to ensure the real perpetrator is apprehended. Eyewitnesses provide testimonials of what they have witnessed; often by providing descriptions of the event, answering police enquiries and identifying the potential suspect. Many studies have demonstrated that there are potential errors at each stage of this process. A real-life example of the murder of Sweden's Foreign Minister, Anna Lindh, serves well to illustrate this. Witnesses to this provided information to the police within a month of the attack. Granhag, Ask, Rebelius, Ohman et al. (2013) compared the eyewitness testimonies with footage of the culprit on CCTV and found their descriptions to be flawed, in fact 42 per cent of what they reported was error-ridden.

The repercussions of a jury believing the evidence provided by a single eyewitness can be problematic if there is no other physical corroboratory evidence. Jurors do, however, place much confidence in the accuracy of an eyewitness. As many as 37 per cent of people in the US are of the view that the evidence provided by a confident eyewitness is enough to base a conviction on (Simons and Chabris 2011). Furthermore, even eyewitnesses can be duped by their own confirmation bias; in other words, they have scripts about what to expect in specific events. In the case of a bank robbery script, there are expectations of one or two men wearing balaclavas, holding guns and a money sack. Bartlett (1932), arguably one of the first researchers to study everyday memory, addressed this problem when he illustrated how schemas can adulterate our records of events by reconstructing the original memory trace. This problem can be exacerbated by what happens after the witnessed event; how police questions are framed post-event and how eyewitnesses identify potential suspects (see Box 4.8).

Another area of everyday memory that influences how we organise our daily activities is prospective memory. It is different from other types of memory discussed thus far in that it concerns future, and not past, events (i.e. retrospective). Graf (2012) described prospective memory as, "the cognitive function we use for formulating plans and promises, for retaining them, and for recollecting them subsequently either at the right time or on the occurrence of appropriate cues" (pp. 7–8).

PROSPECTIVE MEMORY

Zogg, Woods, Sauceda, Wiebe et al. (2012) reviewed the literature concerning the formation and execution of intentions in prospective memory and concluded that there are a number of stages (see Figure 4.9).

During the formation of an intention, we often attach a cue that will enable us to remember what it is we want to do. For example, we might want to send an email to a friend and so we set up a cue to trigger the action. An obvious cue to help us remember to send the email would be when we sit at our desk in front of the computer to open our email server. Once the cue is detected, then the intention to send an email is retrieved. There might be competing intentions such as having to send work-related emails which is why we may have to refer to long-term memories; hence, prospective and retrospective memories often interact with one another. Finally, once the intention to email a friend is triggered and the opportunity to do so is present, then sending the email is

BOX 4.8 HOW GOOD ARE WE AS EYEWITNESSES?

Elizabeth Loftus was the prime instigator of a method for studying the impact post-event information has on the original memory trace of an event. She, and her colleagues, demonstrated through a series of experiments the fragility of eyewitness memories. The original memories could be distorted by misleading information often presented accidentally through police questioning. Misleading information was found to interact with the original memory trace such that details originally absent became present. Misleading information can occur through seemingly innocent questions such as, 'did the man you saw have a dark beard?' or 'did you see a large knife?' This phenomenon was labelled the misinformation effect and continues to be studied even after 46 years since the study by Loftus and Palmer (1974) was conducted. The misinformation effect is alive and kicking although it is possible to reduce the size of effect by instructing eyewitnesses to be wary of misleading information. Changes to how police conduct interviews of eyewitnesses was initially driven by Fisher, Geiselman, Holland and MacKinnon (1984) and Fisher and Geiselman (1992) with the introduction of the cognitive interview. This interview technique highlights all the flaws of the standard police interview. This is because the cognitive interview contains a series of phases (that investigators should follow) based on sound memory research which has proven to be the most effective way of attaining unadulterated information from eyewitnesses. The cognitive interview has been improved over the years through the addition of memory enhancing techniques derived from sound memory research (Milne and Bull 2003; Paulo, Albuquerque, Vitorino and Bull 2017). Inappropriately phrased questions (Milne and Bull 1999) and suggestive tactics which have caused eyewitnesses to be swayed by misleading information (Bull 2019), can clearly interfere with the original memory trace of the event.

Although the misinformation effect is an important factor in how well memories are retrieved, there are other reasons for the ineffective retrieval of memories such as levels of intoxication, how long after the event the witness recalls information and what questions are actually asked (Jores, Colloff, Kloft, Smailes et al.

2019). Are we any good at identifying perpetrators? Our memory for faces far exceeds our ability to recall names and other forms of verbal information. And for the most part our performance at recognising faces is reasonably high at 90 per cent. Laboratory based research, however, puts face recognition at 70 per cent when there are changes of pose (Bruce 1982) and context (Watkins, Ho and Tulving 1976). We tend to be confident when recognising faces (Brewer and Wells 2011) as was borne out by a correlation of +0.38 between accuracy and confidence (Odinot, Wolters and van Koppen 2009). Police use line-ups for eyewitnesses to identify a potential suspect from five or so other individuals who may resemble the suspect in terms of height and weight. By considering the data from 314 real life line-ups, Valentine, Pickering and Darling (2003) found that of 640 eyewitnesses, only 40 per cent identified the suspect. While 20 per cent got it wrong, as many as 40 per cent were unable to make a decision. Horry, Halford, Brewer, Milne and Bull (2013) conducted a meta-study of 833 real life line-ups with 709 eye-witnesses based in England. Crimes of a different nature such as robbery and rape were considered. The overall identification rate from line-ups was 46 per cent, with the selection of an innocent person at 18 per cent and non-selection at 36 per cent. These rates are comparable with Valetine et al.'s findings. Line-ups are now largely conducted by showing eyewitnesses footage of a series of faces including the suspect (resembling a line-up). In line with this approach, Taylor, Workman and Hall (2018) showed participants black and white CCTV style footage of a shoplifter followed by a face recognition test. The faces were shown one at a time, which, once all viewed, were repeated as is the norm (this is known as a sequential line-up). They also included a 'lookalike' face which was shown before or after the suspect's face (including its repetition). Their findings showed that the identification rate was higher when the lookalike appeared before the suspect, whereas the misidenti-fication rate was higher when the lookalike appeared after the suspect (hence, later in the sequence). There are problems, albeit of a different nature, with line-ups presented live or using footage.

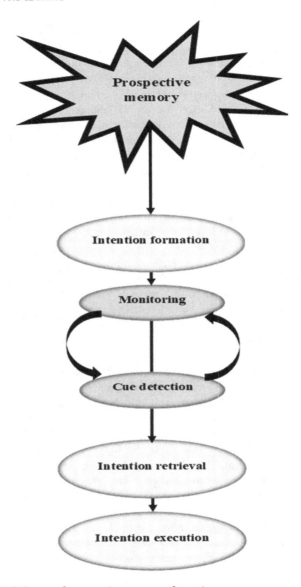

Figure 4.9 Stages of prospective memory formation
Source: Adapted from Zogg, Woods, Sauceda, Wiebe et al. (2012)

executed. Prospective memory can be time-based and/or event-based. For example, a time-based intention might entail the action of being at the airport at a specific time to catch a flight. In the case of an event-based intention, teaching a ballroom formation dance troupe a new step might be triggered when the next rehearsal session is due. Event-based intentions are more likely to be successfully executed than are time-based ones (Cona, Arcara, Tarantino and Bisiacchi 2012). The reasons for this are because event-based actions:

- are easier when externally triggered
- are less demanding
- receive more processing activity

Prospective memory plays an important role in our daily activity and even more so in specific types of occupations (e.g. train drivers, pilots, traffic controllers, those who monitor underground tube systems). In such jobs monitoring controls through focused attention (see Chapter 3) and remembering to execute intended actions is paramount in insuring the safety of passengers on board. An influential explanation of how prospective memory operates is the multi-process theory developed by Einstein and McDaniel in 2005. In the multi-process theory, ongoing tasks are separated according to the amount of focused attention received. They argue that cues play an important role in tasks that do not receive focused attention. Scullin, McDaniel and Shelton, however, expanded this theory in 2013, by invoking the use of top-down and bottom-up processing (see Chapter 3) to explain why some prospective memories require monitoring while others are retrieved automatically. They argue that top-down attention actively searches for cues when intentions are being monitored; in other words, performing tasks where a cue is expected. When a cue has already been triggered, however, bottom-up processing takes over; this induces automatic retrieval to enact the intention. An example of these processes working in tandem is when you are out of the work context, like shopping for clothes, then the need to monitor a cue, such as the boss, is irrelevant. Top-down processing involved with searching for the boss under these circumstances would be a redundant activity. But, once at work, by passing a series of offices, the intention to speak to the boss is enacted and searching for the boss then becomes an active pursuit – hence, top-down processing occurs.

How accurately our intentions are communicated has become an area of interest especially in the light of terrorist security breaches at airports. In 1981, Johnson and Raye outlined the involvement of reality monitoring in the verbal communication of our experiences. This means that our memories are constructed in an organised way by separating the details of events and sub-events and so on based on how we perceived them. When we are asked to describe an experience, we use a reality monitoring approach to access the details accordingly. Johnson and Raye argued that the differentiation between truthful and fabricated accounts of our experiences is down to how memories have been constructed. For instance, in the case of a genuine account of a holiday in Spain, reality monitoring is used to extract the perceptual details. For fabricated accounts, however, there is no perceptual experience to draw upon, and instead these are built using cognitive routes such as making up a story. This line of capturing deception has proven fruitful (see Box 4.9).

All forms of memory require information to be processed so that it can be remembered. The creation of memories occurs when information is encoded and stored. But in order to encode and then store information we need to acquire it. This acquisition of information is what we call learning. Memory and learning, as mentioned in the introduction, are closely entwined. In fact, dividing cognitive processes into memory and learning can be thought of as an arbitrary distinction.

LEARNING

When we think about learning we often envisage various mnemonic techniques that help us to remember facts. **Mnemonics** will be explored later. First, however, we will consider Craik and Lockhart's (1972) levels of processing approach. According to Wheeler (2020) the levels of processing approach is a good example of a learning theory, which is why we will begin with their work.

BOX 4.9   LYING INTENTIONS AS A SOURCE OF CAPTURING DANGEROUS INDIVIDUALS

In the fight against terrorism, prospective memory offers investigators another avenue for detecting deception. Instead of a retrospective approach (e.g. asking questions about an event that has already occurred), suspected individuals can be asked questions tapping into their intentions for travelling to or entering from another country. Prospective memory research has shown that the use of sensory information (in particular auditory and visual) and temporal details (such as the order of when events occurred) helps to establish a truthful from a fabricated account (Masip, Sporer, Garrido and Herrero 2005). The empirical evidence for this success comes from the accuracy rates obtained in separating fabricated from genuine accounts; above chance level between 63- 82 per cent (Vrij, Blank and Fisher 2018). Vrij, Granhag, Mann and Leal (2011) asked passengers at international airports to either give a genuine account about their forthcoming journey or to lie about it. They found that the liars added an abundance of less plausible details about their journey which were also littered with contradictions. Despite a similar amount of details provided by liars and truth-tellers, the latter gave a plausible and stable account. Kleinberg, van der Toolen, Vrij, Arntz et al. (2018) conducted an online study where participants provided either truthful or fabricated statements about their intentions for the coming weekend. They found that those lying included many more references to location and people than those who were telling the truth about what they intended to do over the weekend. Kleinberg et al. concluded that such over detailing can be used as a signal of false accounts. This, they argued, suggests that liars are more likely to over prepare their statement by flourishing it with names of people and places to sound convincing and therefore believable. Liars do this as they are not sure "what a truthful statement about an intended action might look like so that they include unrealistically many specific pieces of information out of precaution to sound believable" (Kleinberg et al. 2018, p. 10). It might be possible, in the future, to ask people passing through security gates at airports questions about their travel intentions. In the future, the instalment of 'names entity recognition' (NER) detectors, could be used to analyse the language content in the responses to questions about travel intentions. And based on the findings from prospective memory research, those with dangerous deceptive intentions might be captured.

LEVELS OF PROCESSING APPROACH

Craik and Lockhart believed that the longevity of information and its transference to LTM depended on how effectively it was processed during learning. During learning, new information is processed further and is eventually encoded. Encoding information is a way of converting it into a construct that can be stored as a memory. The process of encoding involves electrochemical changes in the neurons of the brain such that novel events and sensations we experience become stored as new memories. In other words, the brain can be rewired to accommodate these new memories. For Craik and Lockhart, it is what we do with incoming information that determines how well it is encoded and remembered. They claimed that information can be encoded in different ways. Information can be encoded very superficially such as looking for graphemic features of a written text (is it lower or upper case?). In the case of pictorial information such as a human face, superficial processing (or shallow processing) might mean a simple decision of whether the face is female or male. This shallow processing is not the most effective way of remembering text or faces and unsurprisingly often leads to forgetting. Information processed in this way is less likely to lead to effective encoding and the formation of a memory trace in LTM. The intermediate phonetic level, however, is concerned with how words sound. In many studies, participants are asked to decide whether a series of words rhyme with the target word. This task involves phonetic processing unlike the shallow graphemic level, and, according to Craik and Lockhart, accounts for the higher level of recalled words and reduced forgetting. In the case of pictorial stimuli such as faces, participants are instructed to decide which facial feature is the most distinctive. This leads to increased recognition performance over shallow decisions of the sex of the face shown. Deep semantic levels of processing encourage participants to analyse the information in a meaningful way. This induces elaborative rehearsal that leads to robust encoding of information. Words are compared to other words for their conceptual relatedness, for example, while faces are analysed for their emotional content to inform decisions about the person's personality. Studies where the levels of processing approach was adopted use three different 'orienting tasks'; one for each level (see Box 4.10).

As pointed out in Box 4.10, learning can be incidental or implicit. A quote provided by Cleeremans and Jiménez (2002) defines what is meant by implicit learning:

> ... the process through which we become sensitive to certain regularities in the environment (1) in the absence of intention to learn about these regularities, (2) in the absence of awareness that one is learning, and (3) in such a way that the resulting knowledge is difficult to express.
>
> Cleeremans and Jiménez (2002), p. 20.

IMPLICIT LEARNING

Implicit learning is impervious to differences in age (Simon, Vaidya, Howard and Howard 2012) and IQ (Janacsek and Nemeth 2013). In other words, the course of implicit learning occurs regardless of whether an old or young person has an IQ of 100 or 135. Implicit learning occurs even if an individual has memory problems such as amnesia due to the robustness of systems involved. Brooks and Baddeley (1976) demonstrated deficits in explicit verbal learning in amnesic patients but implicit learning in the solution of specific motor tasks (i.e. the **rotary pursuit task**). Graf and Schacter (1985) found performance on an implicit word completion task showed similar learning across controls and amnesic patients. Implicit learning in this case occurs as missing letters in words are slowly completed as they are presented more than once – this is known as priming. Amnesic patients could complete the words even though they could not remember previously seeing the uncompleted words and being tested (Graf and Schacter 1985). Furthermore, these systems show less individual variability than those systems supporting explicit learning. A technique commonly used to separate implicit from explicit learning is known as the process–dissociation procedure first introduced by Jacoby (1991).

BOX 4.10   IT'S NOT WHAT YOU DO BUT THE WAY THAT YOU DO IT

A multitude of studies have adopted the levels of processing approach using verbal and pictorial material. These studies are designed such that they normally contain three types of orienting task, each used as a way of distracting the participant from the true nature of the experiment (to recall verbal stimuli such as words or sentences or to recognise pictorial stimuli such as objects or unfamiliar faces). This means that participants are instructed to perform the orienting task but are not informed there will be a memory test at the end. In this case, recall or recognition performance during the test are considered to be examples of incidental learning. In other words, learning takes place without awareness (also referred to as implicit learning). A typical design used to test the effectiveness of levels of processing on memory performance for word recall is as follows:

- Intentional versus incidental learning

    - Intentional: participants are instructed to learn the words in preparation for a memory test
    - Incidental: participants perform one of three orienting tasks and are not informed of a memory test

- Orienting tasks

    - Shallow graphemic: participants are instructed to identify whether words are written in upper case or lower case
    - Intermediate phonetic: participants are instructed to identify words which rhyme with the target word
    - Deep semantic: participants are instructed to identify words for their conceptual relatedness

- Test phase

    - All participants are instructed to recall as many of the words as possible

There have been many studies using this basic design, some comparing all three orienting tasks and others concentrating on only two. Hyde and Jenkins (1973) explored intentional versus incidental learning for 24-word lists. They compared deep semantic with shallow graphemic processing and found a deeper processing advantage under both intentional and incidental learning conditions. They demonstrated that the intentionality of learning was not the important factor but rather the orienting task used. Findings such as these have been replicated many times using verbal or pictorial material (Beales and Parkin 1984; Hager 1985). The levels of processing approach has not been without its critics, so much so that Craik and Tulving (1975) made revisions by firstly changing the name to 'elaborate processing'. Another important change was the realisation that even shallow levels of processing involve a degree of simultaneous semantic processing. This minimal core encoding is what enables meaning to be added to words during shallow orienting tasks. Craik and Tulving used the term elaborate processing to mean that the input is related to what is already known about it. Hence, deeper semantic processing involves elaboration which, in turn, increases the retrieval routes, providing easier access to the information. This means the way information is encoded is what facilitates retrieval and the robustness of memory traces in long-term storage.

In his 'false fame' experiment, participants were shown a list of names during the first session. In the second session participants were divided into two groups. For one of the groups, they were informed that none of the names belonged to famous people. Therefore, in the second session they were to respond 'no' to the question of fame (this is the exclusion task). In the other group, participants were told that the names belonged to obscure famous people and when asked if they were famous names during the second session they were to respond 'yes' if they remembered the name from the first session and/or knew them to be famous (this is the inclusion task). According to Jacoby, saying 'yes' in the exclusion condition is likely to be a result of the name being remembered unconsciously (implicit learning). Responding 'yes' in the inclusion condition is a consequence, he argued, of the name being remembered either consciously (explicit learning) or unconsciously. The latter implies an interaction between the two systems. Implicit learning has been studied in relation to how typists learn to navigate the keyboard – do they explicitly or implicitly learn the positions of the keys? (see Box 4.11).

When we intentionally learn information, it is important that we leave time to consolidate what we have learnt. Sometimes we even say, 'think about it' or 'sleep on it'. This alludes to an element of mulling over information which can help with the consolidation process. Consolidation is not a new concept. Hintzman (1974) considered consolidation as an explanation for the deficient processing of the same stimulus when presented immediately after it is first shown. He argued that when the same stimulus is presented in quick succession, there is a time period necessary for the cognitive processes of consolidation to occur. This means that during the second presentation, processing of the first has not yet finished. The moral here is that, when learning a passage from Shakespeare, having a rest from it by reading a different passage might serve as a better learning strategy than to continuously read the same passage. More about this learning technique will be considered in the section on repetition priming, aka the 'spacing effect'.

BOX 4.11   TYPING IMPLICITLY OR EXPLICITLY?

Interestingly, you would think that typists with an average experience of 11.4 years could easily write the letters correctly on a blank keyboard. Snyder, Ashitaka, Shimada, Ulrich et al. (2014) found, however, the level of accuracy to be poor as only 57.3 per cent (translating to 14.9 letters) were correctly located. And yet they must know where the letters are or else their typing would be littered with errors. Snyder et al. substituted the 'QWERTY' keyboard layout for the 'Dvorak' one and asked typists to practise using this keyboard for two hours. Once practice was completed, participants were asked to write the letters correctly on a blank keyboard. Accuracy was at the same level as for the QWERTY keyboard for which they had many years of experience. Snyder et al.'s findings show the importance of implicit learning and how quickly typists can retrieve letter placement on the keyboard without explicit learning and awareness.

CONSOLIDATION

Consolidation can be likened to a backup disk in our hard-drive that we use to store documents. Using this analogy, consolidation is a physiological process that puts related information together and transfers it to LTM. Consolidation theory can account for why we forget information – we simply fail to allow recently learnt information to be consolidated (see Box 4.12). Wixted (2004) claimed that newly acquired memories are still being consolidated which is why they are vulnerable to being forgotten; the forgetting curve for newly learnt information supports this contention (see Figure 4.10).

Earlier, procedural memory was introduced as a type of long-term memory that is non-declarative (no conscious recollection required). Repetition priming, where a stimulus is repeated, is a very effective way of learning material without conscious awareness.

REPETITION PRIMING

There are two forms of repetition priming: perceptual and conceptual. In the case of perceptual priming, the repetition of a stimulus increases the probability of its perceptual characteristics being recognised; contained in pictures or faces. Conceptual priming, alternatively, facilitates the recall of information such as meaning usually contained in stimuli of a verbal nature. Learning without awareness has support from numerous studies of amnesic patients whose memory performance improved under conceptual and perceptual priming (Levy, Stark and Squire 2004). Interestingly, learning can be enhanced depending on how repetition priming is ordered (see Box 4.13).

The use of mnemonics was briefly touched upon at the beginning of this section. Mnemonics has certainly been successful as a memory aid to learning information.

MNEMONICS

Mnemonics are defined as encoding strategies that facilitate the organisation and chunking of novel information. By doing this the to-be-learned information becomes easier to remember as its meaningfulness increases. Bellezza (1996) argued this is due to the

BOX 4.12   DO WE FORGET BECAUSE WE ARE POOR AT LEARNING?

We have seen how easily items in STM can be forgotten, especially if information is not effectively rehearsed so that it can be transferred to LTM. Under these circumstances, information can be lost. Maintenance rehearsal helps in the retention of information in STM long enough for us to take appropriate action, such as dialling an unfamiliar number. Information, however, is lost because it hasn't received sufficient processing for the formation of a memory trace. In other words, the information has not been consolidated. This concept can equally apply to long-term memories. We can ask the question, why do we forget information that has been stored in LTM? Is it a case of sufficient consolidation for information to be transferred to LTM but not enough to be effectively consolidated in an existing network of memories? Understanding forgetting from LTM was first explored by Ebbinghaus in 1885. He is renowned for learning lists of nonsense syllables, known as consonant-vowel-consonant (CVC) trigrams. After learning these lists, he relearned them again between 21 minutes and 31 days later. He recorded the extent of forgetting using a measure he introduced called 'savings'. As Figure 4.10 demonstrates, the savings method enabled Ebbinghaus to ascertain the extent of forgetting by recording how many lists of CVC trigrams he could recall. By relearning the lists and recording the number recalled, the impact of savings was calculated. Ebbinghaus concluded that forgetting newly learnt material occurred very quickly after one hour but slowed gradually with relearning. Relearning the lists allowed him to reconsolidate the information. There have been various explanations of why we forget information from LTM. An early theory was that of decay. This claims that memories fade over time. Despite some biological support for this, many argue that other factors are operating to cause the loss of these memories. It could be that memory traces decay over time when they are no longer retrieved. Hence, they need ongoing consolidation; supporting the adage of 'use it or you lose it'. Interference was another theory put forward. Interference could be proactive (previously learnt information disrupts the consolidation of new information) or retroactive (newly learnt information disrupts the retrieval of old information). Hence, old information interferes with the new and new information interferes with the old respectively. In 2018, Sosic-Vasic, Hille, Kröner, Spitzer et al. investigated how learning can disturb memory. They asked participants to learn lists of German–Japanese paired words. Participants had to recall the Japanese word when its paired German word was presented as a cue. When, however, new lists of German–Japanese paired-words were learnt, recall of the first lists was down by 20 per cent. Hence, retroactive interference damaged the consolidation of previously learnt word-pairings. Tulving (1979) introduced the encoding specificity principle as an explanation of cue-dependent forgetting. If information encapsulated in the memory trace mismatches information available during retrieval, it becomes difficult to recall the required information. Memory traces contain other encoded information such as the context in which information was learnt. Godden and Baddeley (1975) demonstrated this when divers learnt information underwater but had to retrieve it on land. Divers best recalled information when underwater; hence, the context served as a cue for retrieval. This implies that other information is covertly consolidated during learning. It is possible that if information is not effectively consolidated during learning, then other information, such as the context, can be forgotten. Memory traces, however, might be triggered when appropriate cues are reinstated.

intention to learn and the extent of effortful processing used. The information becomes embellished with knowledge encapsulated in existing schemas; in other words, the encoding and retrieval is enhanced through elaboration (Balch 2005). Furthermore, in line with Paivio's (1986) dual-coding theory, the use of mnemonics helps create two or more information codes that increase avenues of retrieval. This means that information codes could be for example, visual or verbal. McDaniel and Einstein (1986) claimed that by mentally visualising interacting bizarre images, the memorability of information can be increased. Bizarre interacting imagery can be used to improve learning words from another language such as a horse kicking an eye. Spanish for horse is 'caballo' and the pronunciation of the second segment overlaps with the English sound for 'eye'.

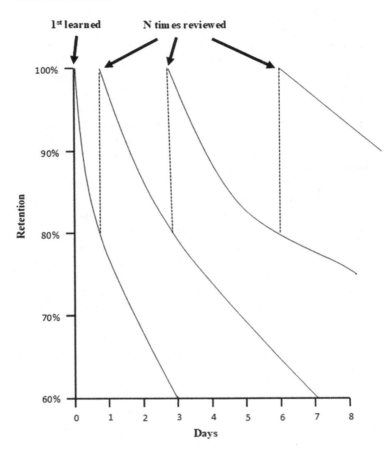

Figure 4.10 Forgetting curve for information learnt
Source: Adapted from Ebbinghaus (1885)

Mnemonics such as acronyms have been used to aid in the learning of reading music. The lines for the treble clef, for example, can be learned by the saying, 'every good boy deserves fruit' (EGBDF). The saying, 'King Phillip came over for good soup', can be used to remember the order of taxonomic categories in biology: kingdom, phylum, class, order, family, genus and species. Keyword mnemonics are found to be useful in remembering difficult words such as harpaxophobia which refers to a fear of robbers. Carney and

BOX 4.13   THE SPACING EFFECT

Both recall and recognition of verbal and visual stimuli can be facilitated by their repetition. Repetition priming can be of a 'massed' or 'distributed' format. When items are presented in the massed format, the first and second presentation occur in quick succession. In the distributed format the second presentation of an item occurs at some point later in a sequence of other items. For example,

A, B, A, C, B or A, B, C, D, E, F, G, A, H, C

When there is one item between the first and second presentation a 'lag1' effect occurs. This increases item memorability from a massed format (e.g. A, A, B, B, C, C). The greater the number of interpolated (in between) items between the first and second presentations, the greater the memorability of the target item. Hence, distributed repetition facilitates learning more than massed repetition. This phenomenon is referred to as the spacing effect. Russo, Parkin, Taylor and Wilks (1998) demonstrated facilitated recall and recognition of words and unfamiliar faces using the spacing effect format. Taylor (2018) adopted the spacing effect to explore the robustness of implicit learning for unfamiliar face-name pairs under conditions of focused and divided attention. Due to the differences in processing (perceptual priming for faces and conceptual priming for names), when attention was divided the recognition of faces remained the same, but the recognition of names was impaired. Moreover, when unfamiliar faces were presented as two different poses during learning, participants did not perform as well, and the advantages incurred under distributed learning were lost. Did they fail to recognise the two poses belonging to the same face? Even when asked to detect whether the second presentation belonged to the same face, those high scorers performed the same as low scorers at test. This implies that it makes no difference whether they identify the two poses as belonging to the same face. In terms of learning where does this leave us? Perceptual repetition priming increases learning when item presentations are the same; in this case faces. Learning that relies on perceptual characteristics is therefore more successful when the material is kept constant.

Levin (2008) conjured up an interactive image of robbers stealing a harp. Those who learnt the word using repetition fared badly in comparison to those using this mnemonic. Shimamura (1984) even introduced an acronym for mnemonics, 'MOVA' – meaningfulness, organisation, visualisation and attention!

The 'peg-word' method is an effective way of remembering new words/concepts by using imagery and an existing structure from which to pin new words as images. A structure consists of a number of 'pegs' which have to be learned first, so that another image or concept encapsulated as an image can be attached, one to each 'peg'. An example of this would be rhyming pegs such as '1 is for bun', '2 is for shoe' and '3 is for tree'. In this case the rhyming facilitates the learning, and the bizarre interactive imagery the learned cues for retrieval. The method of loci is another example of this type of mnemonic. Simonides (c.556 – c.468 BCE), a Greek poet, used a form of mental imagery known as the method of loci. His ability to use mental imagery helped him to identify and locate where people were seated before they were crushed under the collapsed roof of a banqueting hall. The method of loci can be applied by learning a series of objects in different locations. For example, a sofa in the lounge, the breadbin in the kitchen, a sink in the bathroom and a wardrobe in the bedroom could comprise a structure of a house. Once these images are remembered, then further images can be pinned to these locations. Words such as dog, tulip, swimmer and balloon could be visualised as a dog jumping on the sofa, a tulip sticking out of the breadbin, a swimmer sitting in the sink and a balloon attached to the wardrobe.

The use of rhymes, songs and stories has proven to be good mnemonics. Students who learned to sing what VanVoorhis (2002) called 'stat jingles', outperformed those (on a test), who merely read the concepts aloud. The explanation for this lies in the increased chunking of information which is transferred to LTM. VanVoorhis also claimed that the 'stat jingles' were enjoyable and motivated students to learn. Learning and memory are intricately entwined.

SUMMARY

Memory models provide a structured way of conceptualising the flow of information from short-term to long-term storage.

Atkinson and Shiffrin provided the backbone structure of memory from which other components have been added, such as working memory, and to long-term memory, episodic, semantic and procedural. Whereas episodic concerns memories of events and semantic our world knowledge, procedural involves skill acquisition. Both episodic and semantic memory are considered as declarative (involvement of conscious awareness) whereas procedural memory is non-declarative (no involvement of conscious awareness). Episodic and semantic memories can be influenced by schemas. Our memories of events can be embellished by our pre-existing schemas such that we recall details of events that did not actually occur. In the case of semantic memories, knowledge can be added to factual information from schemas. Hence, factual information from a schema about marsupials can embellish limited knowledge concerning kangaroos. Everyday memory has been explored by looking at autobiographical memories throughout the lifespan. Also, memories involving the intention to do something (known as prospective memory) have been studied in relation to being time-based and/or event-based. The involvement of monitoring and cue detection plays an important role in how the intention to perform an action is enacted. Learning is important for remembering. How we engage and learn information influences the longevity of memory traces. The levels of processing approach has shown that when information is processed deeply for meaning, it is less likely to be forgotten from long-term memory. Memories that are encoded efficiently are more likely to be consolidated and remembered. Implicit learning can be achieved through repetition priming. The spacing effect is an effective way of learning without conscious awareness and is often how procedural memories are formed. Other methods of learning include a variety of mnemonic techniques which have proven to be successful aids in learning.

FURTHER READING

Baddeley, A. (2014) *Essentials of Human Memory*. Hove: Psychology Press.

Kandel, E.R. (2007) *In Search of Memory: The emergence of a new science of mind.* New York/London: W.W. Norton and Company.

Luminet, O. (2017) *Flashbulb Memories: New challenges and future perspectives* (2nd edn). London: Taylor and Francis.

Santos, C. (2018) *Mastering Memory: Techniques to turn your brain from a sieve to a sponge.* New York: Puzzle Wright Press.

THINKING: DECISION-MAKING AND PROBLEM-SOLVING

The way in which we define and segregate ourselves from other living organisms is often encapsulated in the philosophical motto introduced by René Descartes, 'I think therefore I am' (*Cogito ergo sum*). Descartes considered the ability to think as an indicator of existence – of being alive. While there are philosophical debates over the accuracy of this phrase, the essence of its meaning does appear to ring true. Psychologists for many years have considered language as a factor differentiating us from other animals, but without the capacity to think, language would be disorganised and incomprehensible. The capacity to think therefore influences how we behave and navigate through our daily lives. The importance of thought processes can readily be seen in babies born with severe or life-threatening chromosomal anomalies that impact on brain development. This generally leads to impairments in cognitive functioning and, in particular, the ability to think. In babies without brain developmental problems, the ability to think becomes apparent soon after birth. As mentioned in Chapter 3, the world appears confusing to the new-born but the ability to form hypotheses about how their immediate world operates is helped by inborn infant competencies. These competencies enable new-borns to navigate their immediate world and develop an understanding using their capacity to think. There are individual differences, however, in how well we can adapt our thinking to solve problems and make judgements and decisions using information available to us. Some individuals are better at using logical deduction when problem-solving and decision-making, whereas others invoke experiential knowledge. Why there are differences and the impact

DOI: 10.4324/9781003014355-5

this has for problem-solving and decision-making for instance, are of interest to cognitive psychologists. Studying thought processes is not new. Plato (427–347 BCE) postulated that the soul is divided into reason (or rational thought), spirit (or emotions) and desire (for excess appetites). It was Aristotle (384–322 BCE), however, who addressed thinking in terms of logic in his treatise, *Organon*. He is particularly known for his logic that revolves around the notion of deduction or *sullogismos* in Greek (hence the derivation of syllogistic logic). Aristotle's writings have an important role in how cognitive psychologists study different types of thinking processes used in problem-solving and decision-making.

THINKING DEFINED

According to the American Psychological Association, thinking is, "cognitive behaviour in which ideas, images, mental representations, or other hypothetical elements of thought are experienced or manipulated .... it is covert ... not directly observable but must be inferred from actions or self-reports .... it is symbolic .... involve operations on mental symbols or representations." (2020).

There are different types of thinking, all of which can be successfully deployed depending on the nature of task. For example, when presented with information about the risks of contracting Covid-19, decisions concerning travelling abroad to a country with a high versus low number of cases can be made by weighing different factors, such as one's age and condition of health. This type of decision will have personal consequences. By travelling to a country with a high case number, there is an increased risk of catching Covid-19 especially if one is old and frail. Under these circumstances, travelling to a low risk country would be a better solution. Eysenck and Keane (2015) outlined six different types of thinking, some of which we might regularly use and others less so:

1   Judgements are considered to be a sub-set of decision-making and involve the careful consideration of how likely events will occur.
2   Decision-making involves the selection of one possible option from more than one.

3   Informal reasoning involves the evaluation of the robustness of an argument by using existing knowledge and personal experience.
4   Inductive reasoning involves making decisions about the truthfulness of a statement using the information available. Unlike deductive reasoning, logical conclusions are not always possible.
5   Deductive reasoning involves forming logical conclusions based on information (such as statements) known to be true.
6   Problem-solving involves, first, the identification of the problem, and second, formulating a stage-by-stage plan of solution. Depending on the nature of the problem, any of the above types of thinking may be used.

These different forms of thinking will be the basic structure for understanding how we think, beginning with making judgements.

JUDGEMENTS

A judgement is defined by Eysenck and Keane (2015) as, "an assessment of the probability of a given event occurred based on incomplete information" (p. 722). Our judgements are not set in stone as we can change our original conclusion when we receive new information. For example, making a judgement of an 80 per cent likelihood that a close friend is seeing a new friend behind one's back can be revised when information verifies the close friend spending some of these occasions with her parents. In these circumstances the judgement might be revised to the odds of a 50:50 per cent likelihood. Hence, the process of forming judgements is often dynamic. Nevertheless, there are situations where judgements made are in error. We are generally poor at considering base-rate information. For example, Kahneman and Tversky (1972) introduced a problem concerning a witness's identification of a 'cab' involved in an accident. On the evening concerned there were cabs operating from two different companies: 85 per cent Green and 15 per cent Blue. The witness said it was a Blue cab but when tested for identification under the same viewing conditions, she was in error 20 per cent of the time (probability of witnessing or seeing the data (D)). The question Kahneman and Tversky posed was, 'what is the likelihood of it being a Blue cab?' Many of us get this wrong because base-rate information fails to be considered in the calculation. Using the formula developed by Bayes for the calculation of the '**odds ratio**' we can use the information available to calculate the probability that the cab was Blue (H_1) or Green (H_2). The formula used to solve the problem posed by Kahneman and Tversky can be seen in Figure 5.1.

The odds ratio therefore is 12:17 and the chance that the cab is Blue is 12/29 (29 is obtained by adding 12 and 17). This means the witness has a 41 per cent chance of being right. This stands in marked contrast to the assumed 80 percent chance of being right.

Base-rates can provide us with important data allowing us to make informed judgements. It has been argued that we do have knowledge about the effects 'A' has on 'B'. This provides us with a knowledge-base of the consequences events have on other events. In other words, we have the knowledge to help ascertain the causal effects of events on other events, or information on the causes of different outcomes. Provided we have full access to information details and the question is framed with all the information present, then we do make good use of base-rates. Using Kahneman and Tversky's cab example, Krynski and Tenenbaum (2007) accounted

H_1 = a probability of 0.15 (as 15 percent were operating)

H_2 = a probability of 0.85 (as 85 percent were operating)

0.15 / 0.85

$p(D/H_1)$ = probability of identifying a Blue cab when it is Blue

$p(D/H_2)$ = probability of identifying a Blue cab when it is Green

0.80 / 0.20

Putting the two elements of the formula together:

$$\frac{0.15}{0.85} \times \frac{0.80}{0.20} = \frac{0.12}{017}$$

Figure 5.1 Formula used to solve the problem posed by Kahneman and Tversky

for why it was difficult for participants to answer the problem correctly. Krynski and Tenenbaum argued that if participants were armed with information that could explain why an identification error was made for 20 per cent of the time, they would correctly solve the problem. Hence, when they were informed that for 20 per cent of the time for both Blue and Green cabs the paint had faded, this offered an explanation for the errors made by the witness. The correct solution increased from 8 per cent to 46 per cent.

When information is incomplete, however, we tend to ignore base-rate data, and instead rely on a 'rule of thumb' approach (Kahneman and Tversky 1972). This rule of thumb known as a **heuristic** provides us with quick accessible guidance on decision-making. One example is the representativeness heuristic. The representativeness heuristic is often used for deciding whether events, individuals or objects belong to a category based on traits that are typical of the category. This means that descriptions of people and what they do can be used to make judgements about them by virtue of the content fitting well with that of a specific category. For example, Mary doesn't drink or smoke and works for the church. She also loves to wear dresses which cover her knees and have a high collar. Is Mary a vicar or an old-fashioned vicar? Most judgements would depict her as an old-fashioned vicar based on how she dresses and by her habits fitting the category 'old-fashioned'. But this can't be right. The error here is that an old-fashioned vicar is a sub-set of vicar. Hence, Mary has to be allocated to the category of vicar before she can be classified as an old-fashioned vicar.

There have been a number of theories put forward to account for how we make judgements. The 'support theory' proposed by Tversky and Koehler (1994) is based on the availability heuristic which claims it is easier to estimate how often an event occurs based on the ease of its retrieval from long-term memory. This means, if the rate of deaths in the UK increased due to the Covid-19 virus, then it is more likely to be considered a common killer. The Covid-19 virus in 2020 becomes readily available in long-term memory as a frequent cause of deaths in the UK. In relation to support theory, Tversky and Kochler argued that the likelihood of an event's frequency depends on the descriptive frame in which a question is asked. If the question is vague without a breakdown of possibilities, then the prediction of something occurring is low. For example, do you think you will inherit your aunt's money next year? The answer is likely to be 'very unlikely'. If the question was framed as: do you think you will inherit your aunt's money next year given how ill she is, and it is now December? Then the answer is likely to be 'very likely'. Hence, the more detail, the higher the probability. This arises as a consequence of increased attention towards heightened aspects of events not provided under vague questioning. Also, by providing such details, aspects of events are made available in memory.

The 'fast-and-frugal' heuristic is another approach proposed by Gigerenzer and Gigerenzer (2011). They argue that we use 'fast-and-frugal' heuristics to make judgements; this helps us to make the best judgement. When using this heuristic three rules are applied: searching, stopping and decision-making. We will continue to engage search cues until the right one helps answer the question. Once the right discriminatory cue is found, it is necessary to know when to stop, as continuing is a waste of time and effort. A decision can then be made. An important model of decision-making incorporates both heuristics and more effortful processing, as does the dual-process model (see Box 5.1).

BOX 5.1 DUAL-PROCESS THEORY

Kahneman (2003) argued that we don't always use heuristics, but under some circumstances we adopt other strategies which engage complicated cognitive operations. In his model there are two processing pathways, one of which involves heuristics and the other more complex processing (see Table 5.1).

Table 5.1 Two processing pathways

System 1	System 2
Includes an automatic, effortless and fast cognitive process that is difficult to stop, control or change. Based on the representativeness heuristic.	Includes a serial, effortful, monitored, directed and slow cognitive process that can be changed or modified at any point. Note this is not a form of heuristics.

There are occasions when the situation demands we make quick decisions based on heuristics. Just because we assume, however, that performing poorly on base-rate problems (mentioned earlier) is on account of using System 1, the errors often made from effortful calculation using System 2 should not be ignored. Errors on base-rate problems can occur equally through cognitive miscalculation based on judgement biases (Le Mens and Denrell 2011). For some types of problem, however, Pennycook and Thompson (2012) have argued that neither Systems 1 nor 2 are used. Furthermore, it depends on how the problem information is presented as to whether Systems 1 or 2 is activated (Chun and Kruglanski 2006). The dual-process model nevertheless has empirical support and provides a successful explanation for individual differences observed in judgement performance.

Making judgements is considered to be a sub-set of decision-making, our next topic.

DECISION-MAKING

Every day we make many decisions. What to wear, who to speak to and who to avoid are just three examples. This makes decision-making a ubiquitous phenomenon. There are, however, different types of decision-making, some of which feature in our professions or as part of our civil duty, as is the case in the process of jury deliberation (see Box 5.2). Making decisions about where we want to go or who we want to befriend are different from making deductive or inductive assumptions. This is because these types of decisions form as a result of the exclusion of one option from another. Furthermore, the decisions we make will have an effect on our lives; hence, the option considered will have personal consequences for us. For example, opting to marry someone who lives abroad might mean that living in a different country determines how often it is possible to visit one's parents. Whereas opting to marry someone who lives in the same country might mean more opportunities to visit one's parents. Hence, some decisions will carry more personal risks or benefits than others.

BOX 5.2 MOCK-JUROR DECISION-MAKING

The 'mock-juror' paradigm is a productive way of investigating how real jurors might engage with court case material when making decisions about a defendant's innocence or guilt. Information can be presented as a transcript or shown as video footage. At the end of the transcript or on viewing the footage, mock-jurors answer a series of questions using a rating scale such as 'extent of guilt' and 'probability of intent'. The mock-juror paradigm is a flexible one, which means that in addition to the case details, information can be manipulated in ways that introduce different levels of intent based on the defendant's account. This type of information is considered to be 'evidential', but non-evidential information can also be included such as a photograph attached to the transcript (either an attractive or unattractive defendant). Non-evidential information has no relevance to the case but instead stereotypes the defendant. Kaplan and Kemmerick (1974) showed how mock-jurors use non-evidential information when the availability of evidential information is limited. Furthermore, Ellison and Munro (2015) found that mock-jurors had difficulty jettisoning their 'common sense' and 'personal experience' when deliberating. Taylor, Alner and Workman (2017) showed how middle-aged mock-jurors, when viewing a video court case enactment of a defendant with Borderline Personality Disorder, would typically rate their behaviour as rude, bad and punishable rather than as a person with mental health issues. The middle-aged mock-jurors rated the defendant as highly guilty, with a high probability of intent rating and a more extreme sentence. Izzett and Fishman (1976) found that defendants with a high justification for their crime were given a lenient sentence. Defendants with a socially attractive profile and with low justification for their crime were given a more lenient sentence than their socially unattractive counterparts. Hence, defendant physical/social attractiveness appears to influence mock-juror sentencing decisions (Korva, Porter, O'Connor, Shaw et al. 2013). Taylor, Lui and Workman (2018) conducted a mock-juror study using three versions of a fictitious theft/handling court case transcript. The three versions varied in the defendant's intent by indirectly considering the differences of motive. A photograph of the defendant was attached (high or low physical attractiveness). Differences across the three intent levels for extent of guilt, probability of intent and sentence occurred. An attractive-leniency effect was not found on any of the ratings. Taylor et al. concluded that when mock-jurors deliberated, they considered the evidential information and paid little credence to physical attractiveness. In this case decision-making was informed by the facts of the case and whether the defendant confessed to the crime (albeit with varying justification of intent) or pleaded not guilty.

In 1944, von Neumann and Morgenstern introduced 'utility theory' as a way of explaining the basis for our decision–making. As the term suggests, utility implies that we try to attain the most benefit to serve our needs – we try to maximise our utility. In other words, we place an arbitrary value to each option in the mix and select the one with the highest return (the utility which benefits us the most). This involves making objective probability calculations of the best option providing us with the optimal utility. Using the previous example of choosing a potential partner to marry, marrying a resident of your own country might be the option offering the best utility, if visiting the parents frequently is a priority.

Von Neumann and Morgenstern had a formula for the utility theory:

Outcome probability × Outcome utility = Expected utility

The expected utility approach has been criticised on the grounds of not being representative of how we normally make our decisions. We rarely estimate objective probabilities when deciding on an option but instead we use subjective probabilities. Most people find the concept of probability difficult to understand, let alone being able to view options collectively and calculate the probabilities of compound options. Moreover, we tend to exclude options immediately by making short-cut decisions using 'rule of thumb' assumptions (see earlier). Another problem for the expected utility approach is that we don't always make the right choices especially when calculating gains and losses (Kahneman and

Tversky 1984). This should appear to be a simple type of decision-making; deciding whether one option leads to gain and the other to loss. Kahneman and Tversky showed how fallible our choices can be. Prospect theory, introduced by Kahneman and Tversky in 1979, highlights the fallible thinking processes involved when making decisions concerning gain or loss.

Prospect theory

Kahneman and Tversky (1979) outlined different types of heuristic. The most commonly used is a simple counting method of how often the same solution worked previously when faced with the same dilemma. Hence, a decision to burgle a house over a commercial property might be based on the number of successful hauls made from burgling residential properties and the narrow escape when fleeing a factory. Experiences such as these make heuristics a quick and computationally simple method of decision-making. It is not uncommon, however, to overweight some outcomes over others by relying on decisions made previously under similar situations. Also, we tend to overweight the small probabilities to protect ourselves against losses. The 'availability' heuristic is also important in prospect theory. This heuristic provides a rough guideline about which option is best. For example, a potential criminal wanting to know the best crime to commit to evade police apprehension, might refer to information available regarding how often perpetrators get caught for committing a specific type of crime.

Kahneman and Tversky predicted that we are more sensitive to potential loss than we are to potential gain; loss–aversion. This means when deciding on an option, we tend to avoid those where we perceive potential loss. According to Kahneman (2003), this is why most people will renounce a 50:50 bet unless circumstances are such that there is a possibility of winning twice as much. (For example, most people would not place a bet of £10 which has a 50:50 chance of winning £10. They probably would, however, place the same bet if they had a 50:50 chance of winning £20.) Kahneman and Tversky proposed a two–phase assessment process for decision-making. In the first phase, options are edited using six types of heuristic: coding, combination, segregation, cancellation, simplification and detection of dominance. Outcomes are valued as losses or gains using coding and this is compared to an individual's current asset situation known as their reference point. Hence, any option outcome below the reference point is considered a loss and is discarded. If, however, it is above, then the option outcome is a gain and might be considered. Calculating compound outcomes are made easier by adding them together using the combination heuristic. For example, if there is a 40 per cent chance of attaining £400 or a 50 per cent chance of attaining £400 for the 'fencing' of stolen television sets, then this prospect will be a 90 per cent chance of £400. In the case of using the segregation heuristic, the options are considered individually rather than together. For example, if there is a 0.6 likelihood of attaining £400 and a 0.4 likelihood of attaining £600, then an individual will reduce the odds of attaining £600 by raising the odds of gaining £200 as an assured sum of money. In this case, fencing stolen goods is the selected option, not for gain but to avoid a loss. The money attained is lower but is more than would be the case if the television sets were not fenced off. Generally, we would prefer to accept a small gain over a larger one if this is a certainty. Occasionally, however, people will cancel outcomes from various options if they were similar in value and likelihood of occurring (Ranyard 1995). Tversky and Kahneman (1987) also observed this whereby people cancelled common elements in compound gambles rather than combining them. By doing this, the cognitive load involved in comparing many options becomes easier to handle. This is similar to an elimination-by-aspects approach which helps to reduce cognitive load. For example, when deciding on a property to buy, it is easier to eliminate properties that do not fit the desired location first. Doing this cancels out common elements such as the design of the house and size of garden. This leaves fewer options of property once a must-have location is selected. In a similar vein, Kaplan, Bekhor and Shiftan (2011) claimed that by retaining options which fit the criteria, it is easier to make detailed comparisons across the remaining ones. The detection of dominance is a heuristic enabling a quick decision about the easiest option to take. For example, a decision over which property to break-and-enter could be as simple as selecting a house with inadequate security such as a hidden and open window. The second phase of the assessment process is the evaluation of the edited prospects considered previously. After consideration of the edited prospects, the prospect with the highest return is selected. Hence, by substituting probabilities for weights, and utilities for subjective values given to all options available, decision–making becomes easier. An interesting alternative to prospect theory is one which has been proposed by Payne (1973). This model, which considers our motivations for doing something, is known as the Simple Contingent Process Model (see Box 5.3).

BOX 5.3 SIMPLE CONTINGENT PROCESS MODEL

According to Payne, individuals make a series of judgements based on their current situation. There are sub-step questions which individuals ask themselves and these are simple, often requiring 'yes' or 'no' answers. An example of how the Simple Contingent Process Model operates is as follows:

1 How much money do I have (lots leads to no need for crime; very little leads to the need for crime)
2 How certain am I of success (low leads to no crime; high leads to crime)
3 How much will I get (low leads to asking question 4; high leads to committing the crime)
4 What are the risks concerned (high leads to no crime; low leads to committing the crime)
5 I will commit the crime but need to decide how, what, where and when

As we can see these questions are quick and easy to answer. The answers very much depend on the individual's situation and motivation for committing a crime. Carroll (1978) asked incarcerated criminals whether they would consider any of the different types of gamble varying on factors such as loss or gain, the amount of gain and type of punishment received if caught. They had difficulty combining the different factors to inform their decision. Instead each factor was considered independently; 60 per cent considered success, 41 per cent likelihood of police capture, 67 per cent focused on punishment severity while 84 per cent were interested in the haul available. These findings indicate how different perpetrators focus on different aspects of committing crime and therefore why deterrents have a differential effect for different perpetrators.

Emotional influences

There are other aspects to decision-making that play an important role, such as our emotions. Emotions can be negative as a consequence of a bad outcome from a decision made that affects us personally. Likewise, we can feel elation after winning a large sum of money on the lottery following a decision to buy a ticket. If we experience the loss of a large amount of money after being swindled, then we are likely to feel unhappy and highly unlikely to be caught out again by a con-person; hence, 'once bitten, twice shy'. Such experiences influence how we behave in future and the decisions we make. Omission bias, for example, is when we decide not to take action under circumstances of risky decision-making.

Omission bias, however, is influenced by emotions. This can be seen when parents were asked whether they are likely to have their children vaccinated. Given the negative media coverage concerning side-effects brought on by some vaccinations, parents were worried about their children being adversely affected (Brown, Kroll, Hudson, Ramsay et al. 2010). Status quo bias occurs when people are reluctant to change a situation even when there are no costs incurred for doing so. More regrets occurred when people decided to change a situation that went wrong afterwards than was the case for maintaining the status quo (even if it were a mistake to do so; Nicolle, Fleming, Bach, Driver et al. 2011).

Influence of selective exposure

Researchers have considered why we often make poor decisions. One reason, it has been argued by Fischer and Greitemeyer (2010),

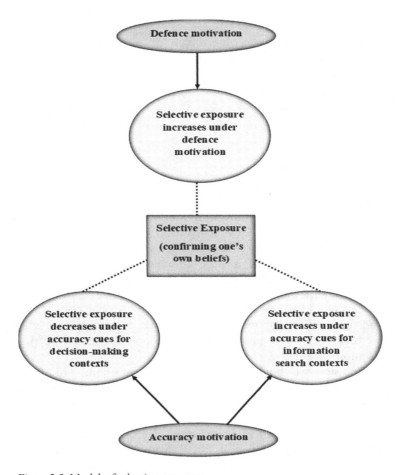

Figure 5.2 Model of selective exposure
Source: Adapted from Fischer and Greitemeyer (2010)

is due to selective exposure (see Figure 5.2). Selective exposure means that we make decisions based on our beliefs. We adhere to these beliefs even when presented with information to the contrary; we continue to use them in our decision-making.

This model suggests that we feel the need to defend our belief system by virtue of the decisions we make. When the need to define our personal stance arises, we enter a defence motivation state which increases selective exposure. When selective exposure increases, we search for information supporting our beliefs. In other words, we find confirmatory information. When the need to make decisions based on optimal choices arises, accuracy motivation reduces the impact of selective exposure. In cases where access to information is limited, but accuracy motivation is high, individuals will resort to searching for data consistent with their beliefs. Doing this increases selective exposure.

Naturalistic decision-making (NDM)

The NDM model consists of five-phases and was proposed by Galotti (2002) to account for how we make decisions about everyday real-life situations. As Figure 5.3 shows, there are four different things that we do before a decision is made and it is not uncommon for us to backtrack and modify plans and goals as a consequence of the information we have found. There is much support for this model from various studies. Moreover, the model is in keeping with predictions from the elimination–by–aspects heuristic approach.

According to Galotti, making decisions can be difficult. We also have a tendency to make biased decisions. This is in part due to the fact that we retrieve information about past experiences and events stored in long-term memory (see Chapter 4). Hence, new information is encoded and compared within a context of pre-existing decisions. As mentioned previously, we often make decisions that maintain the status quo due to this selective exposure. Decisions we make are often appropriate to our needs, but they are by no means perfect. The decisions we make on a daily basis are often bounded by informal reasoning based on our knowledge and experiential learning.

INFORMAL REASONING

Reasoning used on an everyday basis is more likely to be informal rather than the more stringent, logically based, deductive thinking. Informal reasoning has its roots in our knowledge base and our personal experiences. It is also referred to as critical thinking which

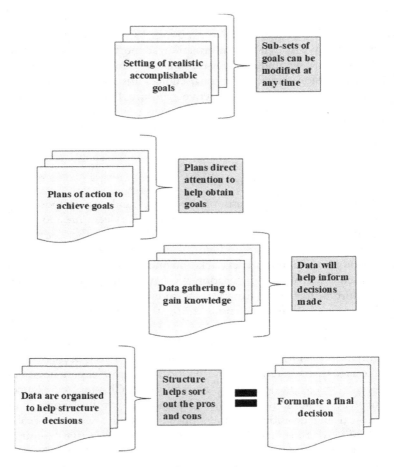

Figure 5.3 Naturalistic decision-making model
Source: Adapted from Galotti (2002)

is a sub-set of logic. It is formal reasoning that is commonly considered to be the route to logical processing, however (see Figure 5.4).

The importance of the content influences the credibility of the argument presented. Moreover, who presents the argument determines the acceptance of it: experts versus non-experts (Walton

Logic		
Informal thinking	**Formal thinking**	
	Deductive	**Inductive**
language	syllogistic	analogy
definition	propositional	generalisation
argument		experimental inquiry
classification		scientific reasoning
problem solving		statistical reasoning
informal fallacies		probabilities

Figure 5.4 The sub-sets of logic

2010). When presented with an argument or statement, we informally reason that the statement, for instance, is probably true or probably false. Hence, we deal with likelihoods rather than certainties (as is the case with formal reasoning; see later). The motivations underlying informal reasoning, according to Mercier and Sperber (2011) are important as a differentiating factor between this type of reasoning and formal thinking. In everyday situations, when we discuss information with others, the intention is to encourage others to see things the same way as we do. For example, when discussing politics, if opinions are incongruent, then discussion turns towards persuading others eventually to agree on the specifics of the argument. According to Mercier and Sperber, "Skilled arguers are not after the truth but after arguments supporting their views" (p. 57). This is considered to be a somewhat pessimistic understanding of how we engage with informal thinking. Its uses can be extrapolated to many other situations such as how we interpret language involved in statements, how we classify information and our ability to plan based on the data-content. We cannot ignore, however, that there are informal fallacies, such as the straw man fallacy. The straw man fallacy is used to depreciate the opinions of others which are at odds with our own. The other person's arguments can be misconstrued as a strategy of reducing any chance of their opinion being considered as correct (Aikin and Casey 2011). This strategy operates at many different levels of society, including academia (see Box 5.4).

BOX 5.4 HOW THE STRAW MAN FALLACY CAN MISCONSTRUE EVOLUTIONARY PSYCHOLOGY

Daly and Wilson (1998) uncovered figures indicating that children living in reconstituted families are 200 times more likely to be abused by the non-biological parent than by residing with two biological parents. This phenomenon is called the 'Cinderella effect'. Importantly, they were not suggesting that abuse will occur in all reconstituted families. In 2005, Buller criticised this finding and claimed that under conditions of a fostered or adopted household (where neither are biological parents), abuse should be much higher than is the case for reconstituted families. Buller argues that this is not the case, as the figures of abuse are lower than that found in one-step-parent households. The conclusion made by Buller is that Daly and Wilson have got it wrong; their claims are false. What is the error in Buller's reasoning? Has he set up a straw man fallacy? First, fostering and adopting is a different scenario from reconstituted family living. He is not comparing like with like. Second, the argument that two non-biological parents should increase the Cinderella effect was never made by Daly and Wilson. This means that Buller makes this argument, on Daly and Wilson's behalf, and then discredits it (Workman and Reader 2016). Now that is a straw man argument.

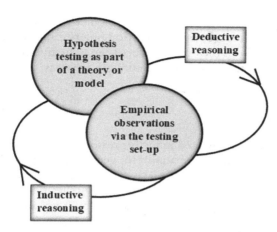

Figure 5.5 Relationship between deductive and inductive reasoning in scientific research

There are other types of informal fallacies which influence reasoning. One in particular known as the 'slippery slope' argument has often been used to account for how low-level deviant behaviour can escalate into something more. For example, if someone smokes cannabis then they have a greater chance of taking harder drugs such as heroin. Stealing from grandmother's purse is the beginning of the slippery slope to a life of crime is another example of this. Regardless of problems associated with informal thinking, it is used more readily in everyday situations than formal thinking such as inductive and deductive reasoning. It is easy to confuse inductive and deductive reasoning, but their involvement in scientific research for example, is equally important as Figure 5.5 demonstrates.

When theories or models are tested for their validity, hypotheses (statements of prediction) are tested using strict scientific methodology (e.g. an experiment with defined testing variables or independent variables (IVs). The results are interpreted by using deductive reasoning (see later) and whether these findings are unlikely to have occurred by chance alone. If the results are not a chance finding, then inductive reasoning is used to generate support of the hypothesis which is fed into an existing theory or model. Hence, in these circumstances inductive reasoning helps generate new ideas based on empirical observations. A simple way of thinking about the difference between inductive and deductive reasoning is that inductive 'indicates' whereas deductive 'deduces'.

INDUCTIVE REASONING

Hamad (2007) considered inductive reasoning as the application of specific cases (or information) to general principles. Inductive reasoning occurs when we make general suppositions from statements referring to specific events. This implies that the suppositions we make are likely to be valid; but this is not always the case. As we saw in Figure 5.5, empirical observations (or results) supporting a hypothesis, can be added to existing knowledge encapsulated in a theory, but there are no rules for performing inductive reasoning. In fact, performing inductive reasoning is very much influenced by the information to hand. Klix (2001) claimed that we use inductive reasoning when a conclusion does not follow with certainty given the available information. Conclusions can change when additional information is in the mix. Modifications to our conclusions can occur as new information alters our subjective probability calculations. A boyfriend accused of cheating, for instance, can be seen differently when new information challenges the likelihood that he was 'playing away from home'. Inductive reasoning, however, falls foul of 'confirmation bias'. This occurs when we entertain a hypothesis (of an everyday event) and then search for information to prove it. According to Cowley and Byrne (2005) we have the tendency to want to maintain our opinions and hypotheses while discrediting those entertained by others; which is achieved through confirmation bias. They found that, even when evidence falsified an original hypothesis, only 25 per cent of participants aborted their own hypothesis. Confirmation bias is less prominent, according to Cowley and Byrne, when the hypothesis tested belongs to another individual. When applying inductive reasoning, there is a tendency to rely on the accumulation of information which supports a theory's validity (Page 2014; see Box 5.5).

BOX 5.5   THE COELACANTH FISH: FACT OR FICTION?

Page (2014) outlined how inductive reasoning has left marine biologists believing the coelacanth fish was extinct. In 1836, fossils found near Durham, north England by Swiss naturalist Louis Agassiz were labelled as belonging to the coelacanth fish. These were dated back to the Cretaceous-Paleogene period. The conclusion drawn was that this fish became extinct as far back as 66 million years. Concluding that the ancient coelacanth fish became extinct was further validated by the fact that it had not been seen in its living form. That is until 1938 when a living coelacanth was caught off the South African coast (others have also been found subsequently). Page argued that scientists fell afoul of the 'out of sight, out of mind' adage and in this case the conclusion drawn using inductive reasoning was incorrect for over 100 years.

Inductive reasoning has been likened to creativity. Hamad (2007) claimed that, in everyday life, inductive reasoning is probably more akin to creativity than to reasoning. Trickett and Trafton (2007) claimed, however, that when scientists explore ideas they often use 'what if' questions while imagining various scenarios. Albert Einstein reportedly did this when he was 16. Imagining hitching a ride on a light beam fuelled his creative thought which led to the development of his theory of relativity. Similarly, using thought experiments engages us in thinking 'outside the box' by allowing us to imagine 'what if' scenarios. Thought experiments enable us to be creative and use inductive reasoning without having to actually test ideas.

DEDUCTIVE REASONING

As we have seen in Figure 5.4, deductive reasoning is formal thinking, which, in turn, is a form of logic. This type of reasoning is often referred to as top–down thinking due to there being a general idea that reaches one possible conclusion. Hence, there is movement from general to specific premises leading to a logical conclusion. For example, in chemistry the first premise might state that 'noble gases are inert' and the second that, 'neon is a noble gas'. The conclusion here is that 'neon must be inert'. There is only one possible correct inference that can be made. There are two types of deductive reasoning: propositional (also referred to as conditional) and syllogistic.

Propositional

In the case of propositional reasoning, there are logical operators that are stated within a proposition. Logical operators include language such as:

- if–then
- if and only if
- or

These logical operators, such as, 'if P then Q', bind the two propositions together so a conclusion can be drawn, where 'P' refers to the first proposition, such as, 'If the sun is out' and 'Q' to the second, 'Then John gets sunburnt'. 'P' can be true or false and there are no in-betweens. There is no entertainment of there being a hazy sun – the sun is out, or it isn't under the conditions of the first proposition. There are two logical argument constructions in propositional reasoning: *modus ponens* and *modus tollens*. These are influential in deciding the validity of the conclusion made from the given propositions. *Modus ponens* is Latin for 'method of affirming' while *modus tollens* refers to 'method of denying'. We tend to find it a challenge to make the correct inference (see Box 5.6).

BOX 5.6   WHY DO WE HAVE PROBLEMS WITH DEDUCTIVE REASONING?

People find it difficult to do deductive reasoning, perhaps because it is generally not the type of problem-solving required in daily life. Having to decide the validity of the 'if P then Q' problem doesn't come naturally. This, in part, is a consequence of using our own knowledge base and previous experiences as a guide to making inferences. Markovits, Brunet, Thompson and Brisson (2013) found that some types of propositional problem were more likely to be considered valid than others despite being invalid. An example from Markovits (2017) demonstrates how *modus tollens* ('if P then Q. Q is false') should lead to the inference that 'P' is false hence:

> 'If a rock is thrown at a window, then the window will break. A window is broken'. From this one generally concludes that the rock caused the window to break, but what if it was already broken? This falsifies the validity of the proposition, simply because the cause of window breakage could be due to something else.

In the case of another example, 'If a person cuts their finger, then their finger will bleed', there are fewer alternative inferences to be made and this proposition is valid. If, however, the following is added, 'Their finger is bleeding. Therefore, the finger was cut', again there could be an alternative reason for the finger to bleed. With this particular proposition, participants have problems negating. This, Markovits et al. argue, is due to our knowledge of how things work interfering with our reasoning. Participants switch towards relying on their general knowledge of cause-and-effect (blood pours from a cut to the finger). They also use their understanding of how individuals' aspirations and preferences operate by relying on a kind of 'theory of mind'. While these strategies are successful when used in daily life, they distract from logical thinking. Markovits et al. also found support for a dual-processing approach, where under time limitations, participants adopt a statistical reasoning strategy, but a counterexample one when time constraints were removed. In the case of statistical reasoning, statistical information held in general knowledge about the premises enables a quick route for processing the premise content. In effect the estimates generated lead to the validity of the inference. Counterexamples generated, alternatively, are based on the logical structure of the proposition presented and how probable the inference made is (also based on our knowledge of reality). Here, however, we consider the number of counterexamples disproving the inference – such that the more there are the less likely the inference is considered to be valid. According to Markovits, Brisson and de Chantal (2016), this dual-strategy approach considers how logical inferences are made rather than the use of heuristics.

Modus ponens refers to inferences in the form of 'P therefore Q'. The following example illustrates a valid conclusion:

'If it is sunny, then Mary gets sunburnt,
It is sunny.
Then Mary gets sunburnt'.

Modus tollens refers to inferences in the form of 'if P, then Q. Not Q. Therefore, not P'. The following example illustrates a valid conclusion:

'If it is a wheelbarrow, then it has a wheel.
It does not have a wheel.
Then it is not a wheelbarrow'.

A good test of propositional deductive reasoning is the Wason selection task, named after Peter Wason (1960) (see Figure 5.6).

The task is as follows:

- Four cards are presented
- There is a letter on one side of each card and a number on the other side
- The rule is; 'if there is a vowel on one side then there is an even number on the other side of the card'
- Turn over the least number of cards to see if you can disprove the rule
- Which cards do you turn over?

Most people will turn the cards that have 'E' and '4' which is incorrect.

Evans (1998) claimed that this was due to the use of 'matching bias'. In other words, people tend to select the cards mentioned in

Figure 5.6 The Wason selection test example

the Wason task. This is the case even when different letters and numbers were substituted (Evans and Ball 2010). In fact, the cards you should turn over are 'E' and '3'. While the '4' appears to be a card we should turn over, the rule does not specify that if there is an even number on one side there must be a vowel on the other. Astonishingly, only 4 percent of participants got this right when Wason first developed this test.

Syllogistic

Syllogistic reasoning differs from propositional in its presentation. Like propositional there are two premises with a conclusion, but the language (or quantifiers) used differs:

All A are B
No A are B
Some A are B
Some A are not B

In the case of syllogistic reasoning, the premises refer to 'sets' rather than to individuals (Geurts 2003). Geurts gives the example of foresters:

> "At least half of the foresters are vegetarians" (p. 232).

This implies that of the set of foresters, the set who are non-vegetarians is smaller than the set who are. Aristotle presented the earliest case of a universal quantifier (i.e. the use of 'all') using the following example:

All men are mortal.
Socrates is a man.
Socrates is mortal.

If the first and second premises are true, then the conclusion must also be true. If the conclusion was changed to 'Something is mortal' then this is also true. Why this is also true relates to Socrates being an example of at least one thing being mortal. Therefore 'something' implies one thing being mortal, hence it does not contradict the premises. We generally find syllogistic reasoning challenging because statements that are logical can have information that we know to be false. The following example shows this principle in operation:

All adults own dogs.
All males are adults.
Therefore, all males own dogs.

The conclusion drawn is logical, but we know from everyday life that premises 'A' and 'B' are incorrect. Not all adults own dogs and there are males who are children. And we know that not all males own dogs. Our belief bias can interfere with syllogistic reasoning, which means we consider the content of the premises and conclusions to be false instead of structurally being logical. This is borne out by the fact that it takes longer to process unbelievable premises from believable ones (Stupple and Ball 2008). There is also the misconception that 'All As are Bs' is reversible which means that 'All Bs are As'. This we believe applies to the use of other quantifiers such as 'some'.

There are two main theoretical approaches explaining deductive reasoning: mental models and dual-processing (see Boxes 5.1 and 5.6). A mental models approach was first introduced by Johnson-Laird in 1983. The basis of this approach is that we construct mental models when we are given a task involving reasoning. Johnson-Laird claims that we construct mental models all the time and each one represents a possibility of the same thing. Alfred, Connolly, Cetron and Kraemer (2020) argue that to develop a mental model we engage both spatial and non-spatial content. Moreover, brain activity in the superior parietal and anterior prefrontal cortex are involved in the creation and maintenance of such mental models. Hence, when provided with information such as the example below, we form a mental model that reflects and preserves the spatial relationships described which, in turn, helps us to make a conclusion:

The oak tree is to the left of the door,
The swing is to the right of the door,
The dog is sitting in front of the swing,
Therefore, the dog is sitting to the right of the oak tree.

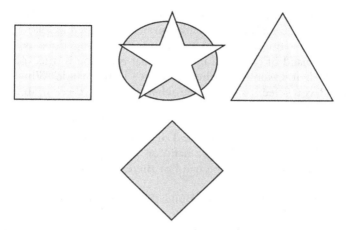

Figure 5.7 Possible premises devised from a visual representation

In the above example, a mental model depicting the spatial relationships using all premises can be constructed using visual imagery. Equally it is possible to construct a series of premises from an existing visual representation (see Figure 5.7).

For example, the star on the circle is between the square and triangle but above the diamond.

Johnson-Laird (1999), however, claimed that we often construct models representing that which is true at the expense of that which is false. We do this to reduce our working memory load (see Chapter 4). This inclusion of 'principle of truth' states, "reasoners represent as little information as possible in explicit models and, in particular, that they represent only information about what is true" (Johnson-Laird and Savary 1996, p. 69). Hence, models tend to be formed for what is true and not false. According to Johnson-Laird, Girotto and Legrenzi (2004) this leads to two fallacies:

1 Illusion of what is possible
2 Illusion of what is impossible

Importantly, Johnson-Laird et al. (2004) argue that we focus on models containing the possible rather than the impossible. This can often lead to fallacious conclusions and to the exclusion of alternative ones. The illusion of the possible can be exemplified as follows:

Suppose you are presented with the following three premises about a hand of cards and informed that only one is true. You are asked, 'Is it possible that there is an ace in the hand?' Which one would you select to determine whether or not there is an ace in the hand?

1 There is a king in the hand or there is an ace, or both
2 There is a queen in the hand or there is an ace, or both
3 There is a jack in the hand or there is a ten, or both

Johnson-Laird et al. (2004) found that 95 per cent of participants concluded there is an ace in the hand. You may be surprised to learn that this is incorrect. Johnson–Laird et al. (2004) explained why this conclusion is wrong using the illusion of possibility. If you selected premise one or two, because you believe that either premise enables the possibility of there being an ace, then you have broken the rule that only one premise is true. Therefore, this implies that the third premise can be true. If so, this means that there can be no ace in the hand. Selecting premise one as being true, means that premise two must be false and vice versa because the task requirement of only one premise being true is contravened. Selecting the third premise means there is no ace (because this means that both one and two must be wrong).

All of the forms of reasoning discussed thus far can be adopted for problem-solving.

PROBLEM-SOLVING

We are presented with different types of problems to solve on a daily basis. While most problems are familiar and can be resolved by referring to similar experiences, some are more challenging. Problems can be classified as well-defined or ill-defined. A well-defined problem has all the information that is needed to resolve it encapsulated in its presentation. This means all the information is there and we just have to use it to resolve the problem. Well-defined problems tend to be 'knowledge-lean', simply because information is inherent in the presentation; hence, there is no need to search our memory for information. This contrasts with an ill-defined problem where information required to solve it is drawn from both knowledge and experience. Such problems are 'knowledge-rich' as they rely on additional information to find a solution. Often these problems require the introduction of benchmarks to help define how and which direction the solution should take. For example, how to become a more assertive person requires further information regarding what assertiveness is so that ways of achieving it can be found. Solutions are not always immediate, so we often adopt a **trial and error** approach. This fits the adage, 'If at first you don't succeed, then try and try again'. Different hypotheses are tried and tested by performing activities to see what works. Thornton (1999) presented school-age children with the 'building a bridge across the river' task. They were provided with a variety of sized, shaped and weighted blocks. On the floor a river was painted. There were only two blocks that, when used together, could form a bridge to cross the river. Only one five-year-old was successful and the solution took time through trial and error; she used the blocks as counterweights. Three different approaches accounting for how we solve problems will be considered.

Gestalt school of thought

Gestalt is probably one of the most renowned approaches – active between 1920–40. Gestaltists differentiated between reproductive and productive thought. In the case of reproductive, thought relied on the recycling of existing knowledge; doing things the same way because it worked previously. Productive, alternatively, involved the reformulation of the problem in a novel way. This, the Gestaltists argued, is like thinking laterally or 'outside of the box'. Insight is considered to be a way of resolving a challenging problem that is new and requires a different outlook. This has been witnessed in chimpanzees who had to restructure the problem so that they could achieve their goal of attaining the banana. Wolfgang Köhler (1925) set problems for chimpanzees to solve, 'How can I get the banana that is out of reach?' Sultan, the chimpanzee, was in an enclosure but could see a banana placed outside of the enclosure which was out of reach. There were two sticks, one short, the other long. The short stick could be used to reach the long stick which could then be used to drag the banana within reach. That is what Sultan did in the moment of an 'ah-ha experience'. This 'ah-ha' experience is known as insight; a flash of sudden inspiration. We humans also experience insight. Maier (1931) presented a problem whereby two cords suspended from the two far ends of a ceiling could not be reached at the same time. There were various objects in the room such as pliers. The task was to work out how these two cords could both be held at the same time. Participants who experienced the 'ah-ha' moment used the pliers to add weight to one of the cords, so that it could be swung like a pendulum. While holding onto the other cord while standing in the centre of the room, they waited for the pendulum to come close enough to grab hold of it. Solved!

Gestaltists have also explored insight in relation to timeframes of problem-solving. For example, we often use the phrase, 'let's sleep on it'. This idea that putting a problem aside for a while will actually help us to resolve it, was considered by Wallas (1926) in his incubation approach. This implies that even when we stop consciously thinking about a problem we continue to do so subconsciously (see Chapter 7). Incubation can easily be tested by giving two groups of participants a problem to solve. The control group is asked to continue working on the problem until it is solved while the experimental group is allowed a 'timeout' period. Sio and Ormerod (2009) performed a meta-analysis and found: a small effect of incubation; a more robust effect using creative problems rather than linguistic problems, and larger effects when more time was spent on the problem before incubation

Moreover, Sio, Monaghan and Ormerod (2013) found that sleep aided the solution of challenging problems. Simon (1966) suggested that sleeping on a problem was a good way of encouraging a fresh look at the problem. Sometimes it is difficult to dispel the ways we consider a problem and we can become stuck in a loop. Sleep helps to break the cycle by forgetting the ways the problem had been thought about. An example of the effectiveness of sleeping on a problem arises from German-born chemist, Friedrich Kekulé, who struggled to identify the structure of a molecule called benzene. The solution fortuitously came to him in a dream where a snake seized its own tail (i.e. the ouroboros).

Kekulé woke up to realise that the benzene molecule has a ring-like structure.

Insight, however, does not occur readily. Gestaltists argued that this is a consequence of how our past experiences interfere with our mind-set and our beliefs about the function of objects (referred to as functional fixedness). Our mental set can be obstructive in problem-solving. We have set strategies for solving problems which in the past may have helped solve specific types of problem. The drawback for applying the same set strategies to different types of problem, is that they may be inappropriate – and yet we still use them. Even experts fall foul of using set strategies that have worked previously at the expense of finding new, efficient and less time-consuming ones. Bilalic, McLeod and Gobet (2008a, 2008b) found this to be the case with expert chess players who maintained a previously successful strategy even at the expense of a more effective one. Furthermore, when their eye movements were tracked, they continued to search in areas of the chessboard consistent with their previous strategy.

In the case of functional fixedness, we focus and adhere to our knowledge about the uses different objects have, instead of creatively changing the object function to help solve a problem. In a classic experiment by Dunker (1945), participants were asked to attach a candle to the wall without it dripping onto the table below. Armed with a candle, strip of matches, a box of tacks and some other objects some participants showed insight by using the box of tacks as a candleholder and using the tacks to attach the box to the wall. According to Challoner (2009) insight can be induced by identifying an obscure object feature and using this to solve the problem.

There are different problem-solving approaches arising from an information-processing approach.

Information-processing

This approach was promoted by Newell and Simon (1972). They described how our limitations in problem-solving stem from a limited memory capacity (see Chapter 4) and cognitive processing based on a step-by-step (serial) approach. One of the well-defined problems set by Newell and Simon is the Tower of Hanoi (see Figure 5.8).

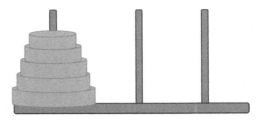

Figure 5.8 The Tower of Hanoi problem
Source: Created by Édouard Lucas (1883)

The objective of this task is to transfer all five disks with the order of size preserved across to the right peg. This can only be done by moving one disk at a time and ensuring that smaller disks are on top of larger ones but not the reverse. The middle peg is a space used for disk manoeuvre. Newell and Simon introduced the notion of a problem space whereby the initial state is the starting point and the goal state defines the problem closure. In between these two states are the moves that are necessary for success. Examples such as the Tower of Hanoi can be solved by using rules – relying more on algorithms (set procedure of steps) than heuristics. The smallest number of moves is actually 31, but most people, if they solve it at all, take many more moves. This is because we tend to use heuristics given the limitations of our information processing capabilities rather than algorithms. There are different types of problem–solving heuristics considered by Newell and Simon (see Box 5.7).

BOX 5.7   PROBLEM-SOLVING HEURISTICS

Although the use of an algorithm will guarantee a solution to a problem, it is generally slower and more effortful than applying a heuristic. For example, using an algorithm to find a painting by Edgar Degas (such as checking every painting in turn) will help eventually locate it in the art gallery, but this might not be the most effective way of finding it. Instead by using a heuristic, containing general knowledge about types of painting styles, looking in the impressionist section will lead to a painting by Degas more quickly. A means-end analysis is an effective heuristic where the problem is broken down by the solver into the ultimate goal and the current situation. The intermediary stages are then thought through. These can be modified as circumstances change, such as taking a different route due to bad weather. The working-forward approach involves trying to solve a problem holistically from start to finish. Alternatively, when working-backward, the solver takes account of the end point and tracks backwards to the starting position. For example, one's flight leaves at 10 a.m. from London, so the aim is to work out what time one needs to arrive at the airport, catch the train, get to the train station and leave the house. The generate-and-test heuristic involves devising different courses of action and deciding for each course whether it can solve the problem. For example, if the route from A to B works then this is used. If not, then a different one is generated. MacGregor, Ormerod and Chronicle (2001) claimed that we often evaluate our progress towards our goal by using the heuristic of progress monitoring. We tend to monitor how well we are progressing towards our goal and will change tactics if this progress is too slow or likely to exceed the allotted number of stages. Newell and Simon (1972) considered planning as a type of heuristic, but claimed we only use planning to solve problems modestly given our limited short-term memory capacity. Interestingly, Paynter, Kotovsky and Reder (2010) demonstrated how many of our problem-solving processes occur subconsciously. By recording ERPs (see Chapter 1) during challenging problem-solving, they found that there was a differential pattern of ERPs between correct and incorrect moves. They concluded that subconscious learning occurs independently of any deliberate planning.

Experience and knowledge play a role in another type of problem–solving known as analogical, considered next.

Experience and knowledge

Our experience and knowledge shape how we understand our immediate environment and the objects therein. This enables us to make comparisons across objects in everyday events. By doing this we are making analogies. This becomes particularly useful when we experience new events. Making analogies across events, such as the new with the old, helps to process information quickly without too much demand on our processing capacity. Furthermore, an analogy can be creative, in that two unalike events are compared. 'Analogical transfer', for instance, involves the retrieval of successful strategies and solutions and applying them to similar problems (Goswami 2006). However, the success of these previously acquired strategies and solutions to new problems, relies on the degree of similarity of the 'deep structure' and superficial features shared. Chen (2002) recognised three levels of similarity that can occur across different problems:

1   Superficial similarity where the details overlapping are often unimportant in the solution.
2   Structural similarity where there are causal connections for some of the shared components of the problems.
3   Procedural similarity where problems can be solved using common operations.

Chen found that the best form of similarity was procedural as this was easier to find and execute. Using analogies is a successful way of solving many different types of problem (see Box 5.8).

BOX 5.8   DIVERSITY OF ANALOGICAL USE

The development of new theories has often come about through using analogies from different domains of knowledge, such as the hydraulic model of the circulatory system and the 'billiard ball' model of different gases (Gick and Holyoak 1980). Experts often draw upon analogies to account for different phenomena such as 'knowledge brokers' who develop social networks among people and organisations through the provision of knowledge sources and linkages (Hargadon 1999). Dunbar (2001) described how molecular biologists used structural analogising to help formulate theories. Experts and novices differ in what they focus on when making analogies. While experts encode information at a deep structural level, novices encode superficially (Klein 1999), although this has been disputed by Dunbar who found that novices could also engage at the structural level. Vogelaar and Resing (2018) examined analogical reasoning and problem-solving in 40 gifted and 95 average ability nine-to-ten-year-old children. Children who were provided with additional training in the application of analogies to problem-solving showed transference of skill more than those who were allowed to practice unguided. Methods of increasing spontaneous analogical problem-solving have been considered across many areas such as education, design and business (Minervino, Olguín and Trench 2017). Encouraging participants to make multiple analogies across many examples before problem-solving has been found to be a successful way of increasing spontaneity. This success is due to the increased focus on abstract structures instead of superficial information.

As we have seen problem-solving involves the use of knowledge stored in memory as well as previous experience of successful problem solution. Moreover, to solve problems we make use of cognitive processors in the brain. Does this mean that changes take place in a child's brain as new information is acquired such as how to solve the 'bridge over the river' task? In Chapter 2, we considered how the brain processes information and the changes incurred at both structural and neurological levels (i.e. the synaptic landscape). The synaptic landscape of the brain changes as we learn and shows plasticity. Herholz and Zatorre (2012) defined plasticity as: "changes in structure and function of the brain that affect behaviour and that are related to experience or training" (p. 486).

The hippocampus, in the temporal lobe of the brain, has an important role in the development of long-term memories through learning. The hippocampus enables us to acquire knowledge through learning and successful problem–solving. Taxi drivers who have been 'on the go' a long time have superior spatial knowledge of street locations; they have been found to have increased grey matter in the hippocampus (Woollett, Spiers and Maguire 2009). Despite research showing changes to brain structure after learning and training, what is actually changing is still speculative (see Chapter 8).

SUMMARY

There are different types of thinking studied by cognitive psychologists: judgements, decision-making, informal reasoning, inductive and deductive reasoning and problem-solving. Judgements involve assessing the probability of something occurring based on limited information. This is why judgements are dynamic and can change as further information is added to the mix. Kahneman, in his dual-process theory, proposed that we have two pathways of processing information, one automatic and based on the representativeness heuristic and the other effortful relying on cognitive processing. Decision-making is ubiquitous and, like judgements, information is considered using different heuristics. Kahneman and Tversky argued that heuristics rely on quick computationally simple calculations of decisions with optimal outcomes. Decision-making can fall afoul of emotional influences such as that seen in omission bias and selective exposure. Informal reasoning is used daily. It is rooted in our knowledge base and our experiences. Sometimes referred to as critical thinking, it is a subset of logic. Such critical thinking enables us to infer whether a statement is probably true or false based on likelihoods rather than certainties. Common errors in this type of reasoning are the straw man fallacy and the slippery slope argument. Inductive reasoning involves applying specific cases or information to general principles. Inductive reasoning is used when a conclusion is restricted by the available information; hence, it is uncertain. However, inductive reasoning is akin to creativity. Deductive reasoning is a form of logic: propositional and syllogistic. The Wason task is a good example of propositional testing. Syllogistic reasoning also presents with two premises and a conclusion, but instead the premises refer to 'sets' rather than individuals. The logic of the premises follow the truth of the conclusion, but the content can contradict our knowledge of how the world operates. Problem-solving can utilise any of the above forms of thinking. Problems can be well- or ill-defined, knowledge-lean or knowledge-rich. Gestaltists argued we generally solve by trial and error but there are occasions of insight. In information processing approaches there is limited cognitive processing capacity which can reduce problem-solving capabilities. Experience and knowledge used when making analogies can help reformulate problems and increase solution.

FURTHER READING

Hardman, D. (2009) *Judgment and Decision Making: Psychological perspectives*. Chichester: Wiley and Sons.

Krawczyk, D. (2017) *Reasoning: The neuroscience of how we think*. Cambridge, MA: Academic Press.

Sternberg, R. (2013) *Thinking and Problem Solving, Volume 2*. Cambridge, MA: Academic Press.

Weisberg, R. (2020) *Rethinking Creativity*. Cambridge: Cambridge University Press.

LANGUAGE AND COMMUNICATION

What makes humans unique? Some might argue it's having a large brain. Unfortunately, many cetaceans and elephants have larger brains than us. Or perhaps it's tool use. But tool use is now known to be quite common in the animal kingdom from chimps to crows, and from dolphins to octopuses. Then perhaps it's bipedal locomotion. No, here again there are many examples observed in the animal kingdom including kangaroos, jerboas and pangolins – not to mention avian species. The thing that makes us unique is language. While some apes and parrots have been taught to put a few words together, they do not come close to the 50,000–100,000 sized vocabulary that the average literate human has. Nor are members of other species able to combine these words into an inestimable number of permutations we observe in our own species. Language allows us to communicate about past, present and future events and to share our innermost thoughts and feelings. In this chapter we examine this remarkable system of communication, including consideration of how language is acquired, whether it is innate, and how reading, writing and speech occur. We also consider how it is that we are able to perceive these forms of language when they are presented to us. Before all of this, however, we must first consider one fundamental question. If all animals exchange information, what is it about language that is different from other forms of communication?

WHAT IS LANGUAGE?

Providing a definition of language which differentiates it from other forms of communication is no easy task. Rather like love, we

DOI: 10.4324/9781003014355-6

all know what it is but defining it is a lot less straightforward than most people appreciate. Fortunately for our purpose, cognitive psychologists define language by its properties or criteria. While there has been a degree of debate about such properties, psycholinguist Jean Aitchison's (1989) list has generally become well accepted. Aitchison suggests 10 properties:

- Use of vocal auditory channel: A language uses verbal communication. While well accepted, this property is also a little controversial today as it appears to exclude sign language. It also excludes written communication. But as Aitchison states, this criterion captures the essence of human language.
- Arbitrariness: Languages makes use of arbitrary symbols which need not bear a resemblance to features of the discussion. Hence, 'cat' bears no resemblance to the animal it conveys. One exception to this is the use of onomatopoeia (where the word sounds like what it refers to such as 'bang' and 'whoosh').
- Semanticity: Semanticity refers to the fact that words convey meaning.
- Cultural transmission: Languages are passed on within and between generations. The words of a language are specific to a culture.
- Spontaneous usage: Language involves motivation, adults do not have to instruct their children to talk. Even young babies attempt to babble as soon as they are able.
- Turn taking: Outside of formal contexts, such as giving a speech, a conversation involves turn taking.
- Duality or double articulation: To say that there is a duality of language means that there are two layers. The first layer consists of the individual letters which are meaningless until combined together to form the second layer. Hence 'p', 'i' and 'g' have no meaning other than the terms for these letters. When put together in this order, however, they form the name of an animal 'pig'.
- Displacement: Language often refers to things not present (either in time or place). Hence, we can talk about a soccer match we watched elsewhere (spatial displacement) and on a previous date (temporal displacement).

- Structure dependence: All languages have rules about the order in which words are used. In English we can say 'cats are furry' or 'are cats furry?' but we can't say 'furry are cats'. In contrast animal vocalisations do not generally require a structure.
- Creativity: To linguistics, creativity refers to aspects of language which allow us to generate an indeterminately large number of novel sentences.

You may find it useful to refer back to these ten points when considering the sections which are coming up in this chapter. We begin with a word that has struck terror in the hearts of many a school student, 'grammar'.

GRAMMAR

In the case of language teachers, grammar refers to the rules of how words can be put together to form sentences. That is, syntax. To a cognitive psychologist, however, the definition is somewhat broader more than this. To them, in addition to syntax, grammar also refers to phonology (sound patterns – see later), semantics (meaning patterns – see above) and the lexicon (the 'dictionary' that each of us holds in our heads) (Aitchison 2008). It is worth noting, at this point, that the lexicon is made up of small units known as lexemes. As we saw in Chapter 2 each lexeme is a minimal meaningful unit of language. Each lexeme can occur in various forms such as drive, driving and driven.

Is language innate?

One of the most enduring debates in psychology is whether features of 'human nature' are innate or learned. This 'nature–nurture ' argument can be traced back at least as far as Plato (427–347 BCE) and Aristotle (384–322 BCE). Plato considered that much of human nature is innate (nature) while in contrast Aristotle considered we have to learn everything (nurture). During the first half of the twentieth century the predominant view in psychology followed Aristotle with humans being considered to be born as 'blank slates' and to have to learn literally everything. This view was due largely to the behaviourist perspective which was predominant at that time (see Chapter 1). The most famous behaviourist was of course Harvard psychologist, B. F.

Skinner. Having suggested that, in effect, there is no such thing as 'human nature' with all responses being learned, in 1957 Skinner published a behaviourist account of language development entitled *Verbal Behavior*. He suggested that language can be explained simply in terms of forming associations between two stimuli (object and sound) that work via trial and error (known as 'operant conditioning') with no need for any complicated innate mental mechanisms.

Linguist Noam Chomsky decided it was time to challenge this behaviourist assumption and, in reviewing *Verbal Behavior*, suggested simply making stimulus associations cannot explain the development of human language (Chomsky 1959). He suggested that this form of learning could not explain language learning with use of the 'argument from the poverty of the stimulus', also known as the 'learnability argument'. The reasoning here is that, given children learn language so rapidly, and given they make so few errors, trial and error, stimulus association learning could not work without there being some form of general learning mechanism. Put differently, we can say that children have innate knowledge which helps them to fill in the blanks.

We can illustrate this by turning a statement into a question (as Chomsky did). Taking the following statement:

(1)   The woman is eating pasta.

Simply by taking the 'is' and moving it to the beginning of the sentence the sentence can be turned into a question.

(2)   Is the woman eating pasta?

Now imagine a child is attempting to induce the rule which changes statements into questions simply by observing instances of the type of statement (1) and question (2) above. Then imagine the child encounters a different sentence that she needs to know how to turn into a question.

(3)   The woman who is wearing a red dress is eating pasta.

The problem here is that the word 'is' appears twice. So, which one should the child move? A child who is familiar with simple sentences such as sentence 1 might be tempted to move the first 'is' to produce:

*(4) Is the woman who wearing a red dress is eating pasta?

Clearly, this is ungrammatical (note linguists flag this up by use of an asterisk). According to Skinner's trial and error conditioning view of language development, we should expect to see this sort of error. And yet we don't. This, according to Chomsky, is because children innately break up (*parse*) sentences into units such as noun phrases and verb phrases.

In sentence (3), the noun phrase is longer: 'the woman who is wearing a red dress' because 'who is wearing a red dress' is saying something about the woman (noun) rather than what she is doing (verb). Since forming a question means the child has to ask what the woman is doing (the verb phrase), the 'is' that is moved needs to be the one that relates to the verb phrase not the noun phrase. (Note, if we were asking a question about the woman (whether she is wearing a dress) then we would need to move the 'is' from the noun phrase to end up with 'is the woman who is eating pasta wearing a red dress?'). Even though most people have never even heard of noun and verb phrases, they appear to know implicitly how to use them in a manner that is grammatically correct. This is also true of quite young children who have yet to study formal grammar.

Universal grammar

The example presented above is a typical one which supports Chomsky's learnability argument. Parents do not explicitly teach their children these rules concerning noun and verb phrases and yet they pick them up implicitly due, according to Chomsky, to the innate ability to learn languages (which contrasts with other species – see Box 6.1). Put simply, we can think of evidence of 'learnability' as being supportive of the conception of the development of language being an innate facility. If we have an innate ability to acquire language, then arguably, we must have innate 'language software'. Chomsky has proposed that children are born with a series of mental switches which he calls 'parameters' that can be turned on by linguistic experience. This is part-and-parcel of a package that he calls '**universal grammar**'. This does not mean that language (or even grammar) is innate but that we naturally respond to vocal input by creating our own grammar and that, while this appears to vary, it is

BOX 6.1   ARE ANIMALS CAPABLE OF LANGUAGE?

As we have seen, Chomsky suggested language is a specific human ability. This raises the question, are we alone in having this special ability? Do any animals have the ability to use language? There are two ways of addressing this question. First, we can ask, do any animals naturally communicate in ways which we might label 'language'? And second, if they don't naturally make use of language, can they be taught to do so?

With regard to the first question, much progress has been made in our understanding of the nature and complexity of animal communication over the last half century. Primates, being our closest relatives, have been studied in some detail. One of the most impressive findings comes from field observations of vervet monkeys. These small old-world monkeys use four different alarm calls to distinguish between different predators (Cheney and Seyfarth 1990). They use a *chutter* call when they see a snake, a *chirp* when they see a lion or leopard, a *rraup* when they see an eagle and finally a *uh!* when they see a spotted hyena. Not only do they use specific calls for specific predators, but also other members of their troop respond in different and appropriate ways (such as standing on their hind legs to look for snakes and climbing trees to avoid lions and leopards). This finding is certainly impressive and suggests monkeys are capable, up to a point, of symbolic communication (see Aitchison's 10-point list earlier). More recently, wild chimpanzees have been shown to make use of a large number of different gestures, each of which appears to have quite specific meaning (Hobaiter and Byrne 2014). Note this suggests that, in addition to making use of symbolic communication, apes are capable of semanticity. Interestingly, not only do chimps make use of quite specific gestures, but 46 of the same gestures have been also been observed in 1–2-year-old toddlers (Cartmill and Hobaiter 2019). This might be taken as suggestive that such gestures are evolutionary, ancient, and arose in a common ancestor prior to our split from the great apes.

Turning to the second question, once again most attempts to teach animals language have involved the great apes. One of the earliest was the case of Washoe, a female chimp who was taught American Sign Language (ASL) by Allen and Beatrix Gardner from the mid-1960s on. There are debates as to how well she was able to learn and make use of ASL. On the one hand, she did learn to use 350 different signs and quite often put a short string of signs together (usually 2- or 3-word strings) (Gardner and Gardner 1969, 1980). On the other hand, the vast majority of 2- or 3-word strings were requests for food and the word order could be seen as random. That is, Washoe would just as likely sign 'GO SWEET' as 'SWEET GO'. So, while there is reasonably strong evidence of semanticity and symbolism, the evidence for creativity is less clear cut (Aitchison, 2008). Greater success was attained with a bonobo (a cousin of common chimps) called Kanzi who was taught to make use of a keyboard containing symbols representing various words. Kanzi not only managed to learn to use over 200 symbols appropriately, he also responded to over 500 words when used by his researcher Sue Savage-Rumbaugh. It is clear that he was able to respond appropriately to novel requests such as 'give pine needles to Kelly' (Savage-Rumbaugh, Murphy, Sevick, Brakke et al. 1993). This is good evidence both of semanticity and of structural dependence. Despite this, he rarely engaged spontaneously in this language beyond, like Washoe, requesting food. This is quite different from human toddlers who appear to be strongly motivated to engage in conversation and, as any parent will be aware, constantly ask questions about the world around them. In summary, some other primates can be taught to make use of a number of aspects of what we define as language, but probably not all of Aitchison's ten features of human language. This might be taken as indirect evidence that language is a specific human ability.

broadly similar between cultures. Languages around the world, for example, are all based around subjects, objects and verbs, even if the specific rules of syntax vary somewhat. Hence, due to universal grammar, children take basic input and very rapidly induce the rules of that specific language.

READING AND SPEECH

Most experts today consider that the roots of human language date well back into prehistorical times (Hauser, Yang, Berwick,

Tattersall et al. 2014). While spoken language, as we understand it, is likely to have arisen with the evolution of *Homo sapiens* around 150,000−200,000 years ago, it is believed that a simple proto-language first evolved around 1.8 million years ago (in a 'proto-human' species called *Homo erectus*; Fitch, 2010). In contrast, written language is a newcomer on the scene with most scholars dating it back to cuneiform writing that arose in Mesopotamia around 5,500 years ago. This means that, while spoken language may, in some sense, be seen as an innate human faculty, written language is more of a recent human cultural invention. This may help to explain why children develop spoken language so rapidly (and appear motivated to do so) but find learning how to write it down so arduous. In fact, recent estimates suggest 10 per cent of the population have some form of **dyslexia** (British Dyslexia Association 2018). Given this high proportion, developing an understanding at a cognitive level of how reading works and why it sometimes doesn't, goes beyond mere academic intrigue.

Reading involves a number of different forms of cognitive processing including phonology (the way that words sound), or-thography (the conventions of how a language is written and in particular, how words are spelled), semantics (the meaning of words) and grammar (as discussed above).

Phonological processing

Phonological processing refers to the idea that when we read words, we are accessing the sounds these words make when spoken. The question is, is this how we read? Two main models have been developed which seek to answer this:

- The strong phonological model − it is necessary to represent words phonologically in order to read them.
- The weak phonological model − because phonological processing is relatively slow it is not vital for word identifi-cation.

The strong phonological model is particularly associated with Ram Frost (1998). Frost proposed that it is necessary to form an inner phonological representation when reading even though this does not always require explicit pronunciation of each word. In contrast, Max Coltheart and co-workers have provided evidence that, when reading, we do not process individual letters, which suggests we do not need to engage in strong phonological representation of the words (Coltheart, Rastle, Perry, Langdon et al. 2001). How, we might ask, do people like Frost and Coltheart study this process? In fact, there are a number of experimental methods that have been devised to study the relationship between seeing written material and the processes then taken to read it.

One method of investigating the psychology of reading is through a process called 'phonological priming'. Priming in cognitive psychology refers to the presentation of a stimulus (usually a word or 'non-word' or a picture; see Chapter 4) prior to a second word in order to influence the reaction to the second word. Hence, in phonological priming, two phonologically overlapping words are presented with the first word (the prime) being used to influence the speed or accuracy of the second (target) word. Some primes are considered as positive if they increase either the speed or the accuracy of the target word. An example of this might be presenting the prime word 'NURSE' followed by target 'DOCTOR'. In this case the prime increases speed and accuracy of reading the target word. Negative primes do quite the opposite by reducing the speed and/or accuracy of the target word. An example of this might be using the prime of 'APPLE' followed by the target word 'DOCTOR'. In this case the prime is likely to reduce speed and accuracy of the target word because, at some level, the participant is likely to expect the next word to be a fruit. This phonological priming paradigm has been used in a number of experiments in order to determine the role of phonology in reading. In some experiments a word is preceded by a phonologically identical non-word. This might sound rather strange – but such non-words can be derived. Think of 'CUP' and 'KUP'. They should have identical pronunciation, but the former is a real word and the latter a non-word. When Rastle and Brysbaert (2006) reviewed a large number of phonological priming studies, they found words are processed more rapidly if phonologically identical non-words were presented first (i.e. used as primes). They took this finding as evidence for the strong phonological model as it suggests phonological processing having occurred to the prime then increased speed and accuracy to the target word. Rastle and Brysbaert suggest this occurs both rapidly and automatically (see also Castles, Rastle and Nation 2018).

Another way of addressing this issue is by studying individuals who have received brain injury which has altered their language abilities. One such study by Hanley and McDonnell (1997) provided evidence that the meaning of written words can be attained without access to phonology. Hanley and McDonnell made a study of PS, a man in his late forties, who following a left hemisphere cerebral infarct (stroke), had quite severe language problems. In particular, assessments showed that PS did not have access to phonological processing. Despite this he was still able to access the meaning of written words. Interestingly, despite his linguistic problems, PS had relatively well-preserved written spelling. Clearly, this case study provides evidence that we do not have to make use of phonetics in order to read. Other case studies have subsequently reported broadly similar findings (Han and Bi 2009). Such studies therefore provide support for Coltheart et al.'s weak phonological model.

Overall, while the evidence suggests phonological processing is normally involved in reading, hence supporting the strong phonological model, specific case studies have demonstrated that this is not essential, thereby providing some support for the weak phonological model.

Reading out loud

Although reading was described earlier as an arduous task to master, once we have mastered it, rather like driving a car, reading out loud appears be have become almost effortless. We should not, however underestimate just how complex a process this really is. We can illustrate this with an example of a couple of sentences that you will no doubt find very easy to read aloud:

> John was stuck in a jam with the shopping. He was concerned about what his wife would say.

We doubt you had any problems reading this sentence aloud and importantly, understanding its meaning. But what you have just done is, in reality, quite astonishing (Castles et al. 2018). Think about it. You see words on a page or screen. You have to identify them individually which involves, among things, distinguishing them from numerous similar other words. You also have to extract meaning from them. This also isn't as simple as it sounds because we determine meaning partly from context. For example, we realise that the 'he' in the second sentence refers to John. We also understand the word 'jam' in this context means that John is stuck in traffic rather than being entrapped in a sticky conserve. Furthermore, we understand from 'what his wife would say' that John's wife is likely to be annoyed that he is late, perhaps suggesting this is not the first time this has happened (or that he has done other things that she is unhappy about). All of this involves integrating information and placing demands on working memory and engaging executive functions (see Chapter 4). And we haven't even begun to consider the demands and skills of reading out loud (see below). All in all, reading even relatively short and straightforward sentences involves undertaking a series of highly complex neurocognitive tasks. How might we understand this process? Over the last 20 years cognitive psychologists have developed computational models of reading in order to describe and understand the cognitively driven operations involved in this process.

Computational models of reading

Computational models of reading are, as the name suggests, computer program-based models which are designed to mimic the human cognitive processing involved in reading a word (see Chapters 1 and 2). The aim of producing a computational model is not only to help understand how we are able to read but also to aid in our understanding of why some individuals have problems of acquiring this skill. That is, those who have been diagnosed with dyslexia. We will consider how each model strives to explain different forms of dyslexia. Currently there are three main computational models of reading:

- Dual–route cascade (DRC) model
- Triangle model
- Connectionist Dual Process models (CDP – hybrids of the DRC and triangle models)

1. THE DUAL-ROUTE CASCADE MODEL

According to the dual-route cascade model, there are two mechanisms or routes involved in reading (Coltheart et al. 2001). One of the routes simply matches the written word as it appears on the page (or screen) to the spelling entries in the individual's personal lexicon (see Figure 6.1). The second route converts the written letters to sounds which are then matched to the auditory representations in the lexicon. One of the positive features of the DRC is that it accounts for the fact that, once we have learned how to read, we can then read words we have not encountered before. Moreover, we can read non-words such as *slet* and *nish*. Given that *slet* and *nish* have no lexical entries, without this second route we would struggle to read them. And yet we are able to read such non-words effortlessly (even though they make no sense). This, of course, raises the question, why do we need the first route (that is, simply matching the word to our spelling entry in the lexicon)? This is necessary because it helps to explain how we are able to read phonetically irregular words such as *pint* and *answer*. That is, words where the second route would not work as we would pronounce the 'w' in *answer* and the 'i' in pint would be pronounced as it is in *pin*.

Looking at Figure 6.1, we can see it is called 'dual-route' because, following detection of the appropriate features for letters, there are then two routes to reading; a left hand one which relies on the lexicon and the right hand one which is a letter-to-phoneme pathway.

The DRC has been used to help to explain the existence of different forms of dyslexia. Most people are aware of the problem that some individuals have with reading known as dyslexia. They may be unaware, however, that there are several different forms of dyslexia (Willingham and Riener 2019). Confusingly, there are a number of different ways of labelling and classifying forms of dyslexia. However, three of the most common and recognised forms are:

- Surface dyslexia – the inability to read 'irregular' words (those with unusual print-to-sound correspondences such as *yacht*)
- Deep dyslexia – a form of acquired (that is, due to brain injury) reading problem where there are semantic errors and the inability to read non-words

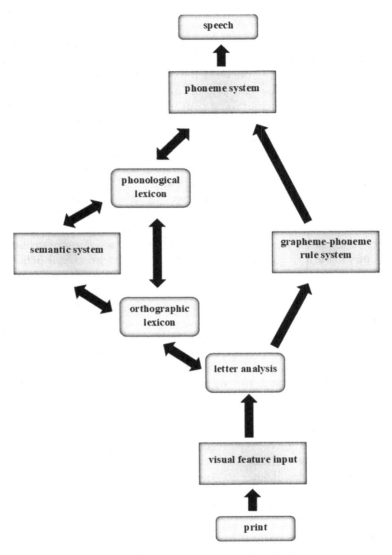

Figure 6.1 The dual-route cascade model of reading aloud
Source: Adapted from Castles et al. (2018)

- Phonological dyslexia – another form of acquired dyslexia; in this case there are serious problems with phonology (that is manipulating the basic sounds of language)

Surface and deep dyslexia, arguably, provide evidence to support the dual-route cascade model of reading (we will consider phonological dyslexia later). Interestingly, those with surface dyslexia are able to read regular words and non-words, but have great difficulty reading irregular words. Hence, they can read and pronounce the words *curse* or *crebe* correctly but have great difficulty with the pronunciation of the irregular *glove* (generally reading it as rhyming with *cove*; Willingham and Riener 2019). With regard to the DRC, this suggests the letter-to-phoneme route (on the right-hand side of Figure 6.1) remains intact but that the orthographic lexicon to phonological lexicon route (left-hand side) is damaged. In contrast, those with deep dyslexia can read both irregular words such as *knife* and regular words such as *dig*, correctly but are unable to read non-words such as *blad*. This suggests the letter-to-phoneme route is damaged, but the phonological lexicon route is unimpaired. Hence, the fact that we observe these two quite different forms of acquired dyslexia appears to be conducive to disruption of the two separate routes of the DRC.

2. THE TRIANGLE MODEL

A second computational model is the 'triangle model' (also known as the 'connectionist triangle model'; Harm and Seidenberg 1999; Seidenberg and McClelland 1989). The three points of the triangle are **orthography** (broadly spelling), phonology (sound patterns) and semantics (meaning). The triangle model proposes there are two routes by which a printed word comes to be read out loud. There is a direct route which involves linking orthography to phonology (spelling to sound). And there is an indirect route via semantics to sound (that is, readers can also use their phonology-semantics system which has previously been developed for spoken language). This means that 'mapping' from orthography to phonology involves simulation of reading out loud, but also involves an indirect route via semantics. Note that in this model these two routes are able to interact making it somewhat different from the DRC (see Figure 6.2).

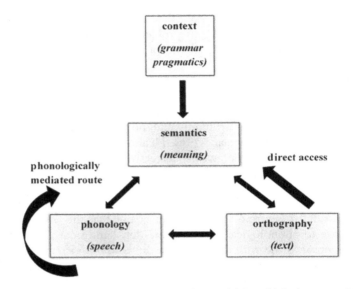

Figure 6.2 An illustration of the 'triangle' model in which three cognitive facilities interact to enable various language skills: known as the 'connectionist framework for lexical processing'

Source: Adapted from Seidenberg and McClelland (1989) and Plaut, McClelland, Seidenberg and Patterson (1996)

Importantly, the DRC model assumes that pronouncing non-words and irregular words involves separate routes. In contrast, according to the triangle model, because all words vary in their consistency, they may be available to all routes, but consistent words and non-words should be read more rapidly than inconsistent words. In a nutshell, there are two main differences between the DRC and the triangle model. First, according to the former, the ability to pronounce irregular words and non-words involves separate routes and second, in the latter, the two routes interact in the process of reading.

Given that computational models of reading were developed in order to help understand reading problems, this raises the question, how does the triangle model explain the dyslexias? The model suggests phonological dyslexia occurs when there is a general impairment in phonological processing. This is why individuals with this condition have difficulty reading both unfamiliar words and non-words. Coltheart (1996) identified a large number of cases of phonological dyslexia where a general phonological impairment was clear. This is at least consistent with the triangle model. Also, when considering both phonological and deep dyslexia participants together, Crisp, Howard and Lambon Ralph (2011) found, as the triangle model predicts, both groups had a substantial impairment in the ability to translate orthography into phonology. This is more conducive to the triangle model than the DRC.

3. CONNECTIONIST DUAL PROCESS MODELS

Because both dual–route cascade and connectionist triangle models have some evidential support, one problem which has arisen is how do we determine which is the better model of reading? One way of resolving this is to attempt to incorporate facets of each into a new model. This is what proponents of the third type of model, the 'connectionist dual process model' (CDP), have attempted to do (Perry, Ziegler and Zorzi 2007; Ziegler, Perry and Zorzi 2014). The term connectionist refers, in this context, to models in which behaviour emerges from a large set of loosely connected units (see Chapter 2). In a sense this can be seen as a division of labour model where lexical and non-lexical processing is conducted by different neural networks. The model makes use of input nodes from feature detectors to letter nodes (that is sub-lexical units). It then passes processed information onto two main routes; a grapheme based one (note, a grapheme is a specific single sound and can be represented either by a single letter such as 'o' or a group of letters such as 'er') and an orthographic and phonological route eventually leading to phoneme output (see Figure 6.3).

Because such models are designed via computer programs, they have seen a number of up-dates. Hence, we have seen the development of the CDP + , the CDP + + and the CDP + + .parser over recent years (just think of the various versions or Microsoft Word or Adobe that have been rolled out over the years). The precise nature of each would be beyond the scope of this text. What they all share in common is the conception of reading being the result of following a set of grapheme–to–phoneme conversion rules. In applying their model to the understanding of various forms of dyslexia, Ziegler et al. (2014) suggest it is visual and phenome deficits in this connectionist dual code approach which are responsible for reading difficulties.

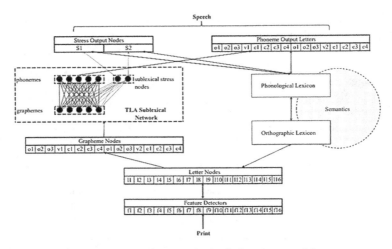

Figure 6.3 Representation of connectionist dual process model
Source: Adapted from Perry, Ziegler and Zorzi (2007)

In summary, the three models of reading which we have briefly presented here may appear complex and even perplexing at times. The important take home message is that all converge on the conception of reading as involving two key cognitive processes or routes. First, there is one route that decodes a word's spelling into its sound and then its meaning. Second, there is another route which involves direct access to meaning from spelling (without having to resort to phonology). (Note, the notion of dual processing is supported by brain scanning findings – see Box 6.2).

SPEECH PERCEPTION

As with reading, the ability to perceive speech is a complex one about which much research has taken place. Speech perception involves a number of stages from hearing through processing to understanding. How this process operates is important not just for our general understanding of speech but also, as in reading, to help us understand why some people have difficulty in this faculty. One influential model of speech perception was outlined by Anne Cutler and Charles Clifton in 1999. They proposed that there are five main stages to speech perception:

BOX 6.2   THE NEURAL BASES OF READING

Recent evidence from brain scanning studies suggests there are two main neural pathways which convert the printed word into the spoken word (Castles et al. 2018). First, there is a dorsal pathway (top of the brain) which underlies phonologically facilitated reading and second, there is a ventral pathway (side of the brain) which underlies direct access from print to meaning (see Figure 6.4). Findings from neuropsychology support this model since it is known that patients suffering from damage to parts of the dorsal pathway have great difficulty reading non-words, whereas those with damage to parts of the ventral pathway have much difficulty reading irregular words (Castles et al. 2018; Rastle 2019). Note that such findings add weight to the computational models of reading.

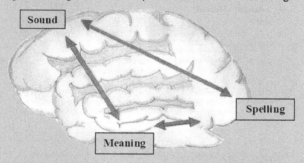

Figure 6.4 Dorsal and ventral pathways from print to spoken word
Source: Adapted from Rastle (2019)

1. Decoding – separating speech from other auditory input (including other voices)
2. Segmentation – of the signal into its component parts
3. Recognition – of words as such
4. Interpretation – of the utterance
5. Integration – of meaning to construct a model of the message

Cutler and Clifton's model is represented in Figure 6.5. As with all auditory information, speech consists of sound waves which reach our ears. Spoken language, however, rarely occurs in isolation of other sounds, meaning that, from the cacophony of noise which our

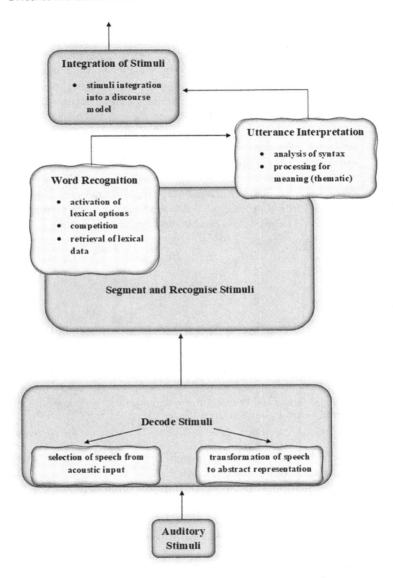

Figure 6.5 The processes involved in speech perception and comprehension
Source: Adapted from Cutler and Clifton (1999)

ears pick up, we must first recognise those which constitute speech. Fortunately, the human auditory system is able to make use of grouping mechanisms such as frequency characteristics which allows us to assign them as speech (this means that speech occurs within certain anticipated frequency parameters; Cutler and Clifton 1999). Isolating the sound components which constitute speech, that is phonemes, is part of the decoding stage. Note that at this stage we also have to transform this input into an abstract representation. Hence, we extract specific phonetic elements that make up the speech we are hearing. There is debate as to whether the next stage involves identification of phonemes or syllables (Eysenck and Keane, 2020) but, in either event, this process is one of segmentation so that language does not appear as a stream of sound. Following segmentation, we begin to recognise words via comparison with our personal lexicon. This is not as easy as it may sound since the indeterminately long list of words in, for example, the English language, is based around a mere 35 phonemes. This means that many words resemble each other and distinguishing between them is no mean feat. Context, of course, helps us here. If, for example, someone says 'one, two three', rather than 'set me free' then, even though the last word of these sentences is very similar, context helps us to recognise the correct word. According to Cutler and Clifton part and parcel of this process is lexical competition. This means that there is competition between candidate words when assessing which word we have heard. This comparison process acts to sharpen up distinctions between candidate words, leading rapidly to rejection of the inappropriate words and acceptance of the appropriate one. Following segmentation and recognition we begin to interpret the utterance by extracting meaning. Finally, the fifth stage involves integrating the meaning of the current utterance with previous ones in order to fully understand the discourse. (Note, some experts consider language to be supported by specific functional modules – see Box 6.3).

LANGUAGE COMPREHENSION

So far, we have considered how we are able to deal with written language and speech as separate processes. Language comprehension goes beyond this, however, as higher level processing involves understanding entire narratives (often by bringing together information

BOX 6.3   FODOR'S CONCEPTION OF A LANGUAGE MODULE

In 1983 the American philosopher of science Jerry Fodor introduced a new concept into our view of cognition. This is the concept of the 'module' or, to be more precise, the 'modular mind'. In his book 'The Modularity of Mind', Fodor proposed that many cognitive processes are self-contained, domain specific modules (see Chapters 1, 8 and 9). Following on from the ideas of Chomsky, Fodor suggested such modules were innate and evolved to serve specific functions. In particular, Fodor perceives modules in relation to perception and language. But what does it mean to say that cognitive processes are modularised? The most important feature of modules is that of domain specificity, which means they process particular forms of input. Hence, according to Fodor, modules react to specific stimuli such as certain aspects of speech. Max Coltheart's proposed dual-route cascade model of reading (see earlier) is an example of a system which contains specific language processing modules (see also Figure 1.5 in Chapter 1). Fodor's original conception of a dedicated language module has not been without its critics. Neuroimaging studies suggest that the human brain demonstrates a relatively high degree of connectivity (Zerilli, 2021). That is, various areas of the brain interact when cognitive processes are engaged. This apparent dispute might be partly resolved if we consider modularity to be more functional rather than structural. This means that while there might not be strict anatomical modularity, there may still be pathways in the brain which are largely devoted to quite specific problem-solving tasks (such as identifying aspects of linguistic input, Fodor, 1983, 2000).

from both written and spoken forms of language). Here we consider this higher level of comprehension through developing an understanding of two important linguistic concepts – parsing and pragmatics. This then leads us on to a consideration of discourse.

Parsing

Parsing, as we saw earlier, consists of breaking down a sentence into its component parts based around syntax and grammar. This

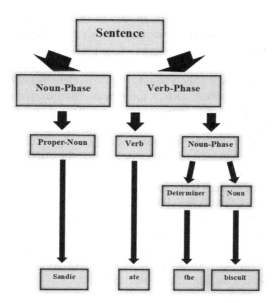

Figure 6.6 Diagram of a parsed sentence

allows us to classify each word by the part it plays in a sentence. Often, as a linguistic exercise, this is illustrated by sentence diagrams. Figure 6.6 presents an example of this.

Here we see that the sentence can first be broken down into a noun phrase (who the person or thing is – in this case Sandie) and a verb phrase (what the person or thing is doing – in this case eating a biscuit). We can then go further by identifying Sandie as a proper noun (that is a specific named entity) and the verb phrase can be sub-divided into a verb – 'ate' and a noun phrase within the verb phrase – 'the biscuit' (which incidentally is a common noun meaning it is a general non-specific thing). The noun phrase embedded in the verb phrase can then be broken down into a determiner (a word that introduces a noun) – in this case 'the' and the common noun – 'biscuit'. Note that in English a determiner always comes before a noun.

While the above provides a formal grammatical explanation of parsing, this is something we do all the time in a less formal manner in order to understand a speaker. That is, we have to know what the noun phrase and the verb phrases are in order to follow the speaker, even if we don't know these are the formal names for such components. This means that parsing involves working out the grammatical and syntactical structure of language. How we parse is a matter of debate. One way that this is achieved is via an understanding of prosodic cues. Prosody concerns elements of speech other than simple phonetics, such as intonation, rhythm, pause, stress and word duration. Hence, prosodic cues are those where differences in these features help us to extract meaning. This can make a big difference when a sentence is ambiguous. If we say, "the children make tasty snacks", then this can mean either that the children are good at preparing a tasty snack or that they are themselves tasty! Prosodic cues help here – although it has to be said that this is an extreme example for the sake of illustration. Researchers have made use of ambiguous statements to help understand the importance of prosodic cues.

An example of this is Gayle DeDe's (2010) research into how individuals with aphasia (language problems which follow brain damage) struggle with ambiguous sentences where the ambiguity can be created by use of a pause, such as:

"While the parents watched (,) the child sang a song."

Note that if we pause between the first four and the last four words it reads as if the parents were watching something, but not necessarily the child. If we exclude the pause, then it becomes clear that the parents are watching the child sing. DeDe found that individuals with aphasia were less able to make use of the prosodic pause cue. So even pausing very briefly can help us to parse a sentence, although this can be difficult for those suffering from aphasia. This suggests that the ability to make use of prosodic cues can be one of the facilities which is disrupted by aphasia.

Pragmatics

Pragmatics concerns how language is used in terms of what the speaker intended to say, rather than the actual words used. Sounds confusing? Here's some examples:

- 'It's raining cats and dogs.' Clearly this is not literally the case, hence pragmatics includes figurative rather than literal language.

- 'You got a mark of 20 per cent on the exam, boy you really put in a lot of effort.' Here the speaker is using irony, with the real meaning being the opposite of the stated meaning.
- 'You failed your driving test 6 times now; you certainly take the biscuit.' This combines both figurative language and irony.

Note that in each of these cases, simply understanding the semantics of what is being said is not enough to follow the speaker's meaning. Hence, pragmatics is very much about context.

Discourse and predictive inference

Thus far we have focused on individual sentences. Most linguistic encounters involve at least several sentences. When we use the term 'discourse', we are normally referring to speech or written language which is at least several sentences long. When a series of sentences is written down and they are related to each other (the normal pattern) researchers refer to this as 'text'. Hence, written discourse concerns extended language or text rather than a simple statement. (Note that 'discourse' means something a little different to social scientists. To sociologists in particular, the term carries connotations about power and politics.) To follow discourse, we need to make inferences about what the speaker (or writer) is attempting to communicate. Discourse allows us to understand a great deal more than stand-alone sentences. Consider the following example:

'Sandie was getting annoyed'
'It took Lance a very long time to make the tea'
'When Sandie saw Lance, she gave him the cold shoulder'

The individual sentences provide us with information, but by putting all three together we are able to make a number of inferences. We infer that Sandie is annoyed with Lance because he took such a long time to make tea for her (note that in this context a 'cold shoulder' is, of course, figurative rather than literal and hence related to pragmatics). We might also infer a great deal more. Perhaps Lance has a history of being slow to make the tea. Perhaps this isn't the case but rather Sandie is a somewhat impatient person. We would also probably infer that Sandie and Lance are an 'item'.

We might be right or wrong in all of these inferences, but without considering all three sentences we would be unlikely to make as many inferences.

As we read or listen to someone speaking, we constantly predict, by inference, what we are about to read or hear. For obvious reasons, cognitive psychologists and linguists call this predictive inference. Cognitivists have shown a great deal of interest in the role that predictive inference plays in comprehending discourse, especially when reading. In particular they have developed two main theories to explain how such inferences are generated (Nahatame 2014):

- The constructionist theory – readers construct a global mental model of events
- The minimalist theory – readers construct a relatively restricted mental model of events

According to the constructionist view many elaborate inferences are drawn as we read (Bransford, Barclay and Franks 1972). This perspective suggests we form elaborate inferences due to embellishing the information as we read. If we look at the sentence above which began with 'Sandie was getting annoyed', it is certain that we immediately begin to wonder why this is the case. Many researchers, however, who subscribe to the minimalist approach, suggest the constructionist approach would open up too many possibilities and that we are likely to make only one or two possible inferences (Nahatame 2014). Graesser, Millis and Zwaan (1997) have attempted to reconcile minimalist and constructionist theories by suggesting we make use of the former when scan reading but move on to the latter when we are reading slowly and consciously attempting to comprehend the discourse.

Note that in either case a reader has to draw on both long-term memory (otherwise much of what we read would be incomprehensible) and working memory (that is, we need to maintain information we have just read in order for us to develop a narrative; see Chapter 4).

Understanding discourse – the construction-integration model

One model of discourse comprehension which builds in the notion of inference, is that of Walter Kintsch (1988, 2005). In his construction-integration (CI) model a number of inferences are activated in parallel, but then the irrelevant ones are rapidly deactivated. (Note that this can be seen as a compromise between constructionist and minimalist theories introduced above.) In order to achieve this both top-down and bottom-up processes are involved (see Chapter 3). According to Kintsch, during initial processing we make use of bottom-up mechanisms as word-meanings are activated and inferences made. Then, we begin to draw on general knowledge, as top-down expectation-driven processes kick in. It is this drawing on top-down knowledge which keeps us on the right track and away from blind alleys. In the CI model it is contextual information which allows us to prune irrelevant propositions that we initially develop in order to comprehend the text. It is these top-down processes which give the model the 'integration' part of its name. The model also suggests we develop three separate levels of representation as we read a passage:

1 Surface − the actual text
2 Propositional − propositions are formed as we read (and then elaborated)
3 Situational − a mental model is developed which describes the situation

Put simply, in the CI model we construct meaning and then integrate it with pre-existing knowledge (see Figure 6.7). While Kintsch's CI model is not the only one which has been developed to help explain how we build up an understanding of discourse, it does appear to stand up well to scrutiny. In particular, the pattern of forgetting each of the three progressive levels of representation supports the model. That is, in time we retain the situational information better than the propositional information and this, in turn, is retained better than the surface representation (Eysenck and Keane 2020). For example, if we look at an actual passage of text (surface) such as 'cat sat under the palm tree on the left side of the hut', we form a series of propositions which in turn helps us to form a mental model (see Chapter 5). In this case it is very much a visual image. It is this situational representation which is the most memorable.

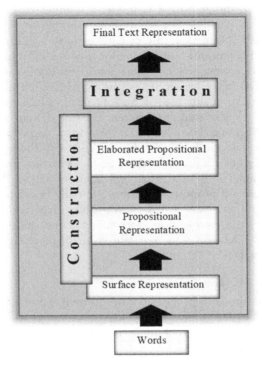

Figure 6.7 Diagram representing Kintsch's construction-integration model

WRITING AND SPELLING

As we saw when we discussed reading and speech, some form of spoken language is considered to have begun to evolve around 1.8 million years ago. In contrast, the first known written language, cuneiform, is believed to date back to around 3,500 BCE. This makes writing a relatively recent cultural invention when compared with speaking. In a sense we can think of writing as having piggybacked on top of talking as a new way of recording events and passing on information. This means that, while we may be well adapted to develop speech (Workman and Reader 2021), writing comes less naturally to us and involves a whole series of complex processes which we need to learn. This raises the question what are these processes? Over the last

40 years cognitivists have developed models to help us understand such processes. A comprehensive review of each model would be out of place here and hence we confine ourselves to the most well accepted (although by no means universally so) model today – Hayes' writing model. Based on earlier work by Chenoweth and Hayes (2001), his model involves three levels plus a task environment (Hayes 2012 – see Figure 6.8).

The three levels that Hayes proposed are:

1   Control level – this involves motivation and goal setting to help form a current plan. In a sense, this level considers why people write and what the intended outcome should be. Your

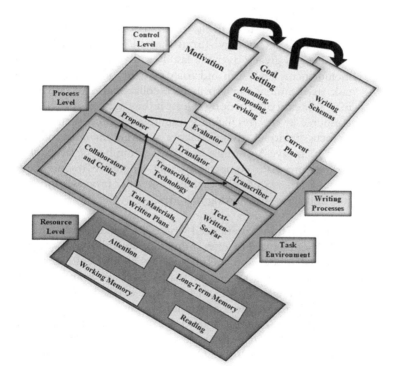

Figure 6.8 Representation of Hayes' writing model
Source: Adapted from Hayes (2012)

motivation might be to revise for or pass an exam, it might be a letter or email to a friend in order to keep them informed or it might be to earn money and gain prominence as a professional writer. Whatever the motivation, in order to achieve a positive outcome, we need to set goals and monitor our progress. The writing schemas represent the writer's views on how writing processes and resources may be used to create the text that is currently planned.

2   Process level – this has two major interactive parts: the writing processes and the task environment. The writing process involves a number of sub-processes (a proposer, evaluator, translator and transcriber) all of which interact with the task environment. Here, transcription (which includes spelling and orthography) is of particular importance as it takes the language and creates the text from it. Transcription draws on the 'transcribing technology' (from the task environment) which has changed greatly over the last 40–50 years. Today this may include pens, keyboards and voice recognition technology. The task environment can also include collaborators or critics who may aid text construction (at least if they are constructive).

3   Resource level – this includes cognitive resources such as ability to focus attention, reading abilities, working memory and long-term memory. According to Hayes, a number of facets of the writing processes compete for such cognitive resources. For example, transcription competes with other processes for attention and access to working memory.

Hayes' model of how experienced writers work can be thought of as a flow chart of mental processes. Note that, in addition to cognitive processes, the model also incorporates social and cultural factors. Hayes' model appears to suggest that, when we write, there is a natural sequence we follow from 1 to 2 to 3 as discussed above. The evidence suggests, however, that while Hayes is broadly correct in this assumption, there are relatively large individual differences in the order with which writers make use of these processes (Eysenck and Keane 2020). Hence, we should not see this sequence as carved in stone, but rather one that allows for back-tracking and at times jumping between stages. It is worth noting, at this stage, that inherent in the ability to write is the ability to spell (see Box 6.4).

BOX 6.4   SPELLING THE DUAL-ROUTE MODEL

In order to write we have to be able to spell. This, of course, is also true when it comes to reading. Hence, spelling is important for both of these language abilities. You won't be surprised to learn that cognitive psychologists have developed complex models of spelling. As with reading (see earlier on) a dual-route model of spelling has been developed (Eysenck and Keane 2020). In this case we have:

1   A lexical route which retrieves spellings of known words from our personal lexicon.
2   A non-lexical (or assembled) route which uses a sound-to-spelling process.

These two processing systems are considered to operate in parallel. In the case of the lexical route, three facets of processing are brought into the mix: phonology (sound), semantics (meaning) and orthography (reading). This means that the lexical route contains information required to connect the sound of a word with both its meaning and how it is read. In this way this route draws heavily on long-term memory of word-specific knowledge. The lexical route is the main one we use when considering familiar words, whether they are regular letter-to-sound (e.g. dog) or irregular (e.g. ewe) words. In contrast, the non-lexical route does not involve retrieval of stored information concerning the sound, meaning and spelling of a word. Rather it makes use of recalled rules which have previously been successful when converting sounds or phonemes into letter groups or graphemes. In this sense it assembles the spelling of the word based on previous experience. This means that the non-lexical (assembled) route is efficient for languages where there are consistent orthographic-to-phonological correspondences (e.g. Italian or Japanese kana which are symbols used to write Japanese phonological units) but is significantly less effective for language where there is inconsistency between orthography and phonology.

Evidence for this dual-route model comes from neurological case studies where various forms of acquired dysgraphia (problems with writing related to brain injury) are observed. Two main forms of dysgraphia are surface and phonological. In the case of surface dysgraphia individuals have problems with orthographic representations of words. This means that they rely very much on sound. In contrast, with phonological dysgraphia it is the spelling of irregular words that is particularly impaired. This means that those with the phonological form have problems spelling by sound. The fact that we see these two forms of dysgraphia provides evidence for the dual-route spelling model with those suffering from phonological dysgraphia having an impairment to the non-lexical route and those suffering from surface dysgraphia having an impairment with the lexical route (Cholewa, Mantey, Heber and Hollweg 2010). Note in cognitive neuropsychology this form of evidence is known as a 'double dissociation' study (see Chapter 1). Double dissociation suggests two related mental processes are observed to function independently of each other because when one route is impaired the other can still operate.

Working memory in writing

Why, we might ask, is writing so effortful compared to talking? At a functional level, as we have emphasised, writing is a relatively new development when considered in the light of human evolution. At a more structural level, we can explain this by referring to the notion that writing draws on so many of our cognitive resources (see 'resource level' in Figure 6.8). While attention and long-term memory are clearly necessary, it has been argued that it is the constant use of working memory which makes it such an effortful process (Kellogg and Whiteford 2012). You may recall from Chapter 4, that working memory is used when we need to store specific information temporarily (Baddeley and Hitch 1974). Clearly this is an important facet of writing. Working memory has four main components: a central executive, phonological loop, visuo-spatial sketchpad and episodic buffer (Baddeley 2000; see Figure 4.3). Of these, the central executive is particularly important due to the attentional processes. Additionally, the phonological loop is used for verbal rehearsal and the visuo-spatial sketchpad is required for visual processing (Eysenck and Keane 2020). Given this massive load on working memory and all of its components, it is hardly surprising writing is so effortful!

SUMMARY

Most psycholinguists agree crucial features of human language include arbitrariness, semanticity, syntax, cultural transmission, displacement and creativity. Grammar consists of syntax (rules about word order), phonology (sound patterns), semantics (the meaning of words) and the lexicon (the 'dictionary' we hold in our heads). Chomsky suggested language has a universal grammar and is an innate ability in humans. While some apes demonstrate evidence of semanticity, their linguistic abilities fall far short of those of humans. Reading involves phonology, orthography (conventions of how a language is written), semantics and grammar. There are two main phonological models of reading: strong models where it is necessary to represent words phonologically in order to read them and weak models where this isn't necessary. Three computational models of reading have been derived. The dual-route cascade model suggests there are two routes to reading (one which relies on the lexicon and one which uses a letter-to-phoneme pathway). The triangle model suggests there is a direct route linking spelling to sound and an indirect route via semantics to sound. Finally, the connectionist dual process model conceives of reading as being the result of following a set of grapheme-to-phoneme conversion rules. Speech perception is considered to involve five stages: decoding (separating speech from other sounds), segmentation (of the signal into its parts), recognition (of words), interpretation (of utterance) and integration (constructing meaning). Language comprehension involves the processes of parsing (breaking down a sentence into its parts), and of understanding pragmatics (the intention of the speaker). During discourse we make inferences about the message. Cognitivists have developed two main theories to explain how inferences are generated. These are the constructionist theory where readers construct a global mental model of events and the minimalist theory where readers construct a restricted mental model of events. The construction-integration model suggests a number of inferences are activated in parallel, but then irrelevant ones are discarded. The model suggests, when reading, we develop three levels of representation: surface (the actual text), propositional (propositions are formed) and situational (a mental model to describe the situation). The Hayes model of writing suggests the process has three levels: a control level (involving planning), a process level (involving actual writing) and a resource level (involving cognitive resources).

FURTHER READING

Aitchison, J. (2008) *The Articulate Mammal.* (5th edn). London: Routledge.

Harley, T. (2017) *Talking the Talk: Language, psychology and science.* Hove: Psychology Press.

Seidenberg, M. (2017) *Language at the Speed of Sight: How we read, why so many can't, and what can be done about it.* New York, NY: Basic Books.

Zerilli, J. (2021) *The Adaptable Mind: What neuroplasticity and neural reuse tell us about Language and Cognition.* Oxford: Oxford University Press.

CONSCIOUSNESS AND METACOGNITION

'Cogito ergo sum' – translating to, 'I think therefore I am', a quote by philosopher René Descartes, was considered in Chapter 5 as key to understanding how important thought is to our existence. Is there, however, a deeper meaning encapsulated in Descartes' quote? Is the ability to think an aspect of consciousness? When we are in thought we use a hypothetical mental system resembling a language shorthand known as mentalese. Mentalese enables us to put concepts into pictorial form without the need of words; as used in speech. When we think about information presented to us, when we recall memories and even when we enjoy what we are seeing, we mark the occasion using self-commentary. This self-commentary can be simplistic such as, 'Oh this is nice' or it can be quite complicated such as 'I wonder if Tom thinks Mary is annoyed with me?' Is the ability to do this a sign of being conscious? Whilst reading this, you are likely to be attending to the words and their meaning, which you later reflect and churn over in your mind to attain the sense of what you have just read. This reflecting is known as metacognition. Koriat (2007) defined it thus: "Metacognition research concerns the processes by which people self-reflect on their own cognitive and memory processes (monitoring) and how they put their metaknowledge to use in regulating their information processing and behavior (control)" (p. 289). Consciousness and metacognition, it seems, go hand in hand. Koriat (2000) further argued that it is consciousness which unites our knowledge and metaknowledge together. Defining consciousness is not straightforward but it is generally considered to refer to a unique individual awareness of one's memories,

DOI: 10.4324/9781003014355-7

sensations, thoughts, emotions and the external world. This awareness extends to how the 'self' interacts with the external world. William James (1890) compared consciousness to a continuous and uninterrupted stream, despite changes of direction and shifts of current. This is a good analogy given that we can attend to one thing and change our attention to something else, and yet at the same time experience unbroken consciousness. This suggests that our consciousness is a dynamic process. We can also experience different natural states of consciousness such as when we sleep, dream, hallucinate or undergo hypnosis or meditation. There are of course other altered states of consciousness experienced through underlying mental conditions such as delirium, disorientation, confusion, lethargy, stupor and coma. James (1890) also described the experience of the new-born as a "blooming, buzzing confusion" (p. 462; see Chapter 3). What kind of consciousness does this suggest? It is clear that new-borns are conscious as they appear to be aware and attentive at times. We might also ask, what is the conscious experience of individuals who are in a coma? Unlike new-borns they appear to be unaware of their surroundings and fail to show behavioural signs of attention. But does this imply that they lack an internal conscious state? It is interesting how moving away from traditional behavioural measures of consciousness towards neurocognitive ones, provides a new perspective on the role of consciousness. To understand how we got here, however, it is important to review the definitions of consciousness and the different forms it takes.

CONSCIOUSNESS

There are different perspectives regarding what consciousness is. For some academics, consciousness is an illusion, and our inner world merely a commentary on what we should do next (Dennett 1988). Dennett (2003) poses the question of whether the underlying mechanisms of consciousness can be revealed by researching this illusion. Alternatively, Oakley and Halligan (2017) conceive consciousness as a passive observer of our inner and outer world experience instead of a controlling mechanism for our actions. They also consider consciousness as an epiphenomenon; an effect resulting as a by-product from some other process. Meese (2018) said of Oakley and Halligan's approach that, "They suggest it is the internal broadcasting ... of a selective personal narrative that defines the wick of our life during its transfer to memory" (p. 2). According to Miles (2015) it provides an intuitive review of how we perceive the world and ourselves. Even Oakley and Halligan's understanding of consciousness, however, has been criticised on account of the fact that consciousness has causal feedback whereas an epiphenomenon does not (Robinson 2015). Causal feedback provides us with information about the current situation and what would be the appropriate action to take next (see Figure 7.1).

Bor and Seth (2012) claim that we should be making a distinction between conscious content and conscious level. This distinction could be used to clarify how consciousness might be studied. In the case of consciousness, Coleman (2001) defines it as, "the experience of perceptions, thoughts, feelings, awareness of the external world, and often in humans ... self-awareness" (p. 160). This fits in with Bor and Seth's description of what conscious content is as it implies that we are aware of information at any point in time. Conscious level, however, describes the different states of consciousness, which we established earlier can be

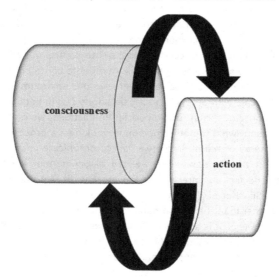

Figure 7.1 A causal feedback loop between consciousness and action

numerous (from being alert to comatose). Further distinctions have been made – access and phenomenal consciousness. As the name implies, the access element of consciousness enables us to review contents and pass this on to memory. Private experiences that are difficult to present in an available form comprise phenomenal consciousness. Yet another distinction was made by Baumeister and Masicampo (2010). In this case phenomenal consciousness is accessible and refers to our sensations and feelings of the moment; a basic type of consciousness. Alternatively, the higher form of consciousness enables us to reason and reflect about past, present and future life events and the self. By this description, the higher form of consciousness is analogous to **metacognition**. To help establish what behavioural measures can be used to understand consciousness the functions of consciousness are outlined below (see Box 7.1).

BOX 7.1 WHAT FUNCTIONS DOES CONSCIOUSNESS SERVE?

There has been controversy over the issue of free will. The fact that we can make our own decisions rather than being subservient to controlling environmental and internally driven factors seems important to us as humans. Therefore, it is not surprising that one of the functions of consciousness is to control our actions. By doing this we are displaying free will. In order to control our actions, however, we need to be able to perceive our environment and to communicate with others in social situations (again both controlled by our consciousness). During social interactions, we make judgements about what the other person is thinking – a process referred to as 'theory of mind'. While we can communicate information to others in the here-and-now, we can also entertain ideas about events and factors unrelated to the present. In fact, Kane, Brown, McVay, Siliva et al. (2007) found that we consciously think about things other than the task at hand for about 30 per cent of the time. Consciousness, it is argued by Tononi and Koch (2015), provides us with valuable information about our circumstances. Given that we can only be in one conscious state at a time, the current state of consciousness excludes other states of consciousness. This means that specific types of information are available, integrated and combined; ultimately packaged in a useable form and directed by the current state of our conscious mind. Consciousness can therefore be regarded as a form of information processing (Fingelkurts and Fingelkurts 2017). Some argue that it is in fact a special way of processing information (Marchetti 2018).

BEHAVIOURAL MEASURES OF CONSCIOUSNESS

Consciousness is measured by considering our conscious experience in relation to the world around us. Gamez (2014) claims that consciousness can only be measured using first person reports. This is problematic for various reasons such as accuracy of reporting and the failure to verbalise non-reportable elements of consciousness. Much of our conscious experiences appear to be lost in translation due to being unreportable. This implies that a part of our actual conscious experiences remains hidden such that what we do report is limited and lacks intensity (Lamme 2010). Furthermore, Lamme argues that, in order to report our conscious experiences, we resort to other cognitive processes such as mentalese, memory and attention, all of which can interfere with verbalising experience. It is this, Lamme argues, that acts as a limiting factor and not the conscious experience *per se*. When we consider consciousness, we often state that we are aware of events occurring. For example, we use words such as, 'I saw', 'I felt' or 'I heard' – all descriptors implying a sense of being aware of an event and being 'tuned in' or attending to it. It is not surprising therefore that many behavioural measures used to study consciousness draw upon our ability to attend to stimuli. This was demonstrated in an experiment by Sperling in 1960 (see Chapter 4). Sperling presented participants with a three-by-four array of letters displayed for 50 milliseconds. Typically, only four-to-five letters were reported. The explanation for such underreporting lay with the degradation of the presentation before participants could report all the letters. When, however, participants were cued to recall a part of the presentation, recall performance increased. A similar result was found by Lamme using the same system of cueing by pointing to a particular object only two seconds before the array disappeared and before the second presentation of the same array. Such findings suggest that participants do have *conscious* access to all the stimuli presented for a while after the array presentation disappears.

An interesting phenomenon called subliminal perception supports the idea of having access to information and yet being unable to recall it. This information is presented below the threshold of conscious perception. This raises the question of how we determine the threshold of conscious perception. In fact, there are two ways in which this can be ascertained: objective and subjective threshold. The objective threshold is determined by the participant's failure to accurately select the correct stimulus from a **forced-choice procedure**. Using this procedure, when participants perform at or below chance level then objective threshold is achieved. In the case of subjective threshold, participants are unable to report being consciously aware of a stimulus presented and fail to select the correct stimulus in a forced-choice design. The subjective threshold is typically 30–50 milliseconds slower than the objective threshold, suggesting that participants are able to detect the stimulus before their perceived accuracy ratings indicate (Chessman and Merikle 1984). Whether awareness of information presented to us is a necessary prerequisite for control over our actions was investigated by Persaud and McLeod (2008). A letter of the alphabet was presented visually at two-time intervals: a short interval of 10 milliseconds and a long interval of 15 milliseconds. Participants were asked not to respond to the letter presented but to provide a different letter. The idea behind this was that if they perceived the letter then they would provide a different letter of the alphabet. If they had not perceived the letter, then they would not know whether the letter they provided was the letter presented or not. For the 15-millisecond presentation, participants correctly responded for 83 per cent of trials, but this decreased to 43 per cent for 10 millisecond presentations. The latter was below chance level and suggested that processing had occurred but was devoid of conscious awareness. Windey, Vermeiren, Atas and Cleeremans (2014) provided evidence for there being a grading of perceptual awareness for simple tasks, but an all-or-none effect for complex tasks.

Subliminal messaging has been used as a marketing ploy for many years. In addition to marketing, it has also been used in music, games and Disney and Pixar animations. According to

Kardes, Cronley and Cline (2011) the subliminal message is processed unconsciously and is unperceived by being masked by
images presented for longer and is therefore consciously perceived.
But can this still have an impact on our behaviour? The evidence
appears to suggest that a subliminal message can influence our
behaviour provided it remains simple. Perloff (2010) claimed that
perception can occur without awareness as seen in the perception
of the subliminal. Such findings as Sperling's experiments and
subliminal perception indicate that understanding the way consciousness operates is far from straightforward. Block (2012) argues
that these findings support his view that there is a difference between access and phenomenal consciousness. Block considers
phenomenal consciousness to be far more extensive than access
consciousness. The reporting of access consciousness, however,
fails to encapsulate the richness of detail found in phenomenal
consciousness. This point of view is not supported by some academics such as Kouider, Sackur and de Gardelle (2012), who refute
the existence of phenomenal consciousness. They consider the
notion of a rich conscious experience as illusory. At the same time,
they suggest we can overestimate the richness of our experiences as
a consequence of our expectation bias. By adapting the Sperling
task, de Gardelle, Sackur and Kouider (2009) demonstrated how
expectations interfere with reporting what was seen in the arrays.
De Gardelle et al. rotated and flipped letters and introduced
pseudo-letters but these were rarely identified by participants. They
concluded that we exaggerate the profundity and richness of our
conscious experience and recall inaccurately.

Whichever way we interpret consciousness and our reporting of
conscious experiences, the role played in social communication and
the control over our actions is difficult to ignore. We find it difficult
to socially isolate from others. This has recently been borne out from
the Covid-19 pandemic. People across the world find it difficult to
avoid communicating with family and friends, which demonstrates
the adaptive role of social communication. Interacting with other
people not only helps us to gauge their intentions but also serves to
develop a sense of self which is rooted in our conscious experiences of
the social and physical world. Marchetti (2018) argued that consciousness does more than merely transmit information, it also produces it. Hence, when we attend to stimuli, we are not just

transmitting what we experience but we are also responding to the information thereby creating new information. To do this effectively and to report our conscious experiences, Marchetti argues that consciousness draws upon attention (see Chapter 3) and working memory (see Chapter 4) to create new information which influences the self (see Figure 7.2). When communicating with a friend, for example, we focus on what they are saying and all other manner of non-verbal communication (such as gestures and eye direction) to interpret what the intention behind the utterance might be. Such interpretations rely on the use of working memory and long-term

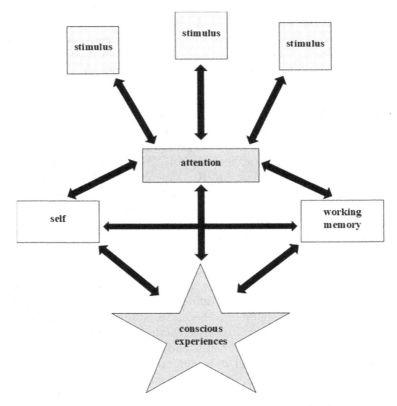

Figure 7.2 Role of self, attention and working memory in the formation of conscious experiences
Source: Adapted from Marchetti (2018)

memories of what, for instance, a gesture might mean. Moreover, what the interpreted intention means for the self, will generate new information – all processed by our conscious mind. When we try to make sense of another person's awareness, we also depend on neural mechanisms such as sensorimotor neurons (also known as mirror neurons; see Chapter 8).

Our conscious mind it seems can be passive and active. The information generated is meaningful and adds to our catalogue of conscious experiences. It also fits in with our plans and goals (Zlatev 2002).This implies that our experiences are continuously transformed as we interact with our environment and it is the self which provides the data for our conscious experiences. When reporting our conscious experiences, we assume that our thoughts to perform an action are of our own free volition. As pointed out by Aarts and van den Bos (2011), our own free will involves, "the ability to make choices and to determine one's own outcomes free from constraints" (p. 532). Thus, when we decide to eat a piece of cake, we do so because it is the choice of food we have selected. Conscious **implementation intentions** are those which determine when, where and how our goals will be achieved, and we use these in everyday life. Gollwitzer and Sheeran (2006) studied implementation intentions by considering the findings from numerous studies (that is, a meta-analysis). The findings from the meta-analysis highlighted how increased goal achievement occurred when intentions were of the implementation type rather than less defined. They concluded that behaviour can be manipulated by conscious intentions, provided we can break away from the cycle of habitual behaviours such as putting the radio on when preparing a salad. Implementation intentions suggest we have free will. Can we make participants believe they have free will when in actual fact the experiment was rigged? (see Box 7.2).

Behavioural measures of reporting conscious experience can be inaccurate and difficult to extract from other factors acting as interference or noise. For this reason, cognitive psychologists use experiments which rely on brain activity indicators.

BRAIN INDICATORS OF CONSCIOUSNESS

Given that when we think of consciousness, we associate it with attention, many studies have focused on what happens in terms of

BOX 7.2   FAKE FREE WILL

Van der Weiden, Ruys and Aarts (2013) designed an experiment to investigate whether participants can be duped into believing that they *magically* made something happen. Participants were presented with a sequence of words shown rapidly on a computer screen. They had the option to press a button causing the word sequence to stop at their goal word. When they pressed the stop button and the word displayed matched their word goal, participants' perception of self-advocacy was higher than when the word mismatched the word goal. In reality there was no control over which word was frozen on the screen – it was all computer generated unbeknownst to the participants. This study highlights how easy it is to be duped into believing we have control over outcomes, when in fact it is a fake free will set-up.

brain activity when we attend to visual stimuli. Lamme (2010) has studied how conscious experience of visual objects activates areas of the visual cortex of the brain automatically. Early activation initially occurs at the visual cortex but progresses rapidly to higher centres of the brain within a 100–150 millisecond timeframe. As previously discussed in Box 3.5, information flows through the hierarchy of visual neurons on a feedforward basis. This means that information progresses on a 'bottom–up' processing basis (see Chapter 3). As pointed out by Gilbert and Li (2013), however, information can also be based on feedback processing; in this case 'top–down'. Lamme claims it is the feedback processing where information passes from higher to lower areas of the brain that conscious experience co-occurs. In other words, it is top–down and not bottom–up processing that is involved with our conscious experience. Banich and Compton (2018) emphasise "that there is not one brain region that is the seat of consciousness, but rather consciousness is an emergent phenomenon that arises from the interaction of brain mechanisms and regions" (p. 330). This implies that in feedback processing, information about objects is integrated to a high level thus providing the complexity of detail required for conscious experience (see Box 7.3). There are different methods for preventing feedback processing but enabling feedforward

BOX 7.3   IS THERE ANY PROCESSING OCCURRING IN UNCONSCIOUS PATIENTS?

There are different states of consciousness. When we are asleep, we are unaware of what is going on around us. When we are in a lecture, we listen to what is being said and read the PowerPoint slides – we are alert and attending to our surroundings. Patients who are in a vegetative state (VS) and those who are in a minimally conscious state (MCS), are believed to be non-responsive and non-attentive to what is going on around them. But is there some kind of processing occurring in the brain? If so, is this feedforward or feedback or both? Boly, Garrido, Gosseries, Bruno et al. (2011) hypothesised that impairment to top-down processing (feedback) is a reliable indicator of consciousness. The frontoparietal cortex (see Chapter 2) plays an important role in awareness through the explicit processing of stimuli. Boly et al. studied three groups: VS, MCS and a healthy control group. They used event-related potentials (ERPs; see Chapter 1) as a measure of brain activity during the presentation of auditory stimuli. Feedforward processing was similar for all three groups. Feedback processing, however, was disrupted in the brain damaged patients which indicated a loss of consciousness. Nevertheless, this measure usefully differentiated between the VS and MCS patients, and could, Boly et al. argued, be reliably used as a diagnostic tool to quantify the level of consciousness. Hence, such electrophysiological measures could separate MCS patients from their VS counterparts.

processing as a means of investigating what happens to conscious experience. One method adopted by Koivisto, Railo, Revonsuo, Vanni et al. (2011) was to cease feedback processing using transcranial magnetic stimulation (TMS; see Chapter 1). TMS enabled feedforward processing to continue such that participants could process the natural scenes and animals embedded but could not integrate information further using feedback processing. The result was that participants could not make decisions as to whether animals were present in the natural scenes. In other words, their TMS interfered with feedback processing and was detrimental to their conscious visual perception.

But can conscious visual perception occur without feedback processing, in other words top-down processing? Empirical findings suggest it can. When a stimulus is presented briefly and immediately followed by another stimulus, known as a masking stimulus, the second stimulus blocks any feedback processing of the first one. When Koivisto, Kastrati and Revonsuo (2014) used this masking approach for some of the target photographs (those containing animals), performance rate for responding failed to be significantly different regardless of being masked (86 per cent) or unmasked (88 per cent). Despite this, however, the participants reported being less aware of the masked photographs. Koivisto et al. concluded that feedback processing enhances perception, but it is not always necessary. Interestingly, feedback processing can occur without there being conscious awareness of it (Scholte, Wittreveen, Soekreijse and Lamme 2006) and yet neural activity in the brain occurs (Thakral 2011).

Understanding the role of consciousness and feedforward and feedback processing is best exemplified by studying brain-damaged individuals. When studying brain-damaged individuals, the level of consciousness can be categorised according to the severity of damage to the brain. Three levels have been identified; coma, vegetative state (VS) and minimally conscious state (MCS). The most severe brain damage is coma, and whilst under a coma the individual experiences no wakefulness or conscious awareness. In contrast, VS individuals show wakefulness but no conscious awareness. For MCS individuals there is evidence supporting consciousness. VS individuals have been of particular interest to academics, given that in some cases, neuroimaging has shown conscious awareness when performing specific cognitive tasks (Owen 2013). This occurs despite an exterior presentation of non-responsivity to behavioural measures (see Box 7.4).

When describing consciousness, we have alluded to the importance of attention operating in tandem. In fact, Eysenck and Keane (2015) likened attention to our choice of television channel and consciousness to the picture seen on the television set. As we have seen some individuals in a VS demonstrate consciousness by the ability to attend to questions asked using the medium of imagery. Those in a coma show no attention nor consciousness. So, what is the relationship between the two?

BOX 7.4 ARE INDIVIDUALS IN A VEGETATIVE STATE (VS) RESPONSIVE?

The cognitive tasks that VS individuals have been subjected to appear simple enough but, when the processing involved is broken down, it becomes apparent that the level of cognition required is multifaceted. For example, these tasks involve working memory, focused attention, understanding of language and choice of response. Imagery is often used to enable response selection. In one case a 23-year-old woman in a vegetative state was requested to imagine either playing tennis or moving through the rooms of her house. The two different forms of imagery can be tracked by the pattern of brain activity evoked which had been established in healthy participants. This particular VS individual was found to be able to respond by producing the appropriate brain activity. Using the same method of imagery, another individual was able to answer the question concerning his father's name. In this case, imagining playing tennis corresponded to 'yes' while moving through the rooms of his house meant 'no'. His pattern of brain activity corresponded to the correct answer. Monti, Pickard and Owen (2013) found it was possible for an individual with a profound disorder of consciousness to shift attention from superimposed pictures of houses to faces and vice versa. This shifting of attention was mirrored by distinct brain activity comparable to that seen in healthy participants. What is of significance here is that brain activity changes were driven by the individual's intention to shift attention. It seems to be the case that individuals who show the most *consciousness* make the best recovery and performance on later behavioural measures. Although enlightening, sadly some 81 per cent of individuals fail to show signs of brain activity when presented with cognitive tasks.

CONSCIOUSNESS AND ATTENTION

The global workspace theory emphasises the role of selective attention (see Chapter 3) in influencing which information we become consciously aware of. This theory also outlines how our conscious awareness is directed through early and integrated processing of information. Event related potentials (ERPs) indicate that during the early stage of processing visual information, individuals do so without conscious awareness. This is equivalent to feedforward or 'bottom–up' processing. Hence, when Lamy, Salti and Bar-Haim (2009) instructed participants to locate a target and vocalise the point at which they were aware of it, ERP amplitudes occurred independently of conscious awareness. ERP amplitudes, however, showed an increase of activity once conscious awareness of the target was realised. Integrated processing is synonymous with conscious awareness. This is borne out by a study using electro-encephalography (EEG; see Chapter 1) to measure brain activity using auditory stimuli (King, Sitt, Faugeras, Rohaut et al. 2013). King et al. compared four groups of individuals: VS (no conscious awareness); MCS; those recovering from VS or MCS and healthy controls. Integrated brain activity varied across the four groups such that those individuals with higher levels of conscious awareness demonstrated the most integrated brain activity. This is what would be predicted. Explaining what actually caused the brain activity (is it conscious awareness or pre- or post–neural activation?) is a difficult problem to overcome. Also, areas of the brain that become activated (such as the prefrontal cortex; see Chapter 2) overlap for attention and conscious awareness. Hence, separating brain activation for attention from conscious awareness is difficult and cognitivists have to resort to clever methods of design and technology such as using TMS. We often consider attention as being important for conscious awareness and vice versa. But is it? (See Box 7.5.)

BOX 7.5 THE ATTENTION-CONSCIOUS AWARENESS CONNECTION

Can attention influence how we behave without being consciously aware? In one study it was demonstrated that unseen nude pictures did influence the processes involved in attention (Jiang, Costello, Fang, Huang et al. 2006). They found that heterosexual men attended to pictures of naked women even though they were presented too rapidly for conscious awareness (and vice versa for heterosexual women). Similarly, Troiani, Price and Schultz (2014) found that the amygdala and connected neural networks involved in attention became active when 'unseen' fearful faces were presented. These findings suggest that we do not have to be consciously aware of stimuli for them to influence our behaviour. The global workspace theory assumes that attention occurs before conscious awareness. Some cognitive psychologists, however, contend that conscious awareness is independent of prior attention. It has been argued that the global workspace theory has much empirical support, but this is limited to visual perception. Different results might be found when the emphasis is on the self and self-knowledge.

An interesting question, and related to attention–conscious awareness, is whether consciousness is a continuous stream ('one stream') or are there 'two streams'? In Chapter 2, symptoms of a discontinuous consciousness were discussed in relation to split-brain patients. As a reminder, split-brain patients had their corpus callosum severed by a callosotomy in order to eradicate the occurrence of their detrimental epileptic *grand mal* seizures. Sperry (1968) argued that split-brain patients showed behaviours suggestive of a consciousness consisting of two streams. In 2000, Baynes and Gazzaniga reported, "She [VJ] .... is frequently dismayed by the independent performance of her right and left hands. She is discomfited by the fluent writing of her left hand to unseen stimuli and distressed by the inability of her right hand to write out words she can read out loud and spell" (p. 1362). There is evidence that the left and right hemispheres can function independently. Numerous studies using cognitive behavioural measures have shown this to be the case (Schiffer, Zaidel, Bogen and Chasan-Taber 1998; Trevarthen 2004). According to Gazzaniga (2013) there is only one stream of consciousness which resides in the left hemisphere (which is usually the dominant one). He accepts that both hemispheres process information and have their processing niches, but the left hemisphere plays a more pivotal role in streaming our consciousness. He uses the example of patient Paul S, who appeared to have two streams of consciousness but would typically interpret behaviour exhibited by the right hemisphere using the left dominant hemisphere. Support for this comes from anarchic–hand syndrome (see Box 7.6). Colvin and Gazzaniga

BOX 7.6   STRANGE CASE OF ANARCHIC-HAND SYNDROME

Sixty-nine-year-old GH endured damage to his corpus callosum which resulted in his left hand not knowing what the right hand was doing – literally. This condition is known as anarchic-hand syndrome. It was reported that he would present money with his left hand on the shop counter, only to put it back into his pocket with the right hand. When a stimulus, to which he was asked to respond, was presented to the right hemisphere, he responded poorly in terms of speed of response and the number of mistakes made using his left hand. ERP measurements supported this poorer performance by showing reduced P3 readings in the range of 300–400 milliseconds. P3 is one aspect of an ERP reading and is specifically involved in attention. The normal response range for P3 is 250–280 milliseconds. In the case of stimuli presentations to the left hemisphere, the right hand responded more quickly and accurately. This suggests that the control of processing involved in attention and the ability to attend resided in the left hemisphere.

(2007), however, claimed that, "No split-brain patient has ever woken up following callostomy … and felt as though his/her experience of self had fundamentally changed or that two selves now inhabited the same body" (p. 189).

Conscious awareness is only useful if we can make sense of it and our conscious experiences can be reflected upon for their meaning and consequences. This is what metacognition enables us to do.

METACOGNITION

Schunk (2006) defined metacognition as, "the deliberate conscious control of cognitive activity" (p. 180). However, Norman, Pfuhl, Saele, Svartdal et al. (2019) added to this that occasionally metacognition is automatic and occurs involuntarily which means we are unaware of it happening. More often than not, however, it is within our control and allows us to reflect upon our own thinking. There are at least two functions that metacognition serves:

1   To monitor our current cognitive activity
2   To control our current cognitive activity

These two functions are interdependently entwined such that metacognitive control is influenced by the cognitive activity monitored and monitored activity needs to be regulated by methods of control. Monitoring and control can influence both self-regulatory (such as controlling thoughts, behaviours and emotions) and introspective processes (such as conscious thoughts and feelings as well as mental states). Hence, cognitive psychologists have outlined three subcomponents of metacognition (Efklides 2011):

- knowledge
- strategies
- experience

Originally defined by Flavell (1979), knowledge refers to our ability to understand our own and others' cognition and the strategies used to help with this understanding. For example, by using a specific route to travel to work more than once, the route will become engrained in memory. Therefore, a good strategy is to stick with the route that works. In the case of metacognitive strategies, Efklides (2008) outlined how our cognition can be controlled by using different methods to improve our cognitive processing. If, for instance, we find it difficult to understand a passage written in German, then we might use the German-to-English online dictionary. Metacognitive experiences refers to the judgements and emotions occurring simultaneously with the cognitive activities performed. This, in turn, encourages us to reflect on these activities. An example of this would be our feelings accompanying the experience of recording a voiceover on a PowerPoint slide; is it enjoyable or scary?

Koriat (2007) claimed that metacognitive experiences can be divided into information-based and experience-based metacognitive feelings. In the case of information-based metacognitive feelings, an individual's conscious knowledge and past experiences are influential. Having expertise skills in a particular area will increase one's confidence in the accuracy of execution, for instance. Alternatively, experience-based metacognitive feelings can arise from an unconscious route such that the answer popped into one's mind or due to familiarity with a task the response appeared without much thought. Nevertheless experience-based metacognitive feelings can arise both consciously and unconsciously. For Rosenthal (2000) and other researchers, the mere definition of metacognition involves consciousness. Given how metacognition is a form of conscious reflection about our own and other people's cognitive processing (see Figure 7.3), interesting research has been conducted on dysfunctional thoughts (see Box 7.7) and how these can be modified using therapeutic intervention (Matthews 2015).

The theory of Self-Regulatory Executive Function (S-REF) provides an explanation for how dysfunctional metacognitive beliefs reinforce psychopathological thinking and behaviour (Wells 2009). Cognitive attentional syndrome (CAS) for instance, is perpetuated by ongoing rumination, anxiety and inappropriate coping techniques. The negative thoughts held and, just as importantly, the dysfunctional beliefs encompassing these thoughts

Figure 7.3 A metacognitive representation of what makes a person smile

BOX 7.7   DYSFUNCTIONAL METACOGNITION

Dysfunctional metacognition such as deficits in thinking or irrational thoughts have long been associated with psychopathology. The inability to form theories about another person's intentions (i.e. theory of mind), for example, reflects a deficit in processing information about what other individuals' behaviour and communication are telling us. For most of us, understanding of intent becomes apparent very quickly when we see a person checking their pockets and then looking on the ground where they were standing. Such behaviour indicates that the person has lost something and searches for it by looking nearby. We, in effect, form a theory of what is going on in the other person's mind. Some individuals find this very difficult and some fail to do this at all. Baron-Cohen, Leslie and Frith (1985) demonstrated how children on the autistic spectrum fail at this specific type of metacognition. This has also been found to occur in some individuals with schizophrenia (Brüne 2005). Dysfunctional metacognition is common across many mental disorders such as:

- Schizophrenia (Lysaker, Erickson, Ringer, Buck et al. 2011)
- Personality disorders (Dimaggio and Lysaker 2015)
- Depression (Halvorsen, Hagen, Hjemdal, Eriksen et al. 2015)
- Anxiety disorders (Spada, Nikcevic, Moneta and Ireson 2006)
- Dependencies (Saed, Yaghubi and Roshan 2010)
- Obsessive compulsive disorder (Salkovskis, Richards and Forrester 1995)

Dimaggio and Lysaker (2015) consider metacognition as reflecting upon what is occurring moment-by-moment in one's own body and the surrounding environment. Being able to do this involves the conscious experience of the self. This draws upon a host of cognitive activities such as being able to think about one's thinking and interpret one's intentions and feelings and to make connections across different events. All this information is then integrated to form profound mental constructs of the self and other selves. Individuals with schizophrenia, for example, find this difficult to do, and their metacognitive deficits can cause difficulties in understanding both the intent and internal states of others, adopting different perspectives of events and the ability to use metacognitive knowledge. The inability to integrate information is

> considered a likely explanation of the disorganised thought experienced by many individuals with the disorder. Research using EEG measurements has shown the importance of information integration by the brain. Bob, Pec, Mishara, Touskova et al. (2016) claim that, "brain disintegration corresponds to psychological disintegration" (p. 5).
>
> Individuals with psychosis, such as schizophrenia, have been treated using metacognitive therapy, which aims to change the way an individual often thinks and feels about their thoughts. This approach has proven to be successful in a number of cases (Vitzthum, Veckenstedt and Moritz 2014).

contribute towards the development of psychopathology (Sun, Zhu and So 2017; Wells 2009).

Clearly being cognisant of one's awareness and higher order thinking skills (i.e. metacognition) plays a key role in how we reflect on and monitor what is happening around us – and ultimately our consciousness. But can metacognition also be a hindrance?

METACOGNITION: HELP OR HINDRANCE?

Metacognition can facilitate optimal cognitive achievement and our psychological well-being. In the case of cognitive achievement, metacognition can help improve learning and retention, problem-solving and rational and logical reasoning and decision-making. Psychological well-being has been defined in different ways such as being happy and self-fulfilled or living without dysfunction or even as having equilibrium between challenges and resources. Metacognition has been shown to help achieve psychological well-being via cognitive achievement for instance. Siegesmund (2016) commented on how metacognitive awareness can help improve learning in educational settings. In Norway, children of 6–7 years, are actively encouraged at school to make use of metacognition in their learning (Furnes and Norman 2016). Psychological well-being can also be improved through metacognitive awareness, especially by promoting social skill development (Umino and Dammeyer 2016). Its uses in therapeutic settings have been discussed earlier in relation to metacognitive awareness of dysfunctional thought attained through metacognitive therapy (Wells 2011).

Norman (2020), however, outlined three ways metacognition can disrupt optimal cognitive achievement and the health of our very being:

1   Interferes with task performance
2   Costs of enacting metacognitive strategies outweigh the benefits
3   Negative self-evaluations arising from metacognitive judgements and emotions

Taking the first point, that metacognition can interfere with task performance, Schooler, Fiore and Brandimonte (1997) demonstrated how, by verbalising (or verbal overshadowing) about a cognitive task while trying to perform it, a negative effect can result rather than a facilitative one. This has been explained as a consequence of there being a discrepancy between using verbal labels to report on what is occurring, and the properties of the perceptual experience itself. Chin and Schooler (2008) refer to this as a 'processing shift' from global to local processing (see Chapter 3). In some cases, verbal overshadowing works well but in these circumstances it has been argued that metacognition is not involved. In the case of costs outweighing the benefits of using metacognitive strategies, new strategies might need to be acquired. These therefore require initiative and effort. Norman (2020) provides an example where the use of a metacognitive strategy might impair performance: "if reading a novel was part of a student's course requirement in English, a conscious strategy to monitor one's comprehension during reading is unlikely to increase comprehension, but could very well reduce well-being" (p. 4). Having a negative metacognitive belief about one's abilities and self-esteem, could have a detrimental effect on motivation to perform well. The negativity surrounding one's sense of worth can be exacerbated by the metacognitive beliefs held (Tarricone 2011). Engaging excessively in self-reflection can enable opportunities for ruminating over negative appraisals, and, for some people, this could lead to obsessive-compulsive disorder.

It should be highlighted, however, that despite the possible hindrance effects of metacognition, on the whole it has been useful in encouraging cognitive performance insight. There is clearly a robust link between awareness and metacognition. Conscious knowledge, for instance, can be construed as knowledge we know we have whereas knowledge we do not know we possess is within the domain of unconscious knowledge (likely to operate using feedforward processing). This means that metacognition is a controlled and intentional process requiring effortful reflection upon one's mental activity. But is knowledge about something from a textbook the same as experiencing it for oneself? (See Box 7.8.)

BOX 7.8   DOES CONSCIOUSNESS OFFER MORE THAN VICARIOUS KNOWLEDGE EXPERIENCE?

Jackson (1986) introduced the 'well-known knowledge argument', a puzzle that asks whether actual conscious experience offers more than finding something out in a textbook. Jackson provides the example of Mary who resides in a black and white room, and who has therefore never had personal experiences of colour. She is aware of how colour vision operates and has attained knowledge about colour from viewing black and white television. She eventually leaves the confounds of her black and white room and for the first time she sees a red tomato. From her knowledge she knows that this is a tomato and that tomatoes are red. But for the first time she knows what it is like to see red. This can be described as a new learning experience for Mary. Mary learns and experiences what it is like to see the colour red. In other words, Mary learns about what Jackson refers to as *qualia* – the properties characterising what it is like to see red. *Qualia* are individual occurrences of subjective conscious experience. This implies that perhaps consciousness is not reducible to physical processing (bottom-up-feedforward). Hence, how consciousness and the physical world interact is still an open question. Interestingly, Jackson (1998) changed his view about the 'knowledge argument', and now embraces physicalism – in other words, the real world is simply physical. Mary, he states, "acquires a new piece of propositional knowledge, namely, that seeing red is like *this*" (Jackson 2003, p. 439).

Is consciousness more than knowledge? Is Timmermans, Schillbach, Pasquali and Cleeremans' (2012) quote the way forward in thinking about the relationship between metacognition and consciousness?

"...thus, metacognition, or 'cognition about cognition' appears to be fundamental to our understanding of consciousness" (p.1412).

SUMMARY

Consciousness appears to be an obvious phenomenon but when we try to understand it using behavioural measures it can become ethereal. It is easy to categorise different states of consciousness, and this tends to be done by considering different levels of conscious awareness or the ability to attend directly to stimuli. Nevertheless, when individuals in a VS or MCS are studied using behavioural strategies but analysed neurologically, it becomes apparent that some VS cases can answer questions using mental imagery. Neurological measurements of brain activity show that their responses to questions using mental imagery are correct. Hence, even when they outwardly show no signs of attention, the brain is active and 'aware'. This begs the question of how consciousness comes about. When visual stimuli are processed automatically, feedforward processing (or bottom-up) occurs. This information is then processed further by feedback processing, and it is at this point where consciousness becomes apparent as information is integrated (and a top-down processing strategy occurs). Conscious experience is considered as part of our ability to recall memories of events and knowledge. It is also considered to be fuelled by conscious awareness and our ability to attend to stimuli. We are, however, able to reflect upon these experiences and the knowledge we attain using metacognition. Metacognition has been defined as the ability to monitor and control our thoughts and behaviour. It is cognition about our cognition. Although metacognition is widely considered as a positive process, there are times when it can be a hindrance to our task performance and well-being. Consciousness and metacognition appear to go hand in hand such that, in order to reflect on our cognition, we need to be aware of our cognition, and to monitor and control what we do. This only makes sense when we are consciously aware and have conscious experiences and knowledge to reflect upon.

FURTHER READING

Dehaene, S. (2014) *Consciousness and the Brain: Deciphering how the brain codes our thoughts*. New York: Viking Press.

Fleming, S.M. and Frith, C.D. (2014) *The Cognitive Neuroscience of Metacognition.* Berlin: Springer-Verlag.

Koch, C. (2012) *Consciousness: Confessions of a romantic reductionist.* Cambridge, MA: MIT Press.

Shoji, M. (2020) *Self-Consciousness: Human brain as data processor.* Bloomington, IN: iUniverse.

COGNITIVE NEUROPSYCHOLOGY

In cognitive neuropsychology the focus is very much on explaining the mind rather than the brain. In particular, it attempts to explain "the functional architecture of cognition" (Coltheart 2010, p. 4). Caramazza and Coltheart (2006) view cognitive neuropsychology as the exploration of models befitting the cognitive processing deficits seen in brain–damaged individuals. They claim, however, that cognitive neuropsychology "should reach out to cognitive neuroscience in their common effort to understand the mind-brain" (2006, p. 12). While the facts about the brain arise primarily from research in cognitive neuroscience, it is nevertheless important to understand the brain's involvement in how the mind operates (see Chapter 2). In fact, many developments in understanding how our cognition functions stem from studying brain-damaged individuals. The following areas have benefited from such research:

- Production of language (such as speech and reading)
- Memory (such as semantic and working memory)
- Thought (such as problem-solving)
- Social cognition (such as Theory of Mind)
- Perception of motion and action execution
- Attention and visual recognition

As we have seen in Chapter 1, cognitive neuropsychologists use observational methodologies, such as single-case/case-series and dissociation, to derive flowcharts of models demonstrating the structure of cognition. Fodor (1983), for example, developed a model based on modularity to account for how language might operate.

DOI: 10.4324/9781003014355-8

This model involved the 'semantic system' and the interlinking 'modules' of the 'visual input lexicon' and 'speech output lexicon', 'visual analysis system' and 'phoneme level'. When working normally in unison, these modules enable us to understand written words and speech (see Figure 1.5). This model enables cognitive neuropsychologists to identify which modules are damaged by considering patterns of behavioural deficits observed in brain–damaged individuals. In other words, it is possible to speculate on the 'modules' that are not working properly in brain-damaged individuals through a process of elimination. This can be done by simply observing where the specific language behavioural deficits lie. This approach was used to understand the deficits experienced by a well-known brain-damaged case, going by the initials of 'H.M'. H.M. suffered severe seizures due to epilepsy. In 1953 (aged 27 years old) he subsequently underwent surgery. Post-operation, he was unable to form new long-term memories (see Box 8.5). It is from studying patients such as H.M. that model constructs of memory, have helped develop our understanding of the relationship between short-term and long-term memory. Hence, here we see an important crossover between cognitive neuropsychology and cognitive neuroscience. Despite this important crossover, our primary focus will be on the models used by neuropsychologists to account for both 'typical' and 'atypical' patterns of cognition. We will also consider brain anatomy, but only in the context of its effects on behavioural observations and measurements used to account for cognitive phenomena. For example, sensorimotor neurons (a.k.a. **mirror neurons**) in the brain, help us to understand what we think is going on in the minds of others and to copy and perform the actions they enact. From devising experiments and recording brain activity, models describing how we develop a 'theory of mind' (ToM) can be generalised to groups of individuals who have problems with understanding the mental states of others. We will begin with the theory of mind.

SOCIAL COGNITION: TOM, IMITATION AND EMPATHY

Having a theory of mind (ToM) involves being able to recognise what causes people to behave in the way they do. This sounds straightforward and easy to do. It is only when you have a problem interpreting another person's behaviour and the intention behind it, that the complexities involved become apparent. Our own actions are guided by our thoughts, beliefs, goals and emotions. Given that other people's actions are guided by their own thoughts, beliefs, goals and emotions, the equation for predicting the behaviour of others becomes complicated. Yet for most of us, this comes naturally. ToM is very much a cognitive issue and involves how we think about the information presented to us. For example, in solving the following statement, we draw upon our ability to think about the statement and its implications.

Is the following statement 'true' or 'false':

'Isobel believes that kangaroos are giant rodents'

Did you find this difficult to answer? It is difficult to answer because while the content is incorrect, you cannot disagree with Isobel's belief. She believes this, so the statement is true, but kangaroos are marsupials and not rodents. Hence, the content of her belief is false. Many people make the error of assuming such statements are false. Nevertheless, we are aware that people entertain different beliefs or feelings to our own which is why it is possible both to empathise and to deceive others. Telling the truth is less complex than formulating a lie. The fact that we are able to lie, however, provides us with the ability to manipulate others which is known as **Machiavellian intelligence** (Whiten and Byrne 1988). Dennet (1996) claimed there are four orders of understanding intentionality:

1   I believe something
2   I believe you believe something
3   I believe that you believe that I believe something
4   I believe that you believe that I believe that you believe something

So how do we fathom these levels? What mechanisms enable us to understand the mental states of others by decrypting their intentions? Leslie (1994) introduced the 'Theory of Mind Mechanism' (ToMM) that enables us to infer all mental states from other people's behaviour (see Box 8.1).

Having a ToM enables us to be accomplished communicators and plays a pivotal role in social cognition (such as the thinking about social interactions). As we can see in Figure 8.1, cognitive

BOX 8.1 WHAT THE THEORY OF MIND MECHANISM ENABLES US TO DO

The Theory of Mind Mechanism (ToMM) allows us to infer all types of mental states from behaviour, including what Baron-Cohen refers to as epistemic mental states. Examples of epistemic mental states include pretending, knowing, believing, dreaming, guessing, thinking, deceiving and imagining. ToMM highlights how people's actions are robustly related to their mental states. It also allows us to suspend the normal truths encapsulated within propositions, known as 'referential opacity'. Take the following example of Snow White:

Proposition 1: 'Snow White thought the woman selling apples was a kind person'.

Proposition 2: 'Snow White thought her wicked stepmother was a kind person'.

Proposition 1 can be true and proposition 2 false if Snow White was unaware that the woman selling apples is also her wicked stepmother.

Children of four to five years enjoy tales of deception, such as that seen in pantomime and Punch and Judy puppet shows. This suggests that they have developed referential opacity early in childhood. Children of above three and a half to four years are also very good at another aspect of ToMM. This can be demonstrated by considering a series of false-belief experiments, the most famous being the Sally-Anne test (Wimmer and Perner 1983). The test is as follows: 'Sally has a basket and Anne has a box. Sally has a marble and puts it into her basket, then goes out. Anne takes out Sally's marble and puts it into her box. Sally comes back and wants to play with her marble. Where will Sally look for her marble?' The answer is her basket because that is where she left the marble and she has no reason to think differently. Children three and a half years and younger nearly always answer 'in the box' demonstrating that they struggle to understand false-belief. Interestingly, there are other children above the age of three and a half who still fail to perform successfully on false-belief tests – these children are on the autism spectrum. Children on the autism spectrum have problems reading the intentions behind the behaviours of others, known as 'mindblindness' (Baron-Cohen 1997). This is an example of how specific types of assessment can distinguish between 'typical' and 'atypical' behaviour (see Figure 8.1). Models of the mind and, in this case, the mechanisms developed, can be traced to underlying problems of the brain.

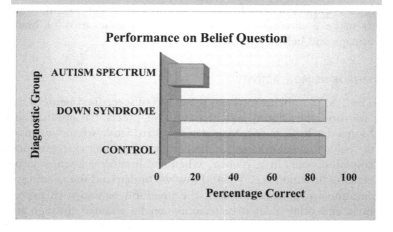

Figure 8.1 Performance on belief question of false belief task
Source: Adapted from Rutter and Lockyer (1967)

neuropsychologists can introduce tasks that help to separate individuals with different diagnoses by using, in this case, specific social cognitive tests. Despite the control group being younger (unimpaired 4–5-year-olds), they out-performed children on the autism spectrum. This is also true of a third group (Down Syndrome group).

There are two biological approaches to understanding ToM: modularity hypothesis and 'mirror neurons'.

MODULARITY HYPOTHESIS

A 30-year-old patient, known as S.M., presented with severe damage to the amygdala (Adolphs, Tranel, Damasio and Damasio 1995). S.M. was shown photographs of faces depicting a range of emotional expressions but failed to recognise the expression of fear and could not experience it. Furthermore, she failed to identify any bodily posturing expressing a fearful state. Not only does this demonstrate the link between perception and action, but also the importance of being in tune with the emotions of others. This case shows how challenging making inferences about intention and emotional state (i.e. fear) from behaviour can be. Hence, despite some facets of ToM remaining intact, there were deficits in the quality and depth of understanding others. Note this case allows us to make a direct observation between specific areas of brain-damage and behavioural deficits.

'MIRROR NEURON' ACTIVITY

The "[M]irror neuron system is a group of specialised neurons that "mirrors" the actions and behaviour of others" (Rajmohan and Mohandas 2007, p. 66). Mirror neurons are active when we imitate the behaviours of others. It is therefore an important aspect of social cognition, and, in particular, when we mentalise about another person's intention (i.e. ToM). How we understand the meaning of emotional expression in faces, the intention behind such expressions and other related behaviours can be attained through mimicry. By imitating facial expressions, we can increase our ability to identify how another person is feeling. Neal and Chartrand (2011) demonstrated this in a study where participants, when given Botox to induce short-term facial muscular paralysis, failed to identify facial expressions portrayed by others. Hence, this demonstrates how important it is to social interactions to be able to display emotional expressions. When we interpret the mental state of another individual, for instance, we interpret emotions expressed in their faces. This, in combination with their other behaviours, helps us make sense of their current mental state. In order to do this, however, we need to ignore our own current mental state and adopt the mental state of the person under observation. The 'Mind-in-the-Eyes' task is used to test whether we can identify the emotional state of a person from very limited information, that is, a strip showing the eyes only. Baron-Cohen, Ring, Wheelwright, Bullmore et al. (1999) used fMRI to examine brain activity when making judgements concerning emotions expressed in the eyes.

fMRI detected activity in the left frontal lobe and the temporoparietal junction (an area where the temporal and parietal lobes meet) for emotional state inferences. In the case of false belief tasks (see Box 8.1), this area is also activated. This implies that the temporoparietal junction is involved in different types of mentalising.

Another important aspect of ToM is the ability to empathise with another person's distress or pain, even though we are not actually experiencing the emotions ourselves. 'Simulation' studies have been devised to see what happens when we imagine the emotions and pain experienced by another person. fMRI scans are used to measure which areas of the brain become active. When participants imitate or observe the emotional expressions portrayed on faces, there is generally an influx of neural activity in areas of the brain involved in understanding emotional facial expression. The premotor cortex (an area of the frontal lobe), however, also shows neural activity. It is mirror neurons that are responsible for this neural activity. In the case of empathising with someone else's pain, the same pattern of mirror neuron activation occurs as that of the person experiencing the pain (Singer, Seymour, O'Doherty, Kaube et al. 2004). When, for example, participants experienced a sharp probe or viewed a video of someone experiencing a needle prick, Singer et al. found the same pattern of neural activation. fMRI scans show activation of the anterior cingulate cortex (ACC) and the insular. The ACC has connections with the limbic system (involved in emotional processing) and the prefrontal cortex (involved in cognitive processing) which makes perfect sense when expressing empathy. Mirror-like neurons can be found in the ACC that encode pain observed in others. According to Ray (2013), the ACC has a pivotal role in both social cognition and emotional regulation. In the case of the insular (located in an area that separates the frontal, parietal and temporal lobes), there are neural connections to the amygdala and the ACC which makes it important in detecting emotions and social emotional responses (Nieuwenhuys 2012).

Mirror neurons appear to be at the heart of understanding the actions of others. Ferrari and Rizzolatti (2014) claim that empathy is a simulative process and is driven by the firing of mirror neurons when we perform an action and when we observe its execution by other individuals. Some mirror neurons are involved only with coding for the inferred goal of the action instead of the performance of it. In ballet dancers the same brain activation and firing of mirror neurons in the premotor and parietal lobes occurs while watching other ballet dancers perform.

Mirror neurons also play a role in attention and perception, more specifically motion perception and action production.

PERCEPTION OF MOTION AND ACTION EXECUTION

The perception of motion is an important aspect of our daily life. Without the ability to perceive the motion of objects, static snapshots of objects in time, like photographs, are what we would see (see Box 8.2).

There are specific areas of the temporal lobes known as MT (i.e. 'middle-temporal'; also known as V5) and MST (i.e. 'medial superior temporal') that are responsible for the perception and representation of motion (Zeki 2015). The MT area receives input from other areas involved in vision (i.e. V1, V2 and V3; see Chapter 2) and then passes information back to these areas as well as feedforward to the MST. Imaging scans have revealed that the MT becomes active when we

BOX 8.2 THE CASE OF NO MOTION PERCEPTION

A patient lost her ability to perceive the motion of objects. This was the only functional deficit concerning the perception of objects, but it profoundly affected her life. For example, the simple task of pouring a cup of tea was difficult because she could not register the movement of the liquid into the cup. The liquid appeared as a snapshot in time. The result of this was that there was no way of monitoring when the cup was full. It is possible that she could work out an algorithm based on time and the angle she held the kettle which would inform her of when to stop pouring, but the whole procedure was not an automatic process like it is for most of us. Crossing the road was problematic too. In her own words, "When I'm looking at the car, first it seems far away. But then, when I want to cross the road, suddenly the car is very near" (Zihl, von Cramon and Mai 1983, p. 315). She solved this problem using her hearing to form a judgement of noise distance.

focus on moving patterns and objects. When there is a lesion to this area of the brain or processing is disrupted using transcranial magnetic stimulation (TMS; see Chapter 1), perception of motion and the faculty to use motion cues to facilitate action become impaired. It is, however, the MST that is responsible for processing more complex motion such as that experienced as we run through a town. Here we have to keep track of what is ahead of us and need to avoid, as well as realising that as we approach objects they appear to increase in size and decrease in size as we pass them. In contrast, MT processes simple movements of objects.

Our visual system (see Chapter 2) and our ability to attend to stimuli (see Chapter 3) are important in informing us of the world around us. Together these facilitate an understanding of objects and their spatial dimensions, as well as how they move around. This provides us with a spatial representation of the external world. This representation, however, is futile unless we can act upon it appropriately. The dorsal network (see Chapter 2) plays an important role in connecting areas such as V1 and V2 and provides us with a neural pathway that contributes towards planning action. The dorsal network has been studied in the laboratory using constructional tasks such as producing a drawing of an abstract representation, known as the 'Rey-Osterrieth Complex'. Individuals with damage to the temporoparietal area of the right hemisphere are unable to identifiably draw the figure. Visually guided action is important for reaching and grasping objects. To reach for an object we need to know its location but to grasp it we need to know its shape. Individuals with optic ataxia can find both reaching and grasping challenging. They generally find it difficult to use visual feedback required for making fine adjustments to their grasping actions (i.e. V6 area closely connected to the ventral network). The main problem lies, however, with the inability of neurons (such as mirror neurons) in the parietal lobe to connect sensory representations of what the action should be, with how it can be executed. In other words, there is a sensory-motor exchange problem that prevents information about the movements needed to perform the action from getting through.

Interestingly, mirror neurons in the premotor area of the frontal lobes evoke stronger activity when participants are shown simple hand and foot movements using the first rather than third person perspective (Jackson, Meltzoff and Decety 2005; see Figure 8.2).

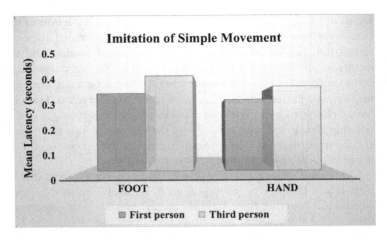

Figure 8.2 Imitation of simple foot and hand movements
Source: Adapted from Jackson, Meltzoff and Decety (2005)

Jackson et al. presented participants with two different visual perspectives of simple hand and foot movements. The first-person perspective was consistent with their own viewpoint, unlike the third-person which was the mirror image. Participants had either to imitate or simply observe the hand and foot movements depicted in five video clips, while in the fMRI scanner. These movements were shown for an equal amount of the time in the first or third-person. Participants found it easier to imitate these movements when shown in the first-person which is reflected in the faster mean latency scores (equivalent to watching the model from behind).

These findings suggest that, while we are good imitators, it is easier to copy the movements observed when they are presented as the same as one's own perspective. Mirror neurons play an important role in action formation, but they are also involved in learning. Learning can alter the structural and neurological landscape of the brain – in particular the synaptic connections made. There are cases, however, where individuals, through disease or accidents, sustain damage to specific areas of the brain and yet make incredible recovery. The brain can show resilience to damage by the ability to modify neural connections or 're-wire' itself. This ability is referred to as neuroplasticity – our next topic.

NEUROPLASTICITY IN LEARNING

As was discussed in Chapter 2, we are able constantly to change the structure and function of the brain through learning. This learning helps us develop our cognitive abilities by making the connections between neurons more effective at relaying information. This ultimately increases the speed of information processing. These neural developments also enable us to continue learning. Hence, this neuroplasticity not only enables learning but is changed by learning and new experiences (see Box 8.3).

BOX 8.3   LEARNING PROTECTS THE BRAIN

It is no surprise to hear that a stimulating environment conducive for learning will help children avoid degenerative brain diseases as they get older. There is evidence to suggest that children who have experienced enriched environments were less likely to develop Alzheimer's disease. Moreover, early exposure to learning increases the body's ability to repair damage incurred to brain cells. But what enables us to learn? The connections among neurons (i.e. synapses) hold our knowledge in the brain. In our early years we have an excess of synaptic connections, some of which are effective, but many are ineffective. In order to improve the synaptic landscape of the brain, two processes occur: proliferation (blooming) and elimination (pruning) (Greenough and Black 1992). The initial proliferation of synapses is adjusted by the elimination of meaningless or useless synaptic connections. This synaptic blooming and pruning become initiated as we experience and learn about our world more effectively. For example, older children are better at categorising objects than are younger children, which, in effect, improves how they learn. This, in turn, facilitates the formation of new and effective synaptic connections. This means that older synaptic connections no longer used are eliminated via pruning. There is evidence that neuroplasticity occurs in adulthood also especially in areas of the brain involved in memory and learning. The hippocampus in the temporal lobe is involved in the formation of new memories via learning. Fotuhi (2015) claimed that the growth and volume of the hippocampus can increase when we eat healthy foods containing omega-3, reduce stress, anxiety and depression, sleep well and have an active lifestyle such as exercising daily. He also found that the hippocampus can shrink in size when these things are not in place. Shrinkage of the hippocampus can have a deleterious effect on our memory and our ability to learn new information. This can increase our chances of developing Alzheimer's disease. MacMaster and Kusumakar (2004) studied 34 teenagers aged 13 to 18 years old. Half of these teenagers suffered from depression. Using fMRI, the volume of their left and right hippocampi were measured. The teenagers suffering from depression had hippocampi that were 17 per cent smaller than the control teenagers. Hence, depression can have an impact on our ability to learn and retain new information.

Draganski, Gaser, Kempermann, Kuhn et al. (2006) studied German medical students who were revising for their medical exams. They had their brains scanned three months prior to the exam date and once they had finished their studies. These students were compared with a control group who were not revising. The scans revealed that learning-induced changes had occurred in the parietal lobes and in the hippocampi for the students who were revising. Such changes to these areas are associated with memory retrieval and learning. These findings provide direct evidence of neuroplasticity when we learn new information. The brain, however, can also compensate after brain damage to these areas by reorganising damaged synaptic connections to form new ones with neurons that are still intact. Again, learning plays an important role in stimulating new synaptic connectivity (see Box 8.4).

There are a combination of factors influencing the extent of recovery from brain injury (see Table 8.1).

An individual's level of cognitive functioning prior to brain damage is important to the likely level of recovery. For instance, a person with a high level of intellect and who has received extensive education is more likely to make a better recovery than someone who has neither of these advantages. In fact, this prediction was made back in 1937 by Symonds, "It is not only the kind of head injury that matters but the kind of head" (p. 1092). Why this is the case relates to two possibilities:

BOX 8.4 ROLE OF MIRROR NEURONS IN POST-STROKE RECOVERY

Mirror neurons become activated in post-stroke patients when they imagine performing an action, such as a hand movement. This motor imagination has been used as part of a treatment regime to activate mirror neurons during training/learning (Garrison, Winstein and Aziz-Zadeh 2010). The underlying reason why such an approach is successful at retraining the brain, is that we have a mechanism enabling us to make mental notes of how different behaviours can be imitated (Martineau, Andersson, Barthelemy, Cottier et al. 2010). Hence, we mentally imitate actions observed before attempting to perform them. fMRI studies show that mirror neurons become activated during this process which indicates their importance in learning. Interestingly, Burns (2008), showed how regaining abilities in post-stroke patients was accelerated after observing motor actions. fMRI scans have shown how their mirror neuron activation increases when watching a video of hand, foot and mouth movements. Mirror neuron activation facilitates neuroplasticity in the premotor region and the parietal lobes, by changing the synaptic landscape in these areas.

1 Such an individual has a greater reserve and therefore has more capacity to draw upon
2 Such an individual may be more resourceful at learning or devising alternative strategies for coping with the challenges resulting from the brain damage

Table 8.1 Factors influencing recovery post brain damage

Nature of Brain Damage	Individual Differences
Severity of damage incurred	Age at time of damage
Frequency of damage to the brain	Individual brain structural differences
Spacing between occurrences of brain damage	Prior level of cognitive functioning
Level of brain intactness	Motivation to recover
Possibility of another area taking over function	Emotional response
	Level and quality of rehabilitation

Source: Adapted from Banich and Compton (2018)

When cognitive neuropsychologists talk about a brain-damaged individual overcoming their challenges, it is necessary to differentiate between 'true' and compensatory recovery. In the case of true recovery, physical and mental functions are restored. For compensatory, the individual overcomes challenges by resorting to other means of achieving their goal targets, such as leaving notes as reminders of tasks to be completed. Unfortunately, the window of opportunity for achieving true recovery using rehabilitation measures is small; the first few months after brain injury (Zeiler and Krakauer 2013). There is no time limit for the implementation of compensatory rehabilitation. According to Banich and Compton (2018) there is an "emphasis on repeated use of the affected function as a tool for recovery in both acute and long-term time frames ... therapies for aphasia emphasize expecting the patient to use spoken language, however difficult it may be, rather than relying upon ... writing or gesturing" (p. 482).

Head injuries can cause specific cognitive dysfunction such as aphasia or amnesia. Damage to the hippocampus in particular, can cause problems in the formation and the ordering of memories. Cognitive neuropsychologists were fortunate in being able to study extensively the memory of H.M. who suffered lesions to various areas of the brain including a region of the temporal lobe and the hippocampus (see Box 8.5).

BOX 8.5   THE MEMORY PROBLEM OF H.M.

H.M. suffered from profound amnesia following removal of three structures positioned near the centre of his brain. It was believed at the time that these areas were concerned with the sense of smell, and a loss of this ability would be a minor imposition. This was not the case. Although his surgeon kept accurate medical notes of the structures excised, it was only following death and post-mortem that the extent of lesion incurred could be understood. Over many years H.M. participated in research examining his memory problems post-surgery. This could be compared to his baseline memory performance before he had undergone surgery. Hence, there was an abundance of information about what happens to memory function when specific areas of the brain endure damage. There were lesions to areas of the temporal lobe, hippocampus and amygdala among many neighbouring areas of the brain. It is well established that the hippocampus plays a major role in the memory of visual, auditory, olfactory and somesthetic (such as touch, pain and temperature) sensory modalities (Corkin 1984). H.M. had substantial loss of memory. He had both retrograde amnesia (loss of memories from before his surgery) and anterograde amnesia (the inability to lay down new memories following surgery). The hippocampus is involved in the formation and consolidation of new memories. The hippocampus also connects memories from different areas of the brain and helps to piece them together in order to make sense.

Lesion damage to the hippocampus suffered by H.M. is different to the problems experienced by individuals who use their hippocampus ineffectively. In the case of depression (see Box 8.3) where the hippocampi of sufferers show signs of shrinkage, once treated for their depression this shrinkage could be reversed. Hence, there was evidence of neuroplasticity. But is it possible to create neuroplasticity in individuals with a lesion to the hippocampus? Currently there is exciting work being undertaken using a drug called CPTX. It is considered to be a 'glue' which promotes synaptic growth. CPTX mimics a protein called Cerebellin-1, responsible for linking neurons that send signals (i.e. pre-synaptic neurons) with those receiving them (i.e. post-synaptic neurons). Individuals with injuries to the spinal cord often become paralysed as a consequence of damage to neural connections. The problems occur when the pre- and post-synaptic neurons can no longer communicate. What would happen if a protein that binds to both was created? Would the signal then get through? Scientists working in collaboration from the UK, Japan and Germany, believe they have created such a protein that can form a 'molecular bridge' across the damaged areas, therefore allowing for new neural growth and synaptic connections. These scientists injected CPTX into the hippocampi of mice with Alzheimer's disease and spinal cord injury. These mice demonstrated improvements to both memory and locomotion respectively (Suzuki, Elegheert, Song, Sasakura et al. 2020). This could be a form of treatment in the future.

Our attention now focuses on research on brain lateralisation (see Chapter 2), in particular, cognition and emotion.

BRAIN LATERALISATION

In Chapter 2, the structure of the brain and how the two hemispheres of the brain are connected via the corpus callosum were explained. Furthermore, specific structures in the left and right hemispheres were highlighted in terms of their role in processing language and non-verbal stimuli respectively. Neural networks and their inter-connections with specific brain structures were also considered. Here, the aim is to consider the relationship between lateralisation, cognition and emotion. Historically, cognitive neuropsychologists have studied individuals with brain damage. By studying the location of brain damage and then testing for cognitive ability, it is possible to make connections between the area of damage and specific deficits. It is through these studies that an understanding of hemispheric specialisation or the lateralisation of function was established. While the left hemisphere is dominant in language processing, the right hemisphere excels in tasks involving non-verbal and spatial stimuli. Gazzaniga (1970), for example, showed how the left hand (controlled by the right hemisphere) excelled at depicting a three-dimensional object in a two-dimensional plane. Moreover, the left hand and not the right fared better at drawing a three-dimensional cube on paper. Prete and Tommasi (2018) considered such motor control at a neurophysiological level and concluded that there is a behavioural preference for using one side of the body that is controlled by the contralateral (the opposite) hemisphere. This is because the neural pathways for motor control emanate from the opposite hemisphere. They argue that this allows for each hemisphere to enhance competencies in its specific domain of function. In 1998, Crow, Crow, Done and Leask, claimed that individuals who are less lateralised for behavioural preference (such as being ambidextrous or left-handed), have a propensity to show cognitive developmental deficits. This suggests that it is necessary to form a good pattern of lateralisation during development. The effects of lateralised motor skill in children can be tested by devising different tasks where the dominant and non-dominant hand can be compared using a variety of performance measures. The preferred hand usually performs more favourably in terms of accuracy, strength and speed than the non-preferred hand, especially for right-handers (Häger-Ross and Rösblad 2002). Bondi, Prete, Malatesta and Robazza (2020) found that children who are right-handed have more asymmetry when performing motor activity such as playing sport than left-handers. They found robust lateralisation in these right-handed children.

Individuals with lesions to the right hemisphere experience different deficits to those with left hemisphere damage. Right hemisphere damage disrupts spatial and visuospatial skills. Other problems present themselves such as:

- recognising objects from different perspectives and angles
- making line orientation judgements
- distinguishing previously seen faces from new ones
- distinguishing variations of pitch in sounds and tones expressed in speech
- interpreting emotional expressions in faces

These challenges faced by individuals with right hemisphere damage, suggest that the right hemisphere is also involved in processing cognitive stimuli. To test for lateralisation, cognitive neuropsychologists resort to measures of speed and accuracy in performing tasks where items are presented to the right visual field (RVF; or to the right ear for auditory presentation) or the left visual field (LVF; or to the left ear for auditory presentation). Where superior performance is shown when items are presented to the LVF, for instance, the right hemisphere is considered to be specialised in processing that information. Many studies have revealed a difference in the perception of stimuli depending on whether it is presented to the LVF or RVF. This difference is referred to as **perceptual asymmetries**. Findings from research on perceptual asymmetries suggest that the left hemisphere is superior at processing words while the right has an advantage processing faces. Non-verbal sounds, such as wildlife noises, a door slamming or musical tones, are processed more accurately when heard by the left ear (right hemisphere) for instance. An interesting question is whether differences in perceptual asymmetries occur across the sexes (see Box 8.6).

BOX 8.6   ARE THERE HEMISPHERIC SEX DIFFERENCES?

If we are to believe the stereotypes about sex differences, such as men being good at navigation and visuospatial skills with women being better at language and reading people's emotions, then we might expect to see performance differences for perceptual asymmetry tasks. Sommer, Aleman, Bouma and Kahn completed a meta-analysis of 14 studies in 2004 and 26 studies in 2008, looking at verbal task performance. They failed to find any significant sex differences in the lateralisation of verbal stimuli. Interestingly, Jordan, Wüstenberg, Heinze, Peters et al. (2002) found that females used both hemispheres when performing a mental rotation task whereas men showed lateralisation of the right hemisphere. This finding, however, was never repeated. In a meta-analysis by Thompson and Voyer (2014), an advantage in emotional perception was found for females. Neuroimaging in a study by Wager, Phan, Liberzon and Taylor (2003), however, showed more lateralisation for emotional activity in males than females. When they focused on specific regions of the brain there were more likely to be sex differences. They concluded that the lateralisation of emotional activity is not straightforward and is likely to be more region-specific. This suggests that, rather than comparing the hemispheres for differences, a region-specific comparison approach might be more fruitful. Furthermore, researchers should be looking for sex differences by comparing performance on same domain-specific tasks such as different aspects of emotional or visuospatial skills.

In a nutshell, the consensus is that the left and right hemispheres simultaneously contribute to almost all forms of complex cognitive activities. This also applies to activities originally believed to be associated only with the left or the right hemisphere. As succinctly put by Banich and Compton (2018), "it means that the right hemisphere is not just taking a nap while we are reading, and the left hemisphere is not just snoozing while we recognize a friend's face. Going around in such a half-brained manner doesn't seem a very good strategy!" (pp. 58–9). We can therefore conceptualise lateralisation in terms of complementary specialisation rather than simply having one hemisphere that is dominant. An example of this specialisation is the perceptual asymmetries which have been found in the processing of facial emotional expressions.

PERCEPTUAL PROCESSING OF FACIAL EMOTIONAL EXPRESSIONS

Ekman and Friesen (1971) claimed we have six facial expressions that can be seen cross-culturally: happiness, pleasant surprise, sadness, anger, fear and disgust. These expressions stem from 'approach-avoid' expressions demonstrated in new-borns by using simple behaviours such as smiling and crying respectively. Traditionally, the processing of facial expressions is considered to be predominantly lateralised to the right hemisphere (Springer and Deutsch 1998). There are two schools of thought, however, regarding the extent of involvement of both the right and left hemispheres:

1   right hemisphere hypothesis which argues this hemisphere processes positive and negative emotions
2   valence hypothesis which proposes a right hemisphere specialisation in processing negative emotions while the left processes positive emotions

Workman, Peters and Taylor (2000) considered whether positive and negative facial expressions are processed to the same extent by the right hemisphere (see Box 8.7).

BOX 8.7   DOES THE RIGHT HEMISPHERE PROCESS ALL FACIAL EMOTIONAL EXPRESSIONS?

By using all six emotional expressions, Workman et al. (2000) devised a series of 'chimeric faces'. These chimeric faces had one side of the face showing a neutral expression while the other side showed one of the six emotional expressions. The emotional expression for half of the faces appeared on the left side with the remainder appearing on the right side (as it appeared to the viewer). Thus, two sides of a face consisted of a neutral and emotional expression in order to create a whole face. The mirror image was created such that the emotional half of the face and the neutral half were represented in both sides of the face. This was then reversed so that both the right and left sides of the face were used. Hence, each emotion expressed in these chimeric faces appeared on the left or right and the mirror image was presented below or above. This meant there were a total of 48 pairs of chimeric faces which breaks down as follows:

> "2 posers X 6 emotions X 2 versions (emotive half-face produced by the left/right side of the poser's face) X 2 positions (once with the mirror image placed at the bottom and once with it placed at the top)"
>
> Workman et al. (2000, p. 241)

Participants were informed of the emotion they expected to see so that they could make an immediate judgement of which representation portrayed the strongest emotional expression (the top or bottom). A quick response was considered to be a robust indicator of the visual field advantage shown. The findings showed a left hemiface perceptual bias. In other words, the involvement of the right hemisphere (RH). This bias increased from happiness to sadness, pleasant surprise, disgust, fear to anger. This means that the strongest left hemiface bias (RH) was with the negative emotions of anger first, followed by fear then disgust. The positive expressions such as happiness and pleasant surprise showed a shift in the direction of the left hemisphere. Although sadness differed from anger and fear, it failed to differ from happiness or pleasant surprise. The data do not definitively support the valence hypothesis, but they do show some separation between positive and negative emotional processing – with a shift towards the left hemisphere for happiness and pleasant surprise. The conclusions drawn propose a quick reacting response from the RH towards negative emotional expressions for survival purposes. In the case of positive emotional expressions, the interpretation is that the face is friendly and in order to engage in communication we need to engage the left hemisphere (LH). According to Borod, Koff and Buck (1986), the RH is likely to be superior in the processing of facial expressions but when the possibility of communication is involved (such as invitation to communicate by a friendly face), the LH may be superimposed onto this pattern of RH superiority. In the case of sadness, we often feel concern towards the person and not repelled by them. Using this same method, it is interesting how for some individuals such as those on the autism spectrum, a RH advantage was only found for 'happiness' and 'anger' (Taylor, Workman and Yeomans 2012). There was a clear developmental deficit for an RH advantage for the remaining emotions. Given the problems of communication experienced by those on the autism spectrum, such a disadvantage in reading emotional expression goes some way towards explaining this.

SUMMARY

Cognitive neuropsychology draws upon neuroscience to explain how the brain functions cognitively. Models of how the brain functions when performing cognitive tasks are often gleaned from what happens when there is damage to specific areas of the brain. This means that to investigate memory or language performance, cognitive neuropsychologists resort to methodologies that enable comparisons across brain-damaged individuals and controls. They also study individuals who have specific types of disorder such as autism or schizophrenia. Developments in brain imagery techniques have helped to see, in real-time, the areas of the brain that become active when specific tasks are performed. fMRI, for example, has been useful in understanding areas of the brain involved in specific cognitive activities such as the frontal lobe and temporoparietal junction in the understanding of the emotional states of others. This is particularly important in the understanding of theory of mind (ToM). Moreover, the neural pathways and types of neurons involved in ToM help us to understand what their behaviour and actions mean. These mirror neurons also help us to imitate the actions of others and to learn how to do things as well as enabling us to empathise with another person's distress. Neuroplasticity, where new neurons and synapses grow, can be facilitated by learning and new experiences. The processes of blooming and pruning of synapses can help to create optimal connections that improve the speed of information processing.

Mirror neurons can help with learning in individuals with brain damage through imitating the actions of others, thereby promoting new synaptic connections. Research on brain lateralisation shows that, while there are some differences in the processing of information, the consensus is that both the left and right brain hemispheres are involved in most forms of processing. The perception of facial expressions, however, is primarily the role of the right hemisphere (RH).

FURTHER READING

Asenova, I.V. (2018) *Brain Lateralization and Developmental Disorders: A new approach to unified research*. New York: Taylor and Francis/Routledge.

Costandi, M. (2016) *Neuroplasticity*. Cambridge, MA: MIT.

Murden, F. (2020) *Mirror Thinking: How role models make us human*. London: Bloomsbury Sigma.

Slotnick, S.D. (2017) *Cognitive Neuroscience of Memory*. Cambridge: Cambridge University Press.

FUTURE DIRECTIONS OF COGNITIVE PSYCHOLOGY

In this book we have covered a range of topics which between them constitute the subject matter of cognitive psychology. We have also considered the contributions of closely associated disciplines such as cognitive neuroscience, cognitive neuropsychology and computational cognitive science. These new and ground-breaking disciplines have helped to revolutionise our understanding of cognitive psychology. Cognitive neuroscience, for instance, has facilitated our understanding of how the brain is structured and functions through the use of developing brain scanning technologies. Such understanding of how the brain is structured and functions clearly has implications for theories and models of cognition. With more extensive clarity of brain structure and function, it is possible to explore how existing theories and models in cognitive psychology fit with neurological-based science. This has generally revealed a good match between cognitive theories and models with the science, although there are those in need of some modification, or even rejection. Cognitive neuropsychology has played an important role in translating how cognition is affected when brain structure and function are compromised in some way. Technological developments, such as that seen in computational cognitive science, have also provided valuable insights into, for example, how memory and logic might operate. An interesting question we may ask is what future directions cognitive psychology is likely to take given developments in these closely related disciplines. Evolutionary psychology has also been making an impact on psychology *per se* and has more recently offered cognitive psychologists new perspectives on how cognition can be considered and researched.

DOI: 10.4324/9781003014355-9

TECHNOLOGICAL DEVELOPMENTS

If we consider past methods of understanding memory, for example, the presentation of stimuli followed by measures of participant response, the limitations become apparent very quickly. Recently, however, developments in computer and media technology have enabled cognitive psychologists to present stimuli in different ways. Such technology has also allowed for different measures of cognitive output and how this can be recorded. This has provided cognitive psychologists with a diversity of ways to present and record stimuli. It is interesting that, despite the different ways in which stimuli are now presented in, for example, memory experiments, many theories and models derived previously have withstood the test of time. For example, the three main components of Atkinson and Shiffrin's (1968) multi-store model of memory, sensory store, short- and long-term memory are still regarded as the foundation stones of the main processes involved in memory formation. These technologies have enabled cognitive psychologists to be more accurate in the way different measurements are recorded. There is also more opportunity of using different stimuli to tap into areas of cognition that were previously difficult to study. An example of this is the fact that neuroimaging has revealed that we use both top-down and bottom-up processing when visually attending to a stimulus. Modifications have, for example, been made to theoretical assumptions and models of attention and memory. These modifications often involve additional components to models as new areas are explored. An example of this is the development of the concept of working memory. Also, our understanding of attention, and, in particular, the way neural networks operate in feedforward and feedback processing has been improved through the use of brain scanning. Such data provide an understanding of the areas activated in the brain when we attend to stimuli and the neurological pathways involved. Furthermore, brain scanning technologies enable a window of observing the brain in real time. This is particularly useful when those being tested have endured brain damage. In particular, studying areas of brain activation during learning has become a hot topic in the rehabilitation of brain-damaged individuals. Understanding the involvement of the hippocampus in memory and learning *per se* has helped to develop existing theories of short-term memory. The importance of learning in the neuroplasticity of the hippocampi has helped cognitive psychologists to understand the impact depression has on cognition. One of the symptoms of depression is a sense of apathy and an inability to engage mentally with many types of task. We learned in Chapter 8 how scanning techniques have shown shrinkage of the hippocampi in depressed teenagers. Hence, this provides a valuable lesson in the relatedness between a disorder and learning and keeping the brain active.

Brain scanning is not only useful for studying memory, attention and learning but in tasks involving language and thought. Fodor argued that there are interdependent modules, each with their own domain of function. The notion of modules has received much support. By observing how individuals with brain damage perform on language-related tasks while under the scanner (i.e. fMRI or PET), areas of the brain failing to show activity can be seen in contrast with those of control participants. It is not just problems of language that can be highlighted in this way, but other modules concerned with many types of cognitive activity. Ineffective mirror neuron firing, for example, provides information about defective modules concerned with the processing of social communication such as that seen in theory of mind (ToM) and in empathy. Although brain scanning techniques provide scientists with a fairly accurate depiction of brain activity, neuroscience has problems with unpicking cause and effect. Is it the case that a person who lacks empathy does so because their brain is 'wired' differently from most other people or is it a consequence of experiencing parental rejection in childhood? What causes what? Can we be 100 per cent certain that a brain deficit is the cause of the behaviour? The answer usually lies in the grey territory of it being a bit of both. Perhaps with more sensitive recordings of neural activity, it might be possible in the future to have a clearer picture of cause and effect; certainly, for motor-based decision-making.

Using an experimental task called **n-back**, it is possible to investigate working memory updating in the solution of insight problems, a feat not possible without the use of sophisticated computer programs. N-back, as used in a study by Nęcka, Żak and Gruszka (2016), involved the presentation of two-digit numbers for 1800 milliseconds that were masked by patterns of dots randomly displayed for 500 milliseconds. Participants were instructed to press the spacebar only if they thought the stimulus had appeared previously either two or four numbers back. Using this design, Nęcka et al. found the function of working memory updating is partly to support insight problem-solving. Such a task, as a means of investigating the efficiency of working memory updating, would be challenging without new computer technologies. Developments in measuring electrode activity in the brain using electrodes that are driven by a computer program such as 'BioPak', have enabled brain response exploration in cognition within the realm of undergraduate research. Technological developments, however, are not restricted to computer, media and brain scanning. Great strides have also been made in technologies measuring eye movement which have proven insightful for researching how we deploy our attention towards environmental objects. It has also provided greater understanding of language related problems such as dyslexia. The use of eye-tracking goggles with sensors measuring when and where we move our eyes to look at events has been successfully applied to eyewitness research. A multi-layered study researching how effectively eyewitnesses attend, encode, remember and recall details of a criminal event, using the cognitive interview, used such goggles to record what was being observed (The OpenLearn Team 2010). This enabled researchers to compare what was actually observed with what eyewitnesses could remember. Interestingly, the eyewitnesses failed to describe the suspects they had observed (as recorded by the eye-tracking goggles) and yet recognised the suspects they had difficulty describing. The use of eye-tracking goggles in this study revealed that what we observe is not always processed definitively. Hence, there can be discrepancy between what we see and what we can recall.

The use of virtual reality systems is another technology providing a creative approach to investigating cognition. Frequently this involves the use of a headset which enables the wearer to experience a virtual environment that has stereoscopic depth. Hence, the brain becomes tricked into believing we are perceiving objects in a virtual space and are therefore present in a different reality. This is achieved by stimulating our visual senses. This technology has already been applied to pain management, treating phobias and controlling motion sickness. **Virtual reality** can be used to improve learning and memory. By increasing the sensory dimensions involved in our interactions with the environment, we are more likely to encode information and form robust memories. The virtual reality headsets have shown promise in facilitating learning and in the creation of robust memories. This technology provides cognitive researchers with the ability to manipulate how stimuli are presented and which responses are measured. Hence, this increases the ecological validity of cognitive research. In other words, cognitive research can become more applied and reflect what we do and see in our natural environment. Rizzo, Schultheis, Kerns and Mateer (2004) claimed that virtual environments are akin to being 'the ultimate Skinner box' where a diverse range of stimuli of varying complexity can be controlled. This, in turn, can help cognitive psychologists to manipulate complex stimuli that would normally be too challenging to create. Moreover, it enables cognitive psychologists to examine performance using other forms of presentation. Also, such stimuli can be explored in different contexts. For example, visual illusions can be presented under conditions where the observer is moving. Bruder, Steinicke, Wieland and Lappe (2012) examined how visual motion illusions are perceived when the observer is moving. They found that the change of light from images can influence judgements concerning self-motion. Recent developments in virtual reality combine eye-tracking technology as a means of researching the effects of mild traumatic brain injury. Horan, Heckenberg, Maruff and Wright (2020) created a virtual reality concussion assessment tool called CONVIRT which incorporates eye-tracking technology. This enables cognitive neuropsychologists to provide assessments of decision-making ability and levels of attention in concussed individuals. With further developments in technology, cognitive psychologists should be able to study cognition at many different levels of analysis. As a discipline, cognitive psychology can expand its horizons by embracing these new technological developments.

Another area that has influenced cognitive psychology is artificial intelligence (AI). This, in combination with developments in cognitive neuroscience, can potentially improve our understanding of how we think; for example, the algorithms we automatically embrace when making deductions and inductions. Models of attention, memory, language and thought, provide byte size flowcharts of information processing. We have seen how connectionist models of memory provide insight into how memories are stored as connections between nodes, and how this enables parallel distributed processing (PDP). The developments in the 'cognition' of robots have provided greater understanding of how neural connections in the human brain might be formed. Despite the development of sophisticated robots with the ability to 'acquire' language and logic, and to respond to human language interactions, they are still in their infancy when compared to what our brain is capable of learning. This, in part, is a consequence of limited algorithmic input. The computational science behind robotics, however, is improving. For example, the seemingly farfetched 'weird science', often appendaged to computational cognitive science, has entered the realm of scientific understanding and investigation (see Box 2.7). Cognitive psychology, in order to dispel any fallacious 'weird science' assumptions concerning cognition, will need to explore these using scientific methods. By doing so, empirical evidence of the plausibility of such claims (like being able to download our minds onto a computer chip) can be discussed scientifically. When empirical evidence, however, repudiates such claims, then 'weird science' can be excluded from the cognitive psychological research agenda.

An area of psychology that has made an impact on how cognitive theories are interpreted, at both an ultimate and proximate level, is evolutionary psychology.

EVOLUTIONARY PSYCHOLOGY

According to evolutionary psychologists, theories of how we operate cognitively have focused primarily on proximate causes instead of ultimate ones. In the case of proximate explanations, behaviour is accounted for by examining the cognitive processes underlying it – how it operates in the 'here and now'. There is little discourse concerning the underlying purpose of the cognitive processing driving the behaviour in the first place. In other words, an ultimate explanation. An ultimate explanation involves the importance of the behaviour being driven by specific cognitive strategies that were once adaptive in our evolutionary past. An ultimate explanation is best understood by asking how cognitive processes helped our ancestors to solve specific problems they had encountered. More succinctly, what purpose does cognitive processing serve? The areas of cognitive psychology that have been considered using ultimate explanations include:

- vision
- memory
- reasoning

VISION

In Chapter 3, Marr's computational model was briefly considered (see Box 3.5). Given the importance of his ultimate explanation of visual perception, it will be discussed further here. He began by simply asking, what our visual system was initially designed to do? Starting with this question, Marr introduced three levels of explanation:

1 Computational theory: What is the visual system for?
2 Representation and algorithm: How does the visual system achieve this purpose computationally?
3 Hardware implementation: What physical substrate is needed (i.e. eyes, optic nerve) for the visual system to achieve its purpose by following a series of computations?

Evolutionary psychologists are primarily interested in the computational theory as this asks an ultimate question. Why do we need the visual system to operate in the way that it does? Levels two and three can then be explored (and indeed level two is often researched by cognitive psychologists). Evolutionary psychologists argue that our visual system is not designed to represent the world as it really is. Our visual system, they argue, evolved to deal with recurrent ancestral challenges. Hence, our brain contrives to differentiate what the retina sees in an adaptive way. Take for example Figure 9.1. What do you see?

Our brain interprets this as a triangle whose points occlude three circles. Hence, according to Workman and Reader (2021), "If our visual system were truly designed to represent the way that the world is then we should see three Pac-Man characters having a chat

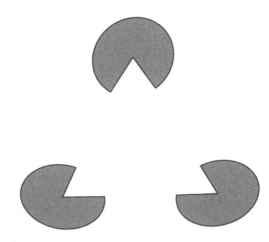

Figure 9.1 A visual illusion

in a triangular configuration..." (p. 226). But we actually perceive a triangle that is not really there. This fits in with Marr's (1982) claim that our visual system produces edited descriptions of our world from a series of images. In so doing, we see a version that has useful information without the extraneous clutter. The outlines of objects, in particular, edges, provide all the information required to make an identification, which is why we see a triangle in Figure 9.1. As discussed in Chapter 3, we have perceptual constancies which act to compensate for variations of object size, colour and illumination.

MEMORY

Evolutionary psychologists consider memory to be optimally adapted for the information we need to suit the environment we frequent. Anderson and Milson (1989) argued that the superior speed of recall for words frequently encountered versus non-frequently experienced words is an adaptive design. It makes sense to be able to formulate intelligent predictions of the words that are useful to us and to access them more speedily than those we encounter infrequently. They further consider the process of repetition priming (see Chapter 4) and how this too enables us to access useful words quickly as we encounter them again. It is the consensus that memory evolved to support how we make decisions (Klein, Cosmides, Tooby and Chance 2002). Decision-making relies on information and this information can be accessed through stored memories. Klein et al. argue that separate memory systems, such as episodic and semantic, are used to process information required for specific types of decisions made. For example, they argue that episodic memories hold different types of information from semantic memories. Episodic memories are associated with personal experiences and often contain emotional content. This makes them likely to be useful for making decisions based on previous experiences (see Box 9.1).

BOX 9.1   WHAT MIGHT EPISODIC MEMORIES BE TELLING US?

Schacter (1999) argued that Post-Traumatic Stress Disorder (PTSD) encourages us to relive negative experiences as a reminder to avoid situations that can be dangerous for our survival. In other words, stay away from such situations that can compromise our safety. When we consider PTSD from this evolutionary angle, how memory interacts with the symptoms of this condition can offer a new way of controlling the constant ruminations experienced by individuals. Interestingly, the existence of flashbulb memories discussed in Chapter 4, also has an ultimate explanation. When we consider our flashbulb memories of the death of Princess Diana (for those of us old enough to have been around at the time), we can recall where we were, what we were doing and possibly even what we were wearing. We may ask the question why evolutionists consider flashbulb memories as having 'fitness' consequences. In other words, such memories enable us to avoid negative events and, in so doing increase our chances of survival and passing on our genes (i.e. increased fitness) to the next generation. But what purpose could the recall of details associated with the death of Princess Diana possibly serve? In order to answer this, we need to consider the environmental conditions under which our prehistoric ancestors lived. In our evolutionary past, living conditions were very different.

It would have paid our ancestors to have such flashbulb memories of how emotional we felt at the time when we saw a pride of lionesses attack one of our family members. In this example it would pay to take heed not to hunt in the vicinity of these lionesses next time. Hence, remembering such an event with all the emotions and actions that had occurred, serves us well in avoiding repeating the unfortunate hunting error. What we see here is an environmental mismatch between our evolutionary past (when such flashbulb memories facilitate good decision-making) and present day. Flashbulb memories can therefore be considered as an adaptation designed to facilitate good decision-making for our ancestors. The mismatch hypothesis, however, argues that it is an adaptation we don't always need today.

Given, that our memory facilitates effective decision-making, it makes perfect sense to store our past experiences. The more we are exposed to the same events, the greater the likelihood that these memories (regardless of being episodic or semantic) will be processed rapidly in comparison to singular events. Suggestions of there being an 'adaptive memory' by evolutionary psychologists can impact on how cognitive psychologists research memory in the future. Perhaps in the future the focus might shift away from analysing the content of what is processed and the structure of short- and long-term memory to understanding how memories served our ancestors in decision-making. In other words, an ultimate explanation of the purpose our memory serves can help us better understand why it appears to malfunction occasionally.

REASONING

The Wason task (see Chapter 5) has been researched using the standard abstract format of 'if a card has a vowel on one side, then it has an even number on the other'. People struggle with having to select two cards to see if the rule is broken. When, however, the problem is less abstract, such as 'if a person is drinking alcohol, then they must be over 19 years of age', we find this an easier task to solve. Evolutionary psychologist, Leda Cosmides in 1989, argued that we can solve the less abstract format because it appeals to our need to spot free riders (those who take without contributing anything). The drinking alcohol and not being over 19 problem can be conceived as a free rider if the rule is contravened. This, in effect, activates a mental module concerned with detecting those who cheat. There are two domains of a mental module, what Sperber (1994) refers to as 'actual' and 'proper'. In the case of the proper domain, a stimulus triggers an action, such as the red belly of a male stickleback triggering an aggressive reaction from another male. The actual domain, in this instance, could be something else that is red thus resembling the male stickleback. So, what has this got to do with the Wason task? The standard Wason task is considered to be an indicative problem in that it is factual and relies on cause and effect. In the case of the underaged drinking scenario, however, the problem is a deontic example – it relates to a moral issue. Hence, the detection of who is breaking the rule and should therefore be reprimanded. According to Cosmides, Barrett and Tooby (2010) the detection of violating a deontic rule should be instigated when the cheater has made gains through cheating; cheating was a deliberate act and it is possible to contravene the rule by cheating. They argue that once these three stipulations are met, then the mental module will become activated as a consequence of the 'cheater-detection algorithm' firing. Hence, the underaged drinking scenario (or deontic rule) will be solved. Cosmides et al. have offered an evolutionarily sound explanation for the differences in solution rate between indicative and deontic representations of the Wason task. We, in effect, have evolved a mechanism to detect cheats which has served our ancestors well for maintaining cooperation and expelling free riders. This ultimate explanation provides an answer as to why we find some versions of the Wason task easier to solve. By considering ultimate explanations, as evolutionary psychology does, studying logic and reasoning can focus less on the analysis of content difficulty and more on why there should be a difference in solution difficulty. Evolutionary psychologists emphasise that our cognition has evolved to facilitate action – our behaviour. With such ultimate explanations in mind, it is possible to explore our cognition using a different perspective.

How our genes on the X chromosomes influence our cognition, has been of interest to geneticists. Given that evolutionary psychologists draw upon the mechanism of sexual selection introduced by

Charles Darwin, any sex differences relating to cognition, ascertained through our sex-determining chromosomes, are worth discussing here.

AN XX ADVANTAGE?

Research has long shown that males are more likely to suffer from specific genetical conditions inherited from the X-chromosome contributed by the mother. To be male (XY), the X chromosome comes from the mother during fertilisation and the Y chromosome from the father. The Y chromosome contains genetical information determining the male developmental pathway. In females (XX), genetical conditions that are carried on the X chromosome, are counteracted by the other X chromosome determining the female pathway of development (provided this X chromosome is functioning normally). In the case of a male, the faulty X chromosome cannot be counteracted by the Y chromosome as it contains far less genetical information. Hence, psychologists talk about the 'gender paradox', whereby more males have sex-linked disorders, but when a female has the same condition (carried by both X chromosomes), she will show more severe symptoms than her male counterparts. And that is the gender paradox. Moalem (2020) explores the genetic advantage females have over males in areas of resilience, stamina, immunity, survival and, important to our discussion here, intellect (see Box 9.2).

BOX 9.2 THE FEMALE ADVANTAGE

Cells in our body contain a genetic/chromosomal blueprint, also known as the karyotype. Therefore, the XX complement for females and the XY pair in males carrying our sex-determining genes, are present in our cells. It was previously believed that only one of the X chromosomes in females was active while the other was a silent partner. This has been shown to be inaccurate, and, in fact, the so-called silent X partner is also active. This helps to explain the high frequency of males experiencing conditions such as haemophilia (a blood clotting disorder) over females. The males, in effect, inherit the faulty gene(s) carried on the X chromosome and show the symptoms while females have their other X chromosome to fall back on – hence, why they are the 'carriers'. Moalem (2020) argues that geneticists are able to track the cause of many intellectual disabilities in males to the X chromosome. He claims that, "An X-linked inheritance pattern on a family tree stands out when only the boys in the family seem to be affected" (p. 62). Taking fragile X syndrome as an example, more often than not, it is males who are severely affected. The X chromosome is prone to breakage and it is the fragile-X mental retardation (FMR1) gene that is the source of the problem. FMR1 is responsible for producing a protein which helps in the formation of synaptic connections (see Chapter 2). In fragile X syndrome, FMR1 fails to initiate the production of this protein which then interferes with the development of the brain. This means that executive functions such as working memory, learning, planning, thought, language and attention fail to operate efficiently and why one of the main symptoms is disruption to cognition. Gissler, Järvelin, Louhiala and Hemminki (1999) looked at the risk of delayed development as a consequence of birthing complications in a sample of 60,254 Finish children born in 1987. Some 31 per cent of the sample who had birthing problems were boys. Moreover, in a sub-set of 14,000 of these children, boys were more likely to be developmentally arrested such that starting school was postponed and special education necessary. In a US study in 2011, boys were more likely to develop learning disabilities and stuttering, Attention Deficit Hyperactivity Disorder and being on the autism spectrum (Boyle, Boulet, Schieve, Cohen et al. 2011). Sex differences in how we learn information and which type of information is learned more easily by males or females needs further investigation. Is it plausible that learning differs across the sexes? We know that there has been a recent trend over the past 30 years of girls out-performing boys as measured by 'GCSE' grades in the UK. Duell (2020) described how schoolgirls are now 14 per cent more likely than their boy counterparts to pass exams in English and maths (64 per cent versus 56 per cent respectively). Miller and Halpern (2014) showed that there are differences between males and females in the type of spatial ability tasks that they excel in. Males out-perform females on reasoning and problem-solving, mental rotation, geometry and statistics while females do better on algebra and comprehending numerical patterns. Liu and Wilson (2009) found that girls are better at solving conventional problems arising from content in textbooks. For boys, their forte is for unconventional problems. This, it is argued, despite the fact that girls out-perform boys at GCSE, means girls have a disadvantage in areas where some standardised tests are based on unconventional problem-solving. There is still much to learn about cognitive differences between the sexes and information assimilation.

SO, WHAT HAVE WE LEARNT ABOUT COGNITIVE PSYCHOLOGY?

CHAPTER 1

Cognitive psychology is the study of mental processing. Areas investigated include attention and perception; memory and learning; thinking and problem-solving and language and communication. Disciplines such as cognitive neuroscience and cognitive neuropsychology have contributed to our knowledge of the brain's involvement in information processing. Brain scanning technology from cognitive neuroscience allows us to understand the areas of the brain involved in cognition. Information about module-specificity, and how cognitive deficits are linked to impaired module function, comes from cognitive neuropsychology. Computational cognitive science offers an understanding of how neurons are interconnected in the brain.

CHAPTER 2

The architecture of the brain is divided into microanatomy and gross anatomy. How neurons in the brain are interconnected and the way that neural pathways pass information to different parts of the brain, is the realm of microanatomy. Gross structure concerns the interrelationship between the lobes of the brain. From the gross anatomy of the brain, it is possible to see how the two hemispheres interact via commissures such as the corpus callosum. By using brain scanning techniques and tasks that help to measure brain function, as well as modelling, understanding the intricate interconnections between structure and function have been studied.

CHAPTER 3

Attention is important to the way the world is perceived. Sensory information guides our attention by what we see, hear, smell, taste or touch. Models of attention frequently include a bottleneck. For those models where there is no bottleneck, it is assumed that we can divide our attention. We can divide our attention across tasks when one is automated, or the demands of the tasks are very simple. The processing of sensory stimuli is enabled during focused attention – this allows for stimuli to be fully processed. Such bottom-up processing is useful in the learning of new information. With increases to our knowledge-base of events, our memory store expands and can be used; hence, adopting top-down processing. Meaning applied to stimuli is known as perception. Our environment is interpreted by the sensation and perception of object interaction.

CHAPTER 4

Shiffrin and Atkinson introduced a basic memory structure of short-term to long-term storage, but other components have since been added – working memory, episodic, semantic and procedural. Memories of events are stored in episodic memory whereas world knowledge resides in semantic memory. Skill acquisition is stored in procedural memory. The involvement of conscious awareness, as occurs in declarative memory, is part of both episodic and semantic memory systems. Alternatively, non-declarative memories (without conscious awareness) are part of procedural memory. Pre-existing schemas embellish our memories of events and can influence recall accuracy. A lifespan of autobiographical memories is considered to be part of everyday memories. Prospective memory can be time-based and/or event-based. This is involved in our intentions to perform actions. Remembering cannot happen without learning. Engaging and learning information impacts on how well we form memory traces. Efficient encoding of memories results in optimal consolidation and recall. Information can be learned using repetition priming without explicit learning (unaware) – hence, implicitly. Mnemonic techniques rely on explicit learning.

CHAPTER 5

Different forms of thinking include judgements, decision-making, informal reasoning, inductive and deductive reasoning and problem-solving. When information is limited, we make judgements about the likelihood of something occurring. Both judgement and decision-making rely on heuristics. Kahneman and Tversky describe heuristics as simple but quick computational calculation of decisions leading to rapid outcomes. Informal reasoning is based on our knowledge-base and experiences. It is considered a sub-set of logic and often referred to as critical thinking. This helps us to conclude if a statement is probably true or false using likelihoods. Inductive reasoning is used when a conclusion is uncertain because the information available is limited. Deductive reasoning divides into two forms of logic: propositional and syllogistic. Both propositional and syllogistic reasoning present two premises and a conclusion. Propositional uses premises referring to individuals whereas syllogistic refers to 'sets'. Problem-solving can present with well- or ill-defined problems, knowledge-lean or knowledge-rich. We solve by trial and error and insight according to Gestaltists. Limited cognitive processing capacity can prevent problem-solving.

CHAPTER 6

According to Chomsky, human language has an innate universal grammar. Computational models of reading suggest there are two routes to reading, one of which is a direct route linking spelling to sound and the other an indirect route via meaning (semantics) to sound. Language comprehension involves breaking down a sentence into its parts (parsing) and understanding the intention of the speaker (pragmatics). During discourse we make inferences about the message. The construction-integration model suggests, during reading, we develop three levels of representation: a surface level (actual text), a propositional level (propositions are formed) and a situational level (a mental model describes the situation). Hayes' model of writing suggests the process has three levels: a planning (control) level, an actual writing (process) level and a (resource) level which draws on cognitive resources.

CHAPTER 7

Different levels of conscious awareness or the ability to attend directly to stimuli, determine category states of consciousness. Individuals in a VS or MCS, when considered neurologically, provide measurements of brain activity to questions using mental imagery. This means that, despite no signs of attention, their brain is active and 'aware'. Feedforward processing (or bottom-up) occurs automatically when visual stimuli are presented. By feedback processing such information is processed further. This is where consciousness occurs as the information becomes integrated through top-down processing. Conscious experience enables us to recall memories of events and knowledge. We can reflect upon these experiences and knowledge using metacognition.

CHAPTER 8

Neuroscience is referred to by cognitive neuropsychologists to understand the brain's role in cognition. Brain-damaged individuals provide information about the involvement of specific areas of the brain in memory and language performance. fMRI helps to examine the role of areas such as the frontal lobes and temporoparietal junction in specific aspects of cognition and emotion (e.g. ToM). fMRI also helps us understand the role of neural pathways and mirror neurons in the imitation of the actions of others. Neuroplasticity is facilitated by learning. This involves the blooming and pruning of synapses to drive optimal connections that will increase the speed of processing.

SUMMARY

Understanding cognition has progressed immensely due to technological advances in brain scanning techniques, computerised data processing and new experimental measurements such as n-back, BioPak, eye-tracking goggles and virtual reality headsets. The way in which the brain operates, and the intricate neural connections and pathways, can be brought to light by adopting these technologies. These enable cognitivists to 'see' inside the brain and how the software is operationalised to perform the many cognitive processing feats that we are unaware of. Artificial intelligence, once a fiction of the movies, is now within our grasp and also provides a window to how neural connectivity forms and influences our cognitive capabilities. Evolutionary psychology is becoming ever more ubiquitous as an explanation of our behaviour in psychology; for which cognitive psychology is no exception. It offers, in addition to proximate explanations, overarching explanations as to why our brain has evolved to function the way it does, and the adaptations to brain structure arising from environmental pressures in our ancestral past. These ultimate explanations also include the impact of mechanisms of sexual selection. In other words, the impact of female choice in mate selection as a driving force in the direction of male development. Evolutionary psychology has provided a different perspective to understanding areas of cognition such as vision, memory and reasoning. Evolutionary psychologists ask what the visual system is for and claim that it provides edited descriptions of the images we see. Memory has evolved to support our decision-making so that our stored episodic memories and experiences help us make optimal decisions that promote our survival. By providing an ultimate explanation for the purpose of memory, a better understanding of why it malfunctions can be derived. The Wason task used to study thinking is presented in an abstract format but once it becomes more concrete (e.g. about underaged drinking), it becomes easier to solve. This is because in our evolutionary history detecting those who violated rules (cheaters) helped to solve ancestral challenges. There is the assumption that having two X chromosomes can provide females with an advantage over males in areas such as intellect. This assumption, however, requires further research.

FURTHER READING

Barkow, J.H., Tooby, J. and Cosmides, L. (1992) *The Adapted Mind: Evolutionary psychology and the generation of culture.* Oxford: Oxford University Press.

Moalem, S. (2020) *The Better Half: On the genetic superiority of women.* UK: Penguin Random House.

Nurit, E. (2011) *Haptic Weight Perception in Virtual Reality.* Germany: Lambert Academic Publishing.

Sutcliffe, A. (2003) *Multimedia and Virtual Reality: Designing multisensory user interfaces.* Hove: Psychology Press.

GLOSSARY

Amnesia: Partial or total inability to recall memories. Two types of amnesia include antegrade (inability to form new memories) and retrograde (loss of pre-existing memories).

Bottom–up processing: Incoming stimuli from our sensory organs initiate processing. These stimuli are passed on for further processing to higher ordered cells involved in stimulus recognition and interpretation. Sometimes called data-driven processing.

Cerebral cortex: This is the largest area of the brain where higher order functions and processing such as perception, memory, language and thought as well as voluntary action occur.

Cognitive algorithms: Algorithms provide step-by-step guidance for solving set problems. In cognitive problem-solving, algorithms provide successful procedures used to solve specific types of problem.

Dyslexia: A general term used to describe those who have problems with reading, writing and spelling yet have a level of general intelligence within the normal range. Various schemes exist for sub-classifications of dyslexia. Three well established forms are: surface (inability to read 'irregular' words), deep (inability to read 'non-words') and phonological (difficulties manipulating the basic sounds of language).

Feedforward–feedback neural processing mechanism: This involves two types of interactive neural processes. In the case of feedforward, specific cells are receptive to specific elements of a stimulus, such as a vertical line. Such information is collectively passed on to other cells that combine the information received to form a reconfiguration of the stimulus. This involves an automatic forward passing and processing of information. However, information about the stimulus is also passed back to other areas of the brain for interpretation. This feedback processing interacts with our existing knowledge about the stimulus for optimal processing and interpretation.

Forced-choice procedure: This procedure forces a decision about a question, opinion or test. For example, there is a 'yes' or 'no' option without any option encouraging indecision.

Global processing: This is where stimuli are processed holistically rather than at the local level (e.g. process 'H' rather than the smaller 's' comprising the letter).

Heuristic: This is a short-cut, 'rule of thumb' approach to solving a problem. Unlike an algorithm, it is a quicker way of informing our decision-making.

Implementation intentions: Often used as a plan for goal attainment, this involves the use of an 'if-then' strategy.

Information processing: This approach concerns the way in which we attend to and perceive, remember, use and manipulate information.

Local processing: Unlike global processing, local processing refers to the attention to specific stimulus detail (e.g. process the smaller 's' forming part of the larger letter 'H').

Machiavellian intelligence: This is used to describe an individual who is able to manipulate social situations to favour their own ambitions, such that they often mask their true personality and emotions to serve them well in deceiving others.

Metacognition: This involves the ability to reflect upon one's own thinking by using processes such as planning, monitoring and assessing.

Mirror neurons: These are sensorimotor neurons involved in our ability to mimic another person's actions. Mirror neurons are activated equally when an action is executed and when we observe others performing the same action. Moreover, this occurs when someone experiences distress which is why we can feel empathy.

Mnemonics: These are memory techniques used to improve encoding, recalling and therefore learning new information.

Modularity: This is the notion that our mind is composed of independent information centres (or modules), each of which have their own domain of processing specific stimuli.

N-back: This is an experimental technique used to measure how working memory and its capacity operate.

Odds ratio: This is used to measure the likelihood of an event occurring in one group in comparison to it occurring in a different group. The comparison pertains to a dichotomous classification.

Orthography: The conventional spelling system of a particular language.

Perceptual asymmetries: A difference in the perception of stimuli occurs depending on whether the presentation occurs to the left or right visual field. When presented to the right visual field, the stimulus is processed by the left hemisphere and by the right when presented in the left visual field. The left hemisphere is superior at word processing whereas the right has an advantage for pictorial formats.

Plasticity: This refers to the brain's capacity to change or modify as a consequence of new experiences, in particular learning. In the case of neuroplasticity, this refers to the neurons comprising the building-blocks of the brain.

Rotary pursuit task: This is a task used to measure motor performance and involves the tracking of a revolving target using a pointer.

Scanning techniques: These technologies (e.g. MRI and PET) are used to provide images of the structure and function of the human brain.

Synapses: These are found where one neuron ends, and another begins. There is a gap between these neurons that allows for the transmission of a signal (impulse) and is enabled by a neurotransmitter.

Top-down processing: While bottom-up processing is involved in building up an interpretation of stimuli, top-down works to process and interpret stimuli using existing knowledge. This acts as a fast-route to understanding stimuli. Sometimes called conceptually-driven processing.

Trial and error: This is a method used in problem-solving where multiple attempts are methodically used and observed until the correct solution is found.

Universal grammar: The hypothesis proposed by Noam Chomsky that language is, in part, an innate faculty.

Virtual reality: By implementing a computer-generated simulation, a 3-D environmental space is created. A person can interact with this fake world by wearing special goggles.

REFERENCES

Aarts, H. and van den Bos, K. (2011) On the foundations of beliefs in free will: Intentional binding and unconscious priming in self- agency. *Psychological Science*, 22, 532–7.

Adolphs, R., Tranel, D., Damasio, H. and Damasio, A. (1994). Impaired recognition of emotion in facial expressions following bilateral damage to the human amygdala. *Nature*, 372, 669–72.

Adolphs, R., Tranel, D., Damasio, H. and Damasio, A.R. (1995) Fear and the human amygdala. *Neuroscience*, 15(9), 5879–91.

Aikin, S.F. and Casey, J. (2011) Straw men, weak men, and hollow men. *Argumentation*, 25, 87–105.

Aitchison, J. (1989) *The Articulate Mammal*. London: Routledge.

Aitchison, J. (2008) *The Articulate Mammal*. (5th edn). London: Routledge.

Alberini, C. and Travaglia, A. (2017) Infantile amnesia: A critical period of learning to learn and remember. *Journal of Neuroscience*, 37, 5783–95.

Alfred, K.L., Connolly, A.C., Cetron, J.S. and Kraemer, D.J.M. (2020) Mental models use common neural spatial structure for spatial and abstract content. *Communications Biology*, 3(1), 17. doi:10.1038/s42003-019-0740-8.

Allen, R.J., Hitch, G.J., Mate, J. and Baddeley, A.D. (2012) Feature binding and attention in working memory: A resolution of previous contradictory findings. *Quarterly Journal of Experimental Psychology*, 65, 2369–83.

American Psychological Association (APA) (2020). Dictionary of Psychology. https://dictionary.apa.org/cognitive-psychology

Ames, A. (1952) *The Ames Demonstrations in Perception*. New York: Hafner Publishing.

Anderson, J.R. and Lebiere, C. (1998) *The Atomic Components of Thought*. Mahwah, NJ: Erlbaum.

Anderson, J.R. and Milson, R. (1989) Human memory: An adaptive perspective. *Psychological Review*, 96(4), 703–19.

Atkinson, A.P., Dittrich, W.H., Gemmel, A.J. and Young, A.W. (2004) Emotion perception from dynamic and static body expressions in point-light and full–light displays. *Perception*, 33, 717–46.

Atkinson, R.C. and Shiffrin, R.M. (1968) Human memory: A proposed system and its control processes. In K.W. Spence and J.T. Spence (eds) *The Psychology of Learning and Motivation (Volume 2)*. New York: Academic Press, pp. 89–195.

Awh, F. and Pashler, H. (2000) Evidence for split attentional foci. *Journal of Experimental Psychology: Human Perception and Performance*, 26, 83–146.

Azevedo, F., Carvalho, L.R.B., Grinberg, L.T., Farfel, J.M., Ferretti, R.E.L., Leite, R.E.P., Filho, W.J., Lent, R. and Herculano-Houzel, S. (2009) Equal numbers of neuronal and nonneuronal cells make the human brain an iso-metrically scaled-up primate brain. *The Journal of Comparative Neurology*, 513(5), 532–41.

Baddeley, A.D. (1996) Exploring the central executive. *Quarterly Journal of Experimental Psychology*, 49A, 5–28.

Baddeley, A.D. (2000) The episodic buffer: A new component of working memory? *Trends in Cognitive Science*, 4, 417–23.

Baddeley, A.D. (2012) Working memory: Theories, models, and con-troversies. *Annual Review of Psychology,* 63, 1–29.

Baddeley, A. and Hitch, G. (1974) Working memory. In G. Bower (ed.) *The Psychology of Learning and Motivation* (pp. 47–89). New York: Academic Press.

Baddeley, A.D., Thomson, N. and Buchanan, M. (1975) Word length and the structure of short-term memory. *Journal of Verbal Learning and Verbal Behavior*, 14, 575–89.

Baddeley, A.D. and Wilson, B. (2002) Prose recall and amnesia: Implications for the structure of working memory. *Neuropsychologia*, 40, 1737–43.

Bahrick, H.P., Bahrick, P.O. and Wittlinger, R.P. (1975) Fifty years of memory for names and faces: A cross–sectional approach. *Journal of Experimental Psychology: General*, 104, 54–75.

Balch, W.R. (2005) Elaborations of introductory psychology terms: Effects on test performance and subjective ratings. *Teaching of Psychology*, 32, 29–34.

Baldo, J.V. and Shimamura, A.P. (1998) Letter and category fluency in pa-tients with frontal lobe lesions. *Neuropsychology*, 12(2), 259–67.

Banich, M.T. and Compton, R.J. (2018) *Cognitive Neuroscience* (4th edn). Cambridge: Cambridge University Press.

Barlow, H.B. (1953) Summation and inhibition in the frog's retina. *The Journal of Physiology*, 119(1), 69–88.

Barsalou, I.W. (2009) Simulation, situated conceptualization, and prediction. *Philosophical Transactions of the Royal Society B: Biological Sciences*, 364, 1281–89.

Bartlett, F. (1932) *Remembering: A study in experimental and social psychology.* Cambridge: Cambridge University Press.

Baron-Cohen, S. (1997) *Mindblindness: An essay on autism and theory of mind.* Cambridge, MA: MIT Press.

Baron-Cohen, S., Leslie, A.M. and Frith, U. (1985) Does the autistic child have a "theory of mind"? *Cognition,* 21(1), 37–46.

Baron-Cohen, S., Ring, H., Wheelwright, S., Bullmore, E., Brammer, M., Simmons, A. and Williams, S. (1999) Social intelligence in the normal and autistic brain: An fMRI study. *European Journal of Neuroscience,* 11, 1891–8.

Baumeister, R.F. and Masicampo, E.J. (2010) Conscious thought is for facilitating social and cultural interactions: How mental simulations serve the animal–culture interface. *Psychology Review,* 117(3), 945–71.

Baynes, K. and Gazzaniga, M. (2000) Consciousness, introspection, and the split brain: The two minds/one body problem. In M.S. Gazzaniga (ed.) *The New Cognitive Neurosciences.* Cambridge, MA: MIT Press.

Beales, S.A. and Parkin, A.J. (1984) Context and facial memory: The influence of different processing strategies. *Human Learning: Journal of Practical Research and Applications,* 3(4), 257–64.

Bechtel, W. and Graham, G. (1998) *A Companion to Cognitive Science.* Cambridge, UK: Blackwell Publishers.

Bellezza, F. (1996) Mnemonic methods to enhance storage and retrieval. In E.L. Bjork and R.A. Bjork (eds) *Memory: Handbook of perception and cognition* (pp. 345–380). San Diego, CA: Academic Press.

Berryhill, M.E. and Olson, I. (2007) Determining parietal involvement in visual working memory: Causal or incidental? *Journal of Visual Abstracts,* 7, 300.

Berryhill, M.E., Phuong, L., Picasso, L., Cabeza, R. and Olson, I.R. (2007) Parietal lobe and episodic memory: Bilateral damage causes impaired free recall of autobiographical memory. *Journal of Neuroscience,* 27(52), 14415–23.

Biederman, I. (1987) Recognition by components: A theory of human image understanding. *Psychological Review,* 94, 115–47.

Bigos, K.L., Hariri, A. and Weinberger, D. (2015) *Neuroimaging Genetics: Principles and Practices.* Oxford: Oxford Press University.

Bilalić, M., McLeod, P. and Gobet, F. (2008a) Why good thoughts block better ones: The mechanism of the pernicious Einstellung effect. *Cognition,* 108, 652–61.

Bilalić, M., McLeod, P. and Gobet, F. (2008b) Inflexibility of experts – Reality or myth? Quantifying the Einstellung effect in chess masters. *Cognitive Psychology,* 56, 73–102.

Bindschaedler, C., Peter-Favre, C., Maeder, P., Hirsbrunner, T. and Clarke, S. (2011) Growing up with bilateral hippocampal atrophy: From childhood to teenager. *Cortex,* 47, 931–44.

Block, N. (2012) Response to Kouider et al.: Which view is better supported by the evidence? *Trends in Cognitive Sciences*, 16, 141–2.

Bob, P., Pec, O., Mishara, A.L., Touskova, T. and Lysaker, P.H. (2016) Conscious brain, metacognition and schizophrenia. *International Journal of Psychophysiology*, 105, 1–8.

Boly, M., Garrido, M.I., Gosseries, O., Bruno, M-A., Boveroux, P., Schnakers, C., Massimini, M., Litvak, V., Laureys, S. and Friston, K. (2011) Preserved feedforward but impaired top-down processes I: The vegetative state. *Science*, 332, 858–62.

Bondi, D., Prete, G., Malatesta, G. and Robazza, C. (2020) Laterality in children: Evidence for task-dependent lateralization of motor functions. *International Journal of Environmental Research and Public Health*, 17, 6705, doi:10.3390/ijerph17186705.

Bor, D. and Seth, A.K. (2012) Consciousness and the prefrontal parietal network: Insights from attention, working memory, and chunking. *Frontiers in Psychology*, 3 (Article 63).

Borod, J., Koff, E. and Buck, R. (1986) The neuropsychology of facial expression in normal and brain-damaged subjects. In P. Blanck, R. Buck and Rosenthal, R. (eds) *Nonverbal Communication in the Clinical Context*. University Park, PA: Pennsylvania State University Press.

Boyle, C.A., Boulet, S., Schieve, L.A., Cohen, R.A., Blumberg, S.J., Yeargin-Allsopp, M., Visser, S. and Kogan, M.D. (2011). Trends in the prevalence of developmental disabilities in US children, 1997–2008. *Pediatrics*, 127, 1034–42.

Bransford, J.D., Barclay, J.R. and Franks, J.J. (1972) Sentence memory: A constructive versus interpretive approach, *Cognitive Psychology*, 3, 193–209.

Brewer, N. and Wells, G.L. (2011) Eyewitness identification. *Current Directions in Psychological Science*, 20, 24–7.

Brewin, C. (2014) Episodic memory, perceptual memory, and their interaction: Foundations for a theory of posttraumatic stress disorder. *Psychological Bulletin*, 140, 69–97.

Bridge, H. (2020) A brain working blind. *The Psychologist*, 4, 41.

British Dyslexia Association (2018) Cited on https://www.bdadyslexia.org.uk/, accessed 7 December 2020.

British Psychological Society (BPS) (2020) *Cognitive Psychology*. https://www.bps.org.uk/subjects/cognitive-psychology

Broadbent, D.E. (1958) *Perception and Communication*. Oxford: Pergamon.

Brooks, D.N. and Baddeley, A.D. (1976) What can amnesic patients learn? *Neuropsychologia*, 14, 111–29.

Brown, K.F., Kroll, S.J., Hudson, M.J., Ramsay, M., Green, J., Vincent, C.A., Fraser, G. and Sevdalis, N. (2010) Omission bias and vaccine rejection by parents of healthy children: Implications for the influenza A/H1N1 vaccination programme. *Vaccine*, 28(25), 4181–5.

Brown, R. and Kulik, J. (1977) Flashbulb memories. *Cognition*, 5, 73–9.

Bruce, V. (1982) Changing faces: Visual and non-visual coding processes in face recognition. *British Journal of Psychology*, 73(1), 105–16.

Bruce, V. and Young, A. (1986) Understanding face recognition. *British Journal of Psychology*, 77, 305–27.

Bruder, G., Steinicke, F., Wieland, P. and M Lappe, M. (2012) Tuning self-motion perception in virtual reality with visual illusions. *IEEE Transactions on Visualization and Computer Graphics*, 18(7), 1068–78.

Brüne, M. (2005) "Theory of mind" in schizophrenia: A review of the literature. *Schizophrenia Bulletin*, 31(1), 21–42.

Bruyer, R. (2011) Configural face processing: A meta-analytic survey. *Perception*, 40, 1478–90.

Brzecki, A., Podemski, R., Kobel-Buys, K. and Buys, G. (2001) Illusions and hallucinations in posterior cerebral artery thrombosis –a case study. *Udar Mózgu*, 3, 71–6.

Bull, R. (2019) Roar or PEACE: Is it a tall story? In R. Bull and I. Blandon-Gitlin (eds) *International Handbook of Legal and Investigative Psychology*. London: Routledge.

Buller, D.J. (2005) *Adapting Minds: Evolutionary psychology and the persistent quest for human nature.* Cambridge, MA: MIT Press.

Bunford, N., Hernández-Pérez, R., Farkas, E.B., Cuaya, L.V., Szabó, D., Szabó, A.G., Gácsi, M., Miklósi, A. and Andics, A. (2020) Comparative brain imaging reveals analogous and divergent patterns of species- and face-sensitivity in humans and dogs. *Journal of Neuroscience*, 10(1523), 1–45.

Burianova, H., McIntosh, A.R. and Grady, C.L. (2010) A common functional brain network for autobiographical, episodic, and semantic memory retrieval. *NeuroImage*, 49, 865–74.

Burns, M.S. (2008) Application of neuroscience to technology in stroke rehabilitation. *Top Stroke Rehabilitation*, 15(6), 570–79.

Caramazza, A. and Coltheart, M. (2006) Cognitive neuropsychology twenty years on. *Cognitive Neuropsychology*, 23, 3–12.

Carney, R.N. and Levin, J.R. (2008) Conquering mnemonophobia, with help from three practical measures of memory and application. *Teaching of Psychology*, 35, 176–83.

Carroll, J.S. (1978) A psychological approach to deterrence: The evaluation of crime opportunities. *Journal of Personality and Social Psychology*, 36(12), 1512–20.

Cartmill, E.A. and Hobalter, C. (2019) Developmental perspectives on primate gesture: 100 years in the making. *Animal Cognition*, 22, 453–59.

Case, R. (1998). The development of conceptual structures. In W. Damon (Series Ed.), D. Kuhn and R. Siegler (eds) *Handbook of Child Psychology* vol.

2, *Cognition, Perception and Language* (5th edn), pp. 745–800). New York: Wiley.

Castles, A., Rastle, K. and Nation, K. (2018) Ending the reading wars: Reading acquisition from novice to expert. *Psychological Science in the Public Interest*, 19, 5–51.

Cave, K.R., Bush, W.S. and Taylor, T.G.G. (2010) Split attention as part of a flexible attentional system for complex scenes: Comment on Jans, Peters and De Weerd (2010). *Psychological Review*, 117, 685–96.

Challoner, J. (2009) *1,001 Inventions That Changed the World*. Hauppauge, NY: Barron's Educational Series.

Chen, Z. (2002) Analogical problem solving: A hierarchical analysis of procedural similarity. *Journal of Experimental Psychology: Learning, Memory, and Cognition*, 28(1), 81–98.

Cheney, D.L. and Seyfarth, R.M. (1990) *How Monkeys See the World: Inside the Mind of Another Species*. Chicago, IL: Chicago University Press.

Chenoweth, N. and Hayes, J.R. (2001) Fluency in writing. *Written Communication*, 18(1), 80–98.

Cherry, E.C. (1953) Some experiments on the recognition of speech with one or two ears. *Journal of the Acoustical Society of America*, 25, 975–9.

Chessman, J. and Merikle, P.M. (1984) Priming with and without awareness. *Perception and Psychophysics*. 36(4): 387–95.

Cheyne, S. and Davies, G. (1999) Perceptual processes. In I. Taylor (ed.) *Active Psychology: A and AS level* (pp. 570–607). London: Longmans.

Chin, J.M. and Schooler, J.W. (2008) Why do words hurt? Content, process, and criterion shift accounts of verbal overshadowing. *Eur. J. Cogn. Psychol.* 20, 396–413.

Cholewa, J., Mantey, S., Heber, S. and Hollweg, W. (2010) Developmental surface and phonological dysgraphia in German 3rd graders. *Reading and Writing*, 23, 97–127.

Chomsky, N. (1959) 'Review of Skinner (1957)', *Language*, 35, 26–58.

Chun, W.Y. and Kruglanski, A.W. (2006) The role of task demands and processing resources in the use of base-rate and individuating information. *Journal of Personality and Social Psychology*, 91(2), 205–17.

Cleeremans, A. and Jiménez, L. (2002) Implicit learning and consciousness: A graded, dynamic perspective. In R.M. French and A. Cleeremans (eds.) *Implicit Learning and consciousness: An empirical, philosophical and computational consensus in the making*. Hove: Psychology Press.

Coleman, A.M. (2001) *Oxford Dictionary of Psychology*. Oxford: Oxford University Press.

Collins English Dictionary (2020) https://www.collinsdictionary.com/dictionary/english/lexeme

Coltheart, M. (1996) *Phonological Dyslexia*. Hove, England: Erlbaum.

Coltheart, M. (2010) Lessons from Cognitive Neuropsychology for Cognitive Science: A Reply to Patterson and Plaut (2009), (p. 4). *Topics in Cognitive Science*, 2, 3–11.

Coltheart, M., Rastle, K., Perry, C., Langdon, R. and Ziegler, J.C. (2001) DRC: A dual-route cascaded model of visual word recognition and reading aloud. *Psychological Review*, 108, 204–56.

Colvin, M.K. and Gazzaniga, M.S. (2007) Split-brain cases. In M. Velmans and S. Schneider (eds) *The Blackwell Companion to Consciousness* (p. 189). Oxford: Blackwell.

Cona, G., Arcara, G., Tarantino, V. and Bisiacchi, P.S. (2012) Electrophysiological correlates of strategic monitoring in event-based and time-based prospective memory. *PLoS ONE*, 7(2), e31659.

Conway, M.A. and Pleydell-Pearce, C.W. (2000) The construction of autobiographical memories in the self-memory system. *Psychological Review*, 107, 262–88.

Conway, M.A., Wang, Q., Hanyu, K. and Haque, S. (2005) A cross-cultural investigation of autobiographical memory. *Journal of Cross-Cultural Psychology*, 36, 739–49.

Corbetta, M., Patel, G. and Shulman, G.L. (2008) The re-orienting system of the human brain: From environment to theory of mind. *Neuron*, 58, 306–24.

Corbetta, M. and Shulman, G.L. (2002) Control of goal-directed and stimulus-driven attention in the brain. *Nature Reviews Neuroscience*, 3, 201–15.

Corbetta, M. and Shulman, G.L. (2011) Spatial neglect and attention networks. *Annual Review of Neuroscience*, 34, 569–99.

Corkin, S. (1984) Lasting consequences of bilateral medial temporal lobectomy – Clinical course and experimental findings in HM. *Seminars in Neurology*, 4, 249–59.

Cosmides, L. (1989) The logic of social exchange: Has natural selection shaped how humans reason? Studies with the Wason selection task. Cognition, *31*(3), 187–276.

Cosmides, L., Barrett, H.C. and Tooby, J. (2010) Adaptive specializations, social exchange, and the evolution of human intelligence. *Proceedings of the National Academy of Sciences*, 107, 9007–14.

Cowley, M. and Byrne, R.M.J. (2005) When falsification is the only path to truth. Paper presented at the Twenty–Seventh Annual Conference of the Cognitive Science Society, *Stresa, Italy*.

Craik, F.I.M. and Lockhart, R.S. (1972) Levels of processing: A framework for memory research. *Journal of Verbal Learning and Verbal Behavior*, 671–84.

Craik, F.I.M., and Tulving, E. (1975). Depth of processing and the retention of words in episodic memory. Journal of Experimental Psychology: General, *104*(3), 268–94.

Creutzfeldt, O.D. (1977) Generality of the functional structure of the neo-cortex. *Naturwissenschaften*, 64, 507–17.

Crisp, J., Howard, D. and Lambon Ralph, M.A. (2011) More evidence for a continuum between phonological and deep dyslexia: Novel data from three measures of direct orthography-to-phonology translation. *Aphasiology*, 25(5), 615–41.

Crow, T.J., Crow, L.R., Done, D.J. and Leask, S. (1998) Relative hand skill predicts academic ability: Global deficits at the point of hemispheric in-decision. *Neuropsychologia*, 36, 1275–82.

Cutler, A. and Clifton, C. (1999) Comprehending spoken language: A blueprint of the listener. In C.M. Brown, and P. Hagoort (eds) *The Neurocognition of Language*. Oxford: Oxford University Press.

Daly, M. and Wilson, M. (1998) *The truth about Cinderella: A Darwinian view of parental love*. London: Yale.

Damasio, H., Grabowski, T., Frank, R., Galaburda, A.M. and Damasio, A.R. (1994) The return of Phineas Gage: Clues about the brain from the skull of a famous patient. *Science*, 264(5162), 1102–5.

DeDe, G. (2010) Utilization of prosodic information in syntactic ambiguity resolution. *Journal of Psycholinguist Research*. 39, 345–74.

de Gardelle, V., Sackur, J. and Kouider, S. (2009) Perceptual illusions in brief visual presentations. *Conscious Cognition*, 18, 569–77.

de Haan, B., Karnath, H-O. and Driver, J. (2012) Mechanisms and anatomy of unilateral extinctions after brain injury. *Neuropsychologia*, 50, 1045–53.

Dennett, D.C. (1988) "Quining qualia." In A. Marcel and E. Bisiach (eds) *Consciousness in Contemporary Science* (381–414). Oxford: Oxford University Press.

Dennett, D.C. (1996) The Science Masters Series. Kinds of Minds: Toward an understanding of consciousness. New York: Basic Books.

Dennett, D.C. (2003) *The Illusion of Consciousness. TED Talk*. Available online at: www.ted.com/talks/dan_dennett_on_our_consciousness

Deutsch, J.A. and Deutsch, D. (1963) Attention: Some theoretical con-siderations. *Psychological Review*, 93, 283–321.

Dimaggio, G. and Lysaker, P.H. (2015) Metacognition and mentalizing in the psychotherapy of patients with psychosis and personality disorders. *Journal of Clinical Psychology*, 71(2), 117–24.

Draganski, B., Gaser, C., Kempermann, G., Kuhn, H.G., Winkler, J., Büchel, C. and May, A. (2006) Temporal and spatial dynamics of brain structure changes during extensive learning. *Journal of Neuroscience*, 26(23), 6314–7.

Duell, M. (6 February 2020) Girls have outperformed boys at GCSE for THREE DECADES and poorer pupils have fallen even further behind richer peers – use our module to see how well your local schools did in

2019 results. Mail Online. www.dailymail.co.uk/news/article-7973933/Englands-GCSE-gender-gap-lasts-30-YEARS.html

Dunbar, K. (2001) The analogy paradox: Why analogy is so easy in naturalistic settings, yet so difficult in the psychological laboratory. In D. Gentner, K.J. Holyoak, and B. Kokinov (eds) *Analogy: Perspectives from Cognitive Science*. Cambridge, MA: MIT Press.

Dunker, K. (1945) On problem solving. *Psychological Monographs*, 58(270), 1–113.

Ebbinghaus, H. (1885) *Memory: A contribution to experimental psychology*. Translated into English by H. Ruger and C. Bussenius in 1913. New York: Columbia University.

Efklides, A. (2008) Metacognition: Defining its facets and levels of functioning in relation to self-regulation and co-regulation. *European Psychologist*, 13(4), 277–87.

Efklides, A. (2011) Interactions of Metacognition with Motivation and Affect in Self–Regulated Learning: The MASRL Model AU –Efklides, Anastasia. *Educational Psychologist*, 46(1), 6–25.

Egly, R., Driver, J. and Rafal, R.D. (1994) Shifting visual attention between objects and locations: Evidence from normal and parietal lesion subjects. *Journal of Experimental Psychology: General*, 123, 161–77.

Ehinger, K.A., Hidalgo-Sotelo, B., Torraiba, A. and Oliva, A. (2009). Modelling search for people in 900 scenes: A combined source model of eye guidance. *Visual Cognition*, 17, 945–78.

Einstein, G.O. and McDaniel, M.A. (2005) Prospective memory: Multiple retrieval processes. *Current Directions in Psychological Science*, 14, 286–90.

Ekman, P. and Friesen, W.V. (1971) Constants across cultures in the face and emotion. *Journal of Personality and Social Psychology*, 17, 124–9.

Elder, J.H. and Goldberg, R.M. (2002) Ecological statistics of Gestalt laws for the perceptual organisation of contours. *Journal of Vision*, 2, 324–53.

Ellis, A.W. and Young, A.W. (1988) *Human Cognitive Neuropsychology*. Hove: Psychology Press.

Ellison, L. and Munro, V.E. (2015) Telling tales: Exploring narratives of life and law within the (mock) jury room. *Legal Studies*, 35(2), 201–25.

Eriksen, C.W. and St James, J.D. (1986) Visual attention within and around the field of focal attention: A zoom lens model. *Perception and Psychophysics*, 40, 225–40.

Evans, J.St, B.T. (1998) Matching bias in conditional reasoning: Do we understand it after 25 years? *Thinking and Reasoning*, 4, 45–82.

Evans, J.St, B.T. and Ball, L.J. (2010) Do people reason on the Wason selection task? A new look at the data of Ball et al. (2003). *Quarterly Journal of Experimental Psychology*, 63, 434–41.

Eysenck, M.W. and Keane, M.T. (2015) *Cognitive Psychology: A Student's Handbook* (7th edn). London: Psychology Press.

Eysenck, M.W. and Keane, M.T. (2020) *Cognitive Psychology: A Student's Handbook* (8th edn). London: Taylor and Francis.

Ferrari, P.F. and Rizzolatti, G. (2014) Mirror neuron research: The past and the future. *Philos. Trans. R. Soc. Lond. B: Biol. Science*, 369, 201210169.

Fingelkurts, A.A. and Fingelkurts, A.A. (2017) Information flow in the brain: Ordered sequences of metastable states. *Information*, 8(1), 22.

Fischer, P. and Greitemeyer, T. (2010) A new look at selective-exposure effects: An integrative model. *Current Directions in Psychological Science*, 19, 384–9.

Fisher, R. and Geiselman, R.E. (1992) *Memory Enhancing Techniques for Investigative Interviewing: The cognitive interview*. Springfield, IL: Thomas.

Fisher, R., Geiselman, R.E., Holland, H. and MacKinnon, D. (1984) Hypnotic and cognitive interviews to enhance the memory of eyewitnesses to crime. *International Journal of Investigative and Forensic Hypnosis*, 7, 28–31.

Fitch, W.T. (2010) *The Evolution of Language*. Cambridge: Cambridge University Press.

Flavell, J.H. (1979) Metacognition and cognitive monitoring: A new area of cognitive–developmental inquiry. *American Psychologist*, 34, 906–11.

Flevaris, A.V., Martinez, A. and Hillyard, S.A. (2014) Attending to global versus local stimulus features modulates neural processing of low versus high spatial frequencies: An analysis with event-related brain potentials. *Frontiers in Psychology*, 5 (Article 277).

Fodor, J. (1983) *The Modularity of Mind*. Cambridge, MA: MIT Press.

Fodor, J. A. (2000) *The Mind Doesn't Work That Way*. Cambridge, MA: MIT Press.

Fotuhi, M. (2015) Systems and methods for creating comprehensive and personalized brain health programs. *US Patent Application, 14/332340*, p. 1–8.

Frost, R. (1998). Toward a strong phonological theory of visual word recognition: True issues and false trails. *Psychological Bulletin*, 123, 71–99.

Furnes, B.R. and Norman, E. (2016) Kunnskap Om Metakognisjon Er Viktig I Skolen. Available at: https://blogg.forskning.no/lesesenteret/kunnskap-ommetakognisjon-er-viktig-i-skolen/1103009 (30 September 2019).

Gainotti, G. and Ciaaffa, F. (2013) Is "object-centred neglect" a homogeneous entity? *Brain and Cognition*, 81, 18–23.

Galotti, K.M. (2002) *Making Decisions That Matter: How people face important life choices*. Mahwah, NJ: Erlbaum.

Gamez, D. (2014) The measurement of consciousness: A framework for the scientific study of consciousness. *Front Psychology*, 5(714), 1–15.

Gardner, B.T. and Gardner, R.A. (1980) Two comparative psychologists look at language acquisition. In K. Nelson (ed.) *Children's Language*, vol. 2. New York: Gardner Press.

Gardner, R.A. and Gardner, B.T. (1969) Teaching sign language to a chimpanzee. *Science*, 165: 664–72.

Garrison, K.A., Winstein, C.J. and Aziz-Zadeh, L. (2010) The mirror neuron system: A neuralsubstrate for methods in stroke rehabilitation. *Neurorehabilitation Neural Repair*, 24(5), 404–12.

Gazzaniga, M.S. (1970) *The Bisected Brain*. New York: Appleton-Century-Crofts.

Gazzaniga, M.S. (2000) Cerebral specialization and interhemispheric communication: Does the corpus callosum enable the human condition? *Brain*, 123(7), 1293–326.

Gazzaniga, M.S. (2013) Shifting gears: Seeking new approaches for mind/brain mechanisms. *Annual Review of Psychology*, 64, 1–20.

Gazzaniga, M.S., Volpe, B.T., Smylie, C.S., Wilson, D.H. and Le Doux, J.E. (1979) Plasticity in speech organization following commissurotomy. *Brain*, 102, 805–15.

Geurts, B. (2003) Reasoning with quantifiers. *Cognition*, 86, 223–51.

Gibson, J.J. (1966) *The Senses Considered as Perceptual Systems*. Boston, MA: Houghton Mifflin.

Gick, M.L. and Holyoak, K.J. (1980) Analogical Problem Solving. *Cognitive Psychology*, 12, 306–55.

Gigerenzer, G. and Gigerenzer, W. (2011) Heuristic decision making. *Annual Review of Psychology*, 62, 451–82.

Gilaie-Dotan, S., Kanai, R., Bahrami, B., Rees, G. and Saygin, A.P. (2013) Neuroanatomical correlates of biological motion detection. *Neuropsychologia*, 51, 457–63.

Gilbert, C.D. and Li, W. (2013) Top-down influences on visual processing. *Nature Reviews Neuroscience*, 14, 350–63.

Gissler, M., Järvelin, M.R., Louhiala, P. and Hemminki, E. (1999) Boys have more health problems in childhood than girls: Follow-up of the 1987 Finnish birth cohort. *Acta Paediatrica*, 88(3), 310–14.

Glanzer, M. and Cunitz, A.R. (1966) Two storage mechanisms in free recall. *Journal of Verbal Learning and Verbal Behavior*, 5(4), 351–60.

Godden, D.R. and Baddeley, A.D. (1975) Context dependent memory in two natural environments: On land and under water. *British Journal of Psychology*, 66, 325–31.

Gollwitzer, P.M. and Sheeran, P. (2006) Implication intentions and goal achievement: A meta-analysis of effects and processes. *Advanced Experimental Social Psychology*, 38, 69–119.

Goswami, U. (2006) *Cognitive Development: Critical concepts in psychology*. London: Routledge.

Graesser, A.C., Millis, K.K. and Zwaan, R.A. (1997) Discourse comprehension. *Annual Review of Psychology*, 48, 163–89.

Graf, P. (2012) Prospective memory: Faulty brain, flaky person. *Canadian Psychology*, 53, 7–13.

Graf, P. and Schacter, D.L. (1985) Implicit and explicit memory for new associations in normal and amnesic subjects. *Journal of Experimental Psychology: Learning, Memory, and Cognition*, 11(3), 501–18.

Granhag, P-A., Ask, K., Rebelius, A., Ohman L. and Giolla, E. (2013). 'I saw the man who killed Anna Lindh!' An archival study of witnesses' offender descriptions. *Psychology, Crime and Law*, 10, 921–31.

Greenough, W.T. and Black, J.E. (1992) Induction of brain structure by experience: Substrates for cognitive development. In M.R. Gunnar and C.A. Nelson (eds) *The Minnesota Symposia on Child Psychology*, vol. 24. *Developmental Behavioral Neuroscience* (pp. 155–200). Mahwah, NJ: Lawrence Erlbaum Associates.

Haber, R.N. and Levin, C.A. (2001) The independence of size perception and distance perception. *Perception and Psychophysics*, 63, 1140–52.

Hager, W. (1985) Methodological and empirical analysis of the interaction of semantic characteristics with learning style and depth of processing. *Zeitschrift für Experimentelle und Angewandte Psychologie*, 32(2), 217–49.

Häger-Ross, C. and Rösblad, B. (2002). Norms for grip strength in children aged 4–16 years. *Acta Paediatrics*, 91, 617–25.

Hall, J. (2011) *Guyton and Hall Textbook of Medical Physiology* (12th edn.). Philadelphia, PA: Saunders/Elsevier.

Halvorsen, M., Hagen, R., Hjemdal, O., Eriksen, M.S., Sørli, Å.J., Waterloo, K. and Wang, C.E.A. (2015) Metacognitions and thought control strategies in unipolar major depression: A comparison of currently depressed, previously depressed, and never-depressed individuals. *Cognitive Therapy and Research*, 39(1), 31–40.

Hamad, S. (2007) Creativity: Method or magic? In H. Cohen and B. Stemmer (eds) *Consciousness and Cognition: Fragments of Mind and Brain* (pp. 127–137). Kidlington, Oxford: Academic Press.

Han, Z.Z. and Bi, Y.C. (2009) Reading comprehension without phonological mediation: Further evidence from a Chinese aphasic individual. *Science in China Series C – Life Sciences*, 52, 492–99.

Hanley, J.R. and McDonnell, V. (1997) Are reading and spelling phonologically mediated? Evidence from a patient with a speech production impairment. *Cognitive Neuropsychology*, 14, 3–33.

Hargadon, A.B. (1999) The theory and practice of knowledge brokering: Case studies of continuous innovation. *Dissertation Abstracts—International Section A: Humanities and Social Science*, 59, 3075.

Harley, T.A. (2013). *The Psychology of Language: From data to theory* (4th edn.). Hove: Psychology Press.

Harley, T.A. (2017) *Talking the Talk: Language, psychology and science.* Hove: Psychology Press.

Harlow, J.M. (1848) Passage of an iron rod through the head. *Boston Medical and Surgical Journal*, 39, 389–93.

Harlow, J.M. (1868) Recovery from the passage of an iron bar through the head. *Publications of the Massachusetts Medical Society*, 2, 327–47.

Harm, M.W. and Seidenberg, M.S. (1999) Phonology, reading acquisition and dyslexia: Insights from connectionist models. *Psychological Review*, 106, 491–28.

Hasher, L. and Zacks, R.T. (1979) Automatic and effortful processes in memory. *Journal of Experimental Psychology: General*, 108, 356–88.

Hauser, M.D., Yang, C., Berwick, R.C., Tattersall, I., Ryan, M., Watumull, J., Chomsky, N. and Lewontin, R. (2014) The mystery of language evolution. *Frontiers of Psychology*, 5, 401. doi:10.3389

Hayes, J.R. (2012) Modeling and remodeling writing. *Written Communication*, 29(3), 369–88.

Hegdé, J. (2008) Time course of visual perception: Coarse-to-fine processing and beyond. *Progress in Neurobiology*, 84, 405–39.

Herholz, S.C. and Zatorre, R.J. (2012) Musical training as a framework for brain plasticity, behaviour, function, and structure. *Neuron*, 76, 486–502.

Hintzman, D.L. (1974) Theoretical implications of the spacing effect. In R.L. Solo (ed.). *Theories in Cognitive Psychology: The Loyola Symposium*. Potomac, MD: Lawrence Erlbaum Associates (pp. 77–99).

Hobaiter, C. and Byrne, R.W. (2014) The meanings of chimpanzee gestures. *Current Biology*, 24, 1596–1600.

Hollingworth, A., Maxcey-Richard, A.M. and Vecera, S.P. (2012) The spatial distribution of attention within and across objects. *Journal of Experimental Psychology: Human Perception and Performance*, 38, 135–51.

Horan, B., Heckenberg, R., Maruff, P. and Wright, B. (2020) Development of a new virtual reality test of cognition: Assessing the test-retest reliability, convergent and ecological validity of CONVIRT. *BMC Psychology*, 8(61), 1–10.

Horry, R., Halford, P., Brewer, N., Milne, R. and Bull, R. (2013) Archival analyses of eyewitness identification test outcomes: What can they tell us about eyewitness memory? *Law and Human Behavior*, 38, 94–108.

Hou, Y. and Liu, T. (2012) Neural correlates of object-based attentional selection in human cortex. *Neuropsychologia*, 50, 2916–25.

Hübel, D.H. and Wiesel, T.N. (1959) Receptive fields of single neurones in the cat's striate cortex. *The Journal of Physiology*, 148, 574–91.

Hyde, T.S. and Jenkins, J.J. (1973) Recall for words as a function of semantic, graphic, and syntactic orienting tasks. *Journal of Verbal Learning and Verbal Behavior*, 12, 471–80.

Izzett, R.R. and Fishman, L. (1976) Defendant sentences as a function of attractiveness and justification for actions. *Journal of Social Psychology*, 100(2), 285–90.

Jack, F. and Hayne, H. (2010) Childhood amnesia: Empirical evidence for a two-stage phenomenon. *Memory*, 18, 831–44.

Jackson, F. (1986) What Mary didn't know. *The Journal of Philosophy*, 83(5), 291–5.

Jackson, F. (1998) *Postscript on Qualia, in his Mind, Method and Conditionals*. London: Routledge.

Jackson, F. (2003) Mind and illusion. In A. O'Hear (ed.) *Minds, Persons: Royal institute of philosophy supplement 53* (pp. 251–71). Cambridge: Cambridge University Press.

Jackson, P., Meltzoff, A. and Decety, J. (2005) How do we perceive the pain of others? A window into the neural processes involved in empathy. *Neuroimage*, 24, 771–9.

Jacoby, L.L. (1991) A process dissociation framework: Separating automatic from intentional uses of memory. *Journal of Memory and Language*, 30(5), 513–41.

Jacobs, A., Pinto, J. and Shiffrar, M. (2004) Experience, context, and the visual perception of human movement. *Journal of Experimental Psychology: Human Perception and Performance*, 30, 833–5.

James, W. (1890) *The Principles of Psychology*. New York: Holt, Rinehart and Winston.

Janacsek, K. and Nemeth, D. (2013) Implicit sequence learning and working memory: Correlated or complicated? *Cortex*, 49, 2001–6.

Jans, B., Peters, J.C. and de Weerd, P. (2010) Visual spatial attention to multiple locations at once: The jury is still out. *Psychological Review*, 117, 637–84.

Jeneson, A. and Squire, L.R. (2011) Working memory, long-term memory, and medial temporal lobe function. *Learn Mem*, 19(1), 15–25.

Jiang, Y., Costello, P., Fang, F., Huang, M. and He, S. (2006) A gender- and sexual orientation-dependent spatial attentional effect of invisible images. *Proceedings of the National Academy of Sciences*, 103, 17048–52.

Johansson, G. (1973) Visual perception of biological motion and a model for its analysis. *Perception and Psychophysics*, 14, 201–11.

Johnson, M. and Raye, C.L. (1981) Reality monitoring. *Psychological Review*, 88(1), 67–85.

Johnson-Laird, P.N. (1983) *Mental Models*. Cambridge: Cambridge University Press.

Johnson-Laird, P.N. (1999) Deductive reasoning. *Annual Reviews*, 109–35.

Johnson-Laird, P.N., Girotto, V. and Legrenzi, P. (2004) Reasoning from inconsistency to consistency. *Psychol Rev*, 11, 640–61.

Johnson-Laird, P. and Savary, F. (1996) Illusory inferences about probabilities. *Acta Psychologica*, 69–90.

Jonas, J., Jacques, C., Liu-Shuang, J., Brissart, H., Colnat-Coulbois, S., Maillard, L., et al. (2016) A face-selective ventral occipito-temporal map of the human brain with intracerebral potentials. *Proc. Natl. Acad. Sci. U.S.A.*, 113, 4088–97.

Jordan, K., Wüstenberg, T., Heinze, H.J., Peters, M. and Jäncke, L. (2002) Women and men exhibit different cortical activation patterns during mental rotation tasks. *Neuropsychologia*, 40, 2397–408.

Jores, T., Colloff, M., Kloft, L., Smailes, H. and Flowe, H. (2019) A meta-analysis of the effects of acute alcohol intoxication on witness recall. *Applied Cognitive Psychology*, 33, 334–43.

Kahneman, D. (2003) A perspective on judgment and choice: Mapping bounded rationality. *American Psychologist*, 58, 697–720.

Kahneman, D. and Tversky, A. (1972) Subjective probability: Judgment of representativeness. *Cognitive Psychology*, 3(3), 430–54.

Kahneman, D. and Tversky, A. (1979) On the psychology of prediction. *Psychological Review*, 80, 237–51.

Kahneman, D. and Tversky, A. (1984) Choices, values and frames. *American Psychologist*, 39, 341–50.

Kane, M.J., Brown, L.H., McVay, J.C., Siliva, P.J., Myin-Germeys, I. and Kwapil, T.R. (2007) For whom the mind wanders, and when: An experimental sampling study of working memory and executive control in daily life. *Psychological Science*, 18, 614–21.

Kaplan, S., Bekhor, S. and Shiftan, Y. (2011) Development and estimation of a semi-compensatory choice model based on explicit choice protocols. *Annals of Regional Science*, 47, 51–80.

Kaplan, M.F. and Kemmerick, G.D. (1974) Juror judgement as information integration: Combining evidential and non-evidential information. *Journal of Personality and Social Psychology*, 30(4), 493–99.

Kardes, F.R., Cronley, M.L. and Cline, T.W. (2011) *Consumer Behavior*. USA: Sothe–Western Cengage Learning.

Kean, S. (2014) Phineas Gage, Neuroscience's most famous patient: Each generation revises his myth. Here's the true story. *Science*, 6 May 2014.. https://slate.com/technology/2014/05/phineas-gage-neuroscience-case-true-story-of-famous-frontal-lobe-patient-is-better-than-textbook-accounts.html

Kellogg, R.T. and Whiteford, A.P. (2012) The development of writing expertise. In E.L. Grigorenko, E. Mambrino and D.D. Preiss (eds) *Writing: A mosaic of new perspectives* (pp. 109–24). New York: Taylor & Francis Group.

Kersten, D., Mamassion, P. and Yuille, A. (2004) Object perception as Bayesian inference. *Annual Review of Psychology,* 55, 271–304.

Kiehl, K.A., Smith, A.M., Hare, R.D., Mendrek, A., Forster, B.B., Brink, J. and Liddle, P.F. (2001) Limbic abnormalities in affective processing by criminal psychopaths as revealed by functional magnetic resonance imaging. *Biological Psychiatry*, 50, 677–84.

Kinchla, R.A. and Wolfe, J.M. (1979) The order of visual processing: "Top-down," "bottom-up," or "middle-out". *Percept. Psychophys.*, 25, 225–31.

King, J-R., Sitt, J.D., Faugeras, F., Rohaut, B., El Karoui, I., Cohen, L., Naccache, L. and Dehaene, S. (2013) Information sharing in the brain indexes consciousness in noncommunicative patients. *Current Biology*, 23, 1914–19.

Kintsch, W. (1988) The use of knowledge in discourse processing: A construction-integration model. *Psychological Review*, 95, 163–82.

Kintsch, W. (2005) An overview of top-down and bottom-up effects in comprehension: The CI perspective. *Discourse Processes*, 39, 125–28.

Klahr, D. and MacWhinney, B. (1998) Information processing. In D. Kuhn and R.S. Siegler (eds) *Handbook of Child Psychology*, vol. 2. *Cognition, Perception, and Language*, (pp. 631–78). New York: John Wiley.

Klein, G. (1999) *Sources of Power: How people make decisions*. Cambridge, MA: MIT Press.

Klein, S.B., Cosmides, L., Tooby, J. and Chance, S. (2002) Decisions and the evolution of memory: Multiple systems, multiple functions. Psychological Review, *109*(2), 306–29.

Kleinberg, B., van der Toolen, Y., Vrij, A., Arntz, A. and Verschuere, B. (2018) Automated verbal credibility assessment of intentions: The model statement technique and predictive modeling. *Applied Cognitive Psychology*, 32, 354–66.

Klix, F. (2001) Problem solving: Deduction, induction, and analogical reasoning. In *International Encyclopedia of the Social and Behavioral Sciences*, 12123–30.

Koene, R.A. (2014) Feasible mind uploading. In R. Blackford and D. Broderick (eds) *Intelligence Unbound: The Future of Uploaded and Machine Minds*. Oxford: Oxford University Press.

Köhler, W. (1925) *Mentality of Apes*. New York, NY: Harcourt, Brace and Company Inc.

Koivisto, M., Kastrati, G. and Revonsuo, A. (2014) Recurrent processing enhances visual awareness but is not necessary for fast categorisation of natural scenes. *Journal of Neuroscience*, 26, 223–31.

Koivisto, M., Railo, H., Revonsuo, A., Vanni, S. and Salminen-Vaparanta, N. (2011) Recurrent processing in V1/V2 contributes to categorisation of natural scenes. *Journal of Neuroscience*, 31, 2488–92.

Konishi, S., Wheeler, M.E., Donaldson, D.I. and Buckner, R.L. (2000) Neural correlates of episodic retrieval success. *Neuroimage*, 12(3), 276–86.

Koppel, J. and Rubin, D. (2016) Recent advances in understanding the reminiscence bump: The importance of cues in guiding recall from autobiographical memory. *Current Directions in Psychological Science*, 25, 135–40.

Koriat, A. (2000) The feeling of knowing: Some metatheoretical implications for consciousness and control. *Consciousness and Cognition*, 9, 149–71.

Koriat, A. (2007) Metacognition and consciousness. In P.D. Zelazo, M. Moscovitch and E. Thompson (eds) *The Cambridge Handbook of Consciousness* (pp. 289–325). New York: Cambridge University Press.

Kouider, S., Sackur, J. and de Gardelle, V. (2012) Do we still need phenomenal consciousness? *Trends in Cognitive Sciences*, 16, 140–41.

Korva, N., Porter, S., O'Connor, B.P., Shaw, J. and ten Brinke, L. (2013) Dangerous decisions: Influence of juror attitudes and defendant appearance on legal decision-making. *Psychiatry, Psychology and Law*, 20(3), 384–98.

Kosslyn, S.M. (1973) Scanning visual images: Some structural implications. *Perception and Psychophysics*, 14, 90–4.

Kosslyn, S.M. (2005) Mental images and the brain. *Cognitive Neuropsychology*, 22, 333–47.

Kosslyn, S.M., Ball, T.M. and Reiser, B.J. (1978) Visual images preserve metric spatial information: Evidence from studies of image scanning. *Journal of Experimental Psychology: Human Perception and Performance*, 4(1), 47–60.

Kravitz, D.J. and Behrmann, M. (2011) Space-, object-, and feature-based attention interact to organise visual scenes. *Attention, Perception and Psychophysics*, 73, 2434–47.

Kringelbach, M.L. and Rolls, E.T. (2004) The functional neuroanatomy of the human orbitofrontal cortex: Evidence from neuroimaging and neuropsychology. *Progress in Neurobiology*, 72, 341–72.

Krynski, T.R. and Tenenbaum, J.B. (2007) The role of causality in judgement under uncertainty. *Journal of Experimental Psychology: General*, 136, 430–50.

Lamme, V.A.F. (2010) How neuroscience will change our view on consciousness. *Cognitive Neuroscience*, 1, 204–40.

Lamy, D., Salti, M. and Bar–Haim, Y. (2009) Neural correlates of subjective awareness and unconscious processing: An ERP study. *Journal of Cognitive Neuroscience*, 21, 1435–46.

Larsen, J.D., Baddeley, A. and Andrade, J. (2000) Phonological similarity and the irrelevant speech effect: Implications for models of short-term memory. *Memory*, 8, 145–57.

Le Mens, G. and Denrell, J. (2011) Rational learning and information sampling: On the "naiverty" assumption in sampling explanations of judgement biases. *Psychological Review*, 118, 379–92.

Lee, M.D., Criss, A., Devezer, B., Donkin, C., Etz, A., Leite, F.P., Matzke, D., Rouder, J.N., Trueblood, J.S., White, C.N. and Vandekerckhove, J.

(2019) Robust modeling in cognitive science. *Computational Brain and Behavior*, 2, 141–53.

Lenneberg, E. (1967) *Biological Foundations of Language*. New York: John Wiley and Sons.

Leslie, A.M. (1994) ToMM, ToBy, and agency: Core architecture and domain specificity in cognition and culture. In S. Baron-Cohen (ed.) *Mindblindness: An essay on autism and theory of mind*. Cambridge, MA: MIT Press.

Lettvin, J.Y., Maturana, H.R., McCulloch, W.S. and Pitts, W.H. (1959) What the frog's eye tells the frog's brain. *Proceedings of the IRE*, 47(11), 1940–51.

Levy, D.A., Stark, C.E.L. and Squire, L.R. (2004) Intact conceptual priming in the absence of declarative memory. *Psychological Science*, 17, 228–35.

Lewis, M. and Brooks-Gunn, J. (1979) *Social Cognition and the Acquisition of Self*. New York: Plenum Press.

Lingnau, A. and Petris, S. (2013) Action understanding within and outside the motor system: The role of task difficulty. *Cerebral Cortex*, 23, 1342–50.

Loftus, E.F. and Palmer, J.C. (1974) Reconstruction of automobile destruction: An example of the interaction between language and memory. *Journal of Verbal Learning and Verbal Behavior*, 13, 585–9.

Logie, R.H. (1995) *Visuo-spatial working memory*, Hove, UK: Lawrence Erlbaum Associates.

Logie, R.H. (2011) The functional organisation and capacity limits of working memory. *Current Directions in Psychological Science*, 20, 240–5.

Liu, O.L. and Wilson, M. (2009) Gender differences in large-scale math assessments: PISA trend 2000 and 2003. *Applied Measurement in Education*, 22(2), 164–84.

Lysaker, P.H., Erickson, M., Ringer, J., Buck, K.D., Semerari, A., Carcione, A. and Dimaggio, G. (2011) Metacognition in schizophrenia: The relationship of mastery to coping, insight, self-esteem, social anxiety, and various facets of neurocognition. *British Journal of Clinical Psychology*, 50(4), 412–24.

Ma, X., Li, T., Li, Z. and Zhou, A-B. (2020) Episodic context reinstatement promotes memory retention in older but not younger elementary school-children. *British Journal of Developmental Psychology*, 38(2), 304–18.

MacGregor, J.N., Ormerod, T.C. and Chronicle, E.P. (2001) Information-processing and insight: A process model of performance on the nine-dot and related problems. *Journal of Experimental Psychology: Learning, Memory, and Cognition*, 27, 176–201.

MacMaster, F. and Kusumakar, V. (2004) Hippocampal volume in early onset depression. *BMC Medicine*, 2, 2.

Maier, N. (1931) Reasoning in humans. I. On direction. *Journal of Comparative Psychology*, 10, 115–43.

Marchetti, G. (2018) Consciousness: A unique way of processing information. *Cognitive Processing*, 19, 435–64.

Markovits, H. (2017) In the beginning stages: Conditional reasoning with category based and causal premises in 8- to 10-year olds. *Cogn. Dev.* 41, 1–9.

Markovits, H., Brisson, J. and de Chantal, P-L. (2016) How do pre-adolescents interpret conditionals? *Psychonomic Bulletin and Review*, 23(6), 1907–12.

Markovits, H., Brunet, M.L., Thompson, V. and Brisson, J. (2013) Direct evidence for a dual process model of deductive inference. *Journal of Experimental Psychology: Learning, Memory, and Cognition*, 39(4), 1213–22.

Marr, D. (1982) *Vision: A Computational Investigation into the Human Representation and Processing of Visual Information*. San Francisco, CA: W.H. Freeman.

Martineau, J., Andersson, F., Barthelemy, C., Cottier, J.P. and Destrieux, C. (2010) A typical activation of the mirror neuron system during perception of hand motion in autism. *Brain Res*, 1320, 168–75.

Masip, J., Sporer, S. L., Garrido, E. and Herrero, C. (2005) The detection of deception with the reality monitoring approach: A review of the empirical evidence. *Psychology, Crime & Law*, 11(1), 99–122.

Matthews, G. (2015) Advancing the theory and practice of metacognitive therapy: A commentary on the special issue. *Cognitive Therapy and Research*, 39(1), 81–7.

McClelland, J.L. and Rumelhart, D.E. (1981) An interactive activation model of context effects in letter perception: Part 1. An account of basic findings. *Psychological Review*, 88, 375–407.

McDaniel, M.A. and Einstein, G.O. (1986) The neuropsychology of prospective memory in normal aging: A componential approach. *Neuropsychologia*, 49, 2147–55.

McDermott, J.H. (2009) The cocktail party problem. *Current Biology*, 19: R1024–R1027.

McLeod, P., Plunkett, K. and Rolls, E.T. (1998) *Introduction to Connectionist Modelling of Cognitive Processes*. Oxford: Oxford University Press.

Meese, T.S. (2018) The how and why of consciousness? *Frontiers in Psychology*, 9, 2173. doi: 10.3389/fpsyg.2018.02173.

Mercier, H. and Sperber, D. (2011) Why do humans reason? Arguments for an argumentative theory. *Behavioral and Brain Sciences*, 34, 57–111.

Miles, J.B. (2015) *The Free Will Delusion*. Kibworth: Matador.

Miller, G.A. (1956) The magic number seven, plus or minus two: Some limits on our capacity for processing information. *Psychological Review*, 63, 81–93.

Miller, D.I. and Halpern, D.F. (2014) The new science of cognitive sex differences. *Trends in Cognitive Sciences*, 18(1), 37–45.

Milne, R. and Bull, R. (1999) *Investigative Interviewing: Psychology and practice*. Chichester: Wiley.

Milne, R. and Bull, R. (2003) Does the cognitive interview help children to resist the effects of suggestive questioning? *Legal and Criminological Psychology*, 8, 21–38.

Minervino, R.A., Olguín, V. and Trench, M. (2017) Promoting interdomain analogical transfer: When creating a problem helps to solve a problem. *Memory and Cognition*, 45(2), 221–32.

Moalem, S. (2020) *The Better Half: On the Genetic Superiority of Women*. UK: Penguin Random House.

Monti, M.M., Pickard, J.D. and Owen, A.M. (2013) Visual cognition in disorders of consciousness: From V1 to top-down attention. *Human Brain Mapping*, 34, 1245–53.

Moors, A. and de Houwer, J. (2006) Automaticity: A theoretical and conceptual analysis. *Psychol. Bull.*, 132, 297–326.

Mottaghy, F.M. (2006) Interfering with working memory in humans. *Neuroscience*, 139, 85–90.

Musel, B., Chauvin, A., Guyader, N., Chokron, S and Perin, C. (2012) Is coarse-to-fine strategy sensitive to normal aging? *PLoS ONE*, 7(6): e38493.

Nahatame, S. (2014) Strategic processing and predictive inference generation in L2 reading. *Reading in a Foreign Language*, 26, 54–77.

Nardini, M. (2020) Learning to see deeper. *The Psychologist*, 4, 42.

Navon, D. (1977) Forest before trees: The precedence of global features in visual perception. *Cogn. Psychol.*, 9, 353–83.

Neal, D.T. and Chartrand, T.L. (2011) Embodied emotion perception: Amplifying and dampening facial feedback modulates emotion perception accuracy. *Social Psychological and Personality Science*, 2(6), 673–8.

Nęcka, E., Żak, P. and Gruszka, A. (2016) Insightful imagery is related to working memory updating. *Frontiers in Psychology*, 7(137). doi: 10.3389/fpsyg.2016.00137.

Neisser, U. (1967) *Cognitive Psychology*. New York: Appleton-Century-Crofts.

Neisser, U. (1996) Remembering as doing. *Behavioral and Brain Sciences*, 19, 203–4.

Neisser, U. and Hyman, I.E. (1982) *Memory Observed: Remembering in natural contexts*. New York: Worth Publishers.

Newell, A. and Simon, H.A. (1972) *Human Problem Solving*. Englewood Cliffs, NJ: Prentice Hall.

Nicolle, A., Fleming, S.M., Bach, D.R., Driver, J. and Dolan, R.J. (2011) A regret-induced status quo bias. *Journal of Neuroscience*, 31, 3320–7.

Nieuwenhuys, R. (2012) The insular cortex: A review. *Prog Brain Res*, 195, 123–63.

Norman, E. (2020) Why metacognition is not always helpful. *Frontiers in Psychology*, 11, 1537. doi: 10.3389/fpsyg.2020.01537.

Norman, E., Pfuhl, G., Sæle, R.G., Svartdal, F., Låg, T. and Dahl, T.I. (2019) Metacognition in psychology. *Review of General Psychology*, 23(4), 403–24.

Oakley, D.A. and Halligan, P.W. (2017) Chasing the rainbow: The non-conscious nature of being (p. 2). *Frontiers in Psychology*, 8, 1924. doi: 10.3389/fpsyg.2017.01924.

Odinot, G., Wolters, G. and van Koppen, P.J. (2009) Eyewitness memory of a supermarket robbery: A case study of accuracy and confidence after 3 months. *Law and Human Behavior*, 33, 506–14.

Owen, A.M. (2013) Detecting consciousness: A unique role for neuroimaging. *Annual Review of Psychology*, 64, 109–33.

Page, M. (2014) Science and forensic science. In C.M. Bowers (ed.) *Forensic Testimony Science, Law and Expert Evidence* (pp. 23–39). Kidlington, Oxford: Academic Press.

Paivio, A. (1986) *Mental Representations: A Dual Coding Approach*. New York: Oxford University Press.

Paradowski, B., Kowalczyk, E., Chojdak-Lukasiewicz, J., Loster-Niewińska, A. and Służewska-Niedźwiedź, M. (2013) Three cases with visual hallucinations following combined ocular and occipital damage. *Case Report / Open Access*, Article ID 450725, 1–5.

Paulo, R., Albuquerque, P., Vitorino, F. and Bull, R. (2017) Enhancing the cognitive interview with an alternative procedure to witness-compatible questioning: Category clustering recall. *Psychology, Crime and Law*, 10, 967–82.

Payne, J.W. (1973) Alternative approaches to decision making under risk: Moments versus risk dimensions. *Psychological Bulletin*, 80, 439–53.

Paynter, C.A., Kotovsky, K. and Reder, L.M. (2010) Problem-solving without awareness: An ERP investigation. *Neuropsychologia*, 48, 3137–44.

Penfield, W. (1930) The radical treatment of traumatic epilepsy and its rationale. *Can. Med. Assoc. Journal*, 23(2), 189–97.

Pennycook, G. and Thompson, V.A. (2012) Reasoning with base rates is routine, relatively effortless, and context dependent. *Psychonomic Bulletin and Review*, 19, 528–34.

Perloff, R.M. (2010) *The Dynamics of Persuasion: Communication and attitudes in the 21st century*. New York: Routledge.

Perry, C., Ziegler, J.C. and Zorzi, M. (2007) Nested incremental modeling in the development of computational theories: The CDP+ model of reading aloud. *Psychological Review*, 114, 273–315.

Persaud, N. and McLeod, P. (2008) Wagering demonstrates subconscious processing in a binary exclusion task. *Consciousness and Cognition*, 17, 565–75.

Pezdek, K. (2003) Event memory and autobiographical memory for the events of September 11, 2001. *Applied Cognitive Psychology*, 17, 1033–45.

Pinto, J. (2006) Developing body representations: A review of infants' responses to biological-motion displays. In G. Knoblich, M. Grosjean, J. Thornton and M. Shiffrar (eds) *Perception of the Human Body from the Inside Out* (pp. 305–22). Oxford: Oxford University Press.

Plaut, D.C., McClelland, J.L., Seidenberg, M.S. and Patterson, K. (1996) Understanding normal and impaired word reading: Computational principles in quasi-regular domains. *Psychological Review*, 103(1), 56–115.

Popper, K.R. (1959). *The Logic of Scientific Discovery*. London: Hutchinson.

Posner, M.I. (1980) Orienting of attention. The VIIth Sir Frederic Bartlett lecture. *Quarterly Journal of Experimental Psychology*, 32A, 3–25.

Prete, G. and Tommasi, L. (2018) Split-brain patients: Visual biases for faces. In G.S. Forrester, W.D. Hopkins, K. Hudry and A. Lindell (eds.). *Cerebral Lateralization and Cognition: Evolutionary and Developmental Investigations of Behavioral Biases*, vol. 238 (pp. 271–91). Amsterdam: Elsevier.

Raine, A., Buchsbaum, M.S., Stanley, J., Lottenberg, S., Abel, L. and Stoddard, S. (1994) Selective reductions in prefrontal glucose metabolism in murderers. *Biological Psychiatry*, 36, 365–73.

Rajmohan, V. and Mohandas, E. (2007) Mirror neuron system (p. 66). *Indian J. Psychiatry*, 49(1), 66–9.

Ranyard, R. (1995) Reversals of preference between simple and compound risks: The role of editing heuristics. *Journal of Risk and Uncertainty*, 11, 159–75.

Rastle, K. (2019) The place of morphology in learning to read in English. *Cortex*. 116, 45–54.

Rastle, K. and Brysbaert, M. (2006) Masked phonological priming effects in English: Are they real? Do they matter? *Cognitive Psychology*, 53, 97–145.

Ratiu, P. and Talos, I-F. (2004) The tale of Phineas Gage, digitally remastered. *The New England Journal of Medicine*, 351, e21.

Ray, W.J. (2013) *Evolutionary Psychology: Neuroscience perspectives concerning human behavior and experience*. Thousand Oaks, CA: Sage Publications.

Rizzo, A., Schultheis, M., Kerns, K.A. and Mateer, C. (2004) Analysis of assets for virtual reality applications in neuropsychology. *Neuropsychological Rehabilitation*, 14(1–2), 207–39.

Robinson, W. (2015) "Epiphenomenalism". In E.N. Zalta (ed.) *The Stanford Encyclopedia of Philosophy*. Stanford, CA: Stanford University Press.

Rorden, C., Hjaltason, H., Fillmore, P., Fridriksasson, J. Kjartansson, O., Magnusdottir, S. and Karnath, H.O. (2012) Allocentric neglect strongly associated with egocentric neglect. *Neuropsychologia*, 50, 1151–7.

Rosch, E., Mervis, C.B., Gray, W.D., Johnson, D.M. and Boyes-Braem, P. (1976) Basic objects in natural categories. *Cognitive Psychology*, 8, 382–439.

Rosenholtz, R., Huang, J. and Ehinger, K.A. (2012) Rethinking the role of top-down attention in vision: Effects attributable to a lossy representation in peripheral vision. *Frontiers in Psychology*, 3 (Article 13).

Rosenthal, D.M. (2000) Consciousness, content, and metacognitive judgments. *Consciousness and Cognition*, 9(2), 203–14.

Rubin, D.C. and Berntsen, D. (2003) Life scripts help to maintain autobiographical memories of highly positive, but not negative events. *Memory and Cognition*, 31, 1–14.

Rubin, D.C. and Schulkind, M.D. (1997) The distribution of important and word-cued autobiographical memories in 20–35-, and 70-year-old adults. *Psychology of Aging*, 12, 524–35.

Rumelhart, D., McClelland, J. and the PDP Research Group (1986) *Parallel Distributed Processing: Explorations in the Microstructures of Cognition.* Cambridge, MA: MIT Press.

Runeson, S. and Frykholm, G. (1983) Kinematic specifications of dynamics as an informational base for person-and-action perception: Expectation, gender recognition, and deceptive intention. *Journal of Experimental Psychology: General*, 112, 585–615.

Russo, R., Parkin, A.J., Taylor, S.R. and Wilks, J. (1998) Revising current two-process accounts of spacing effects in memory. *Journal of Experimental Psychology, Learning, and Memory Cognition*, 24(1), 161–72.

Rutter, M. and Lockyer, L. (1967) A five to fifteen year follow-up study of infantile psychosis: I. Description of sample. *The British Journal of Psychiatry*, 113(504), 1169–82.

Saed, O., Yaghubi, H. and Roshan, R. (2010) The role of meta-cognitive beliefs on substance dependency. *Procedia –Social and Behavioral Sciences*, 5, 1676–80.

Salkovskis, P.M., Richards, H.C. and Forrester, E. (1995) The relationship between obsessional problems and intrusive thoughts. *Behavioural and Cognitive Psychotherapy*, 23(3), 281–99.

Sarikcioglu, L. (2007) Otfrid Foerster (1873–1941): One of the distinguished neuroscientists of his time. *Journal of Neurol. Neurosurg. Psychiatry*, 78(6), 650.

Savage-Rumbaugh, E.S., Murphy, J., Sevick, R.A., Brakke, K.E., Williams, S.L. and Rumbaugh, D. (1993) *Language Comprehension in Ape and Child.* Monographs of the Society for Research in Child Development, 233. Chicago: University of Chicago Press.

Schacter D. L. (1999) The seven sins of memory: Insights from psychology and cognitive neuroscience. *American Psychologist*, 54, 182–203.

Schiffer, F., Zaidel, E., Bogen. J. and Chasan-Taber, S. (1998) Different psychological status in the two hemispheres of two split-brain patients. *Neuropsychiatry, Neuropsychology and Behavioral Neurology*, 11, 151–6.

Scholte, H.S., Wittreveen, S.C., Soekreijse, H. and Lamme, V.A.F. (2006) The influence of inattention on the neural correlates of scene segregation. *Brain Research*, 1076, 106–15.

Schooler, J.W., Fiore, S.M. and Brandimonte, M.A. (1997) At a loss from words: Verbal overshadowing of perceptual memories. In D.L. Medin (ed.) *The Psychology of Learning and Motivation: Advances in research and theory*, vol. 37 (pp. 291–340). San Diego, CA: Academic Press.

Schunk, D.H. (2006) *Learning Theories: An educational perspective* (3rd edn). Upper Saddle River, NJ: Prentice Hall.

Schweppe, J., Grice, M. and Rummer, R. (2011) What models of verbal working memory can learn from phonological theory: Decomposing the phonological similarity effect. *Journal of Memory and Language*, 64, 256–69.

Scullin, M.K., McDaniel, M.A. and Shelton, J.T. (2013) The dynamic multiprocess framework: Evidence from prospective memory with contextual variability. *Cognitive Psychology*, 67, 55–71.

Seidenberg, M.S. (2017) *Language at the Speed of Sight: How we read, why so many can't, and what can be done about it.* New York, NY: Basic Books.

Seidenberg, M.S. and McClelland, J.L. (1989) A distributed developmental model of word recognition and naming. *Psychological Review*, 96, 523–68.

Selfridge, O. (1959) Pandemonium: A paradigm for learning. Paper presented at *Proceedings of the Symposium on Mechanisation of Thought Processes*, National Physical Laboratory, Teddington, (vol. 1, pp. 513–26). London: HMSO.

Selfridge, O. and Neisser, U. (1960) Pattern recognition by machine. *Scientific American*, 203(2), 60–8.

Shah, P. (2020) Processing faces and social situations. *The Psychologist*, 4, 43–4.

Shah, P., Gaule, A., Bird, G. and Cook, R. (2013) Robust orienting to protofacial stimuli in autism. *Current Biology*, 23, 1087–8.

Shepherd, A. (2020) 'Many take visual perception for granted...' *The Psychologist*, 4, 37–9.

Shiffrar, M. and Thomas, J.P. (2013) Beyond the scientific objections of the human body: Differentiated analyses of human motion and object motion. In M. Rutherford and V. Kuhlmeier (eds) *Social Perception: Detection and interpretation of animacy, agency, and intention.* Cambridge, MA: MIT Press/ Bradford Books.

Shiffrin, R.M. and Schneider, W. (1977) Controlled and automatic human information processing: II. Perceptual learning, automatic attending, and a general theory. *Psychological Review*, 84, 127–90.

Shimamura, A.P. (1984) A guide for teaching mnemonic skills. *Teaching of Psychology*, 11, 162–6.

Shimamura, A.P. (2001) Dysexecutive syndromes. *International Encyclopedia of the Social and Behavioral Sciences* (pp. 3911–13). Amsterdam: Elsevier.

Siegesmund, A. (2016) Increasing student metacognition and learning through classroom-based learning communities and self-assessment. *J. Microbiol. Biol. Educ*, 17, 204–14.

Simon, H.A. (1966) Scientific discovery and the psychology of problem solving. In H.A. Simon (ed.) *Mind and Cosmos: Essays in contemporary science and philosophy*. Pittsburgh, PA: University of Pittsburgh Press.

Simon, J.R., Vaidya, C.J., Howard, J.H. and Howard, D.V. (2012) The effects of aging on the neural basis of implicit associative learning in a probabilistic triplets learning task. *Journal of Cognitive Neuroscience*, 24, 451–63.

Simons, D.J. and Chabris, C.F. (2011) What people believe about how memory works: A representative survey of the US population. *Public Library of Science One*, 6, e22757.

Singer, T., Seymour, B., O'Doherty, J., Kaube, H., Dolan, R. and Frith, C. (2004) Empathy for pain involves the affective but not sensory components of pain. *Science*, 303(5661), 1157–61.

Sio, U.N., Monaghan, P. and Ormerod, T. (2013) Sleep on it, but only if it is difficult: Effects of sleep on problem solving. *Memory Cognition*, 41(2), 159–66.

Sio, U.N. and Ormerod, T.C. (2009) Does incubation enhance problem solving? A meta-analytic review. *Psychological Bulletin*, 135(1), 94–120.

Skinner, B.F. (1957) *Verbal Behavior*. New York: Appleton-Century-Crofts.

Snyder, K.M., Ashitaka, Y., Shimada, H., Ulrich, J.E. and Logan, G.D. (2014) What skilled typists don't know about the QWERTY keyboard. *Attention, Perception, and Psychophysics*, 76, 162–71.

Sommer, I.E.C., Aleman, A., Bouma, A. and Kahn, R.S. (2004) Do women really have more bilateral language representation than men? A meta-analysis of functional imaging studies. *Brain*, 127, 1845–52.

Sommer, I.E.C., Aleman, A., Somers, M., Boks, M.P. and Kahn, R.S. (2008) Sex differences in handedness, asymmetry of the Planum Temporale and functional language lateralization. *Brain Research*, 1206, 76–88.

Sosic-Vasic, Z., Hille, K., Kröner, J., Spitzer, M. and Kornmeier, J. (2018) When learning disrupts memory – Temporal profile of retroactive interference of learning on memory formation. *Frontiers in Psychology*, 9, Article 82.

Spada, M.M., Nikcevic, A.V., Moneta, G.B. and Ireson, J. (2006) Metacognition as a mediator of the effect of test anxiety on a surface approach to studying. *Educational Psychology*, 26(5), 615–24.

Sperber, D. (1994) The modularity of thought and the epidemiology of representations. In L.A. Hirschfeld and S.A. Gelman (eds.) *Mapping the Mind: Domain specificity in cognition and culture*. New York: Cambridge University Press.

Sperling, G. (1960) The information that is available in brief visual presentations. *Psychological Monographs*, 74(498), 1–29.

Sperry, R.W. (1968) Hemisphere deconnection and unity in conscious awareness. *American Psychologist*, 23, 723–33.

Spiers, H.J., Maguire, E.A. and Burgess, N. (2001) Hippocampal amnesia. *Neurocase*, 7, 357–82.

Springer, S.P. and Deutsch, G. (1998) Left Brain, Right Brain: Perspectives from cognitive neuroscience (5th edn). New York: W H Freeman.

Stupple, E.J.N. and Ball, L.J. (2008) Belief–logic conflict resolution in syllogistic reasoning: Inspection-time evidence for a parallel process model. *Thinking and Reasoning*, 14(2), 168–81.

Stuss, D.T. (2011) Functions of the frontal lobes: Relation to executive functions. *Journal of the International Neuropsychological Society*, 17, 759–65.

Sun, R. (2008) *The Cambridge Handbook of Computational Psychology*. Cambridge: Cambridge University Press.

Sun, X., Zhu, C. and So, S.H.W. (2017) Dysfunctional metacognition across psychopathologies: A meta-analytic review. *European Psychiatry*, 45, 139–53.

Suzuki, K, Elegheert, J., Song, I., Sasakura, H., Senkov, O., Matsuda, K., Kakegawa, W., Clayton, A.J., Chang, V.T., Ferrer-Ferrer, M., Miura, E., Kaushik, R., Ikeno, M., Morioka, Y., Takeuchi, Y., Shimada, T., Otsuka, S., Stoyanov, S., Watanabe, M., Takeuchi, K., Dityatev, A., Aricescu, A.R. and Yuzaki. M. (2020) A synthetic synaptic organizer protein restores glutamatergic neuronal circuits. *Science*, 369(6507), eabb4853. doi:10.1126/science.abb4853

Symonds, C. (1937) Mental disorder following head injury (p. 1092). *Proceedings of the Royal Society of Medicine*, 3, 1081–92.

Talarico, J.M. and Rubin, D.C. (2003) Confidence, not consistency, characterizes flashbulb memories. *Psychological Science*, 14, 455–61.

Talarico, J.M. and Rubin, D.C. (2019) Flashbulb memories result from ordinary memory processes and extraordinary event characteristics. In O. Luminet and A. Curci (eds) *Flashbulb Memories: New issues and new perspectives* (pp. 79–97). Hove: Psychology Press.

Talsma, D., Coe, B.C., Munoz, D.P. and Theeuwes, J. (2010) Brain structures involved in visual search in the presence and absence of color singletons. *Journal of Cognitive Neuroscience*, 22(4), 761–4.

Tarricone, P. (2011) *The Taxonomy of Metacognition*. New York, NY: Psychology Press.

Taylor, S. (2015) *Crime and Criminality: A multidisciplinary approach*. Abingdon, UK: Routledge, Taylor and Francis Group.

Taylor, S. (2018) Spacing effects for face recognition as a function of study-phase retrieval: Divided attention and age as a criteria for automaticity. *OAJ Behavioural Sci Psych*, 1(1), 180001.

Taylor, S., Alner, E. and Workman, L. (2017) Mock juror age influences judgement of guilt and harshness of sentence on defendants with a record of 'Borderline Personality Disorder'. *Forensic Res. Criminol. Int. J.*, 5(4): 00166. DOI: 10.15406/frcij.2017.05.00166.

Taylor, S., Lui, Y.L. and Workman, L. (2018) Defendant's mens rea or attractiveness: Which influences mock juror decisions? *Forensic Res. Criminol. Int. J.*, 6(2): 00185. DOI: 10.15406/frcij.2018.06.00185.5

Taylor, S., Workman, L. and Hall, R. (2018) To be or not to be – Culprit or Lookalike that is the question: Effects of order on single, repetition and culprit-absent sequential line-ups. *Journal of Forensic Research and Analysis*, 2(1): dx.doi.org/ 10.16966/jfra.107.

Taylor, S., Workman, L. and Yeomans, H. (2012) Abnormal patterns of cerebral lateralisation as revealed by the universal chimeric faces task in individuals with autistic disorder. *Laterality: Asymmetries of Body, Brain and Cognition*, 17(4), 428–37.

Thakral, P.P. (2011) The neural substrates associated with inattentional blindness. *Consciousness and Cognition*, 20, 1768–75.

The OpenLearn Team (2010) *OU on the BBC: Eyewitness*. Milton Keynes: The Open University www.open.edu/openlearn/body-mind/ou-on-the-bbc-eyewitness

Thompson, A.E. and Voyer, D. (2014) Sex differences in the ability to recognise nonverbal displays of emotion: A meta-analysis. *Cognition and Emotion*. Advance online publication. doi:10.1080/02699931.2013.875889.

Thorton, S. (1999) Creating conditions for cognitive change: The interaction between task structures and specific strategies. *Child Development*, 70, 588–603.

Toates, F. (2014) *How Sexual Desire Works: The Enigmatic Urge*. Cambridge: Cambridge University Press.

Tomasello, M. (2019) *Becoming Human: A theory of ontogeny*. Belknap Press.

Tononi, G. and Koch, C. (2015) Consciousness: here, there and everywhere? *Philos. Trans. R. Soc. Lond. B Biol. Sci.*, 370(1668), 20140167.

Treisman, A.M. (1964) Verbal cues, language, and meaning in selective attention. *American Journal of Psychology*, 77, 206–19.

Treisman, A.M. and Davies, A. (1973) Divided attention in ear and eye. In S. Kornblum (ed.). *Attention and Performance*, vol. IV. London: Academic Press.

Treisman, A.M. and Gelade, G. (1980) A feature integration theory of attention. *Cognitive Psychology*, 12, 97–136.

Trevarthen, C. (2004) Split-brain and the mind. In R. Gregory (ed.) *The Oxford Companion to the Mind*. (2nd edn). Oxford: Oxford University Press.

Trickett, S.B. and Trafton, J.G. (2007) "What if…": The use of conceptual simulations in scientific reasoning. *Cognitive Science*, 31(5), 843–75.

Troiani, V., Price, E.T. and Schultz, R.T. (2014) Unseen fearful faces promote amygdala guidance of attention. *Social Cognition, and Affective Neuroscience*, 9, 133–40.

Tsao, D.Y. and Livingstone, M.S. (2008) Mechanisms of face perception. *Annual Review of Neuroscience*, 31, 411–37.

Tulving, E. (1972) Episodic and semantic memory. In E. Tulving and W. Donaldson (eds) *Organisation of Memory*. London: Academic Press.

Tulving, E. (1979) Relation between encoding specificity and levels of processing. In L.C. Cermak and F.I.M. Craik (eds) *Levels of Processing in Human Memory*. Hillsdale, NJ: Lawrence Erlbaum Associates.

Tulving, E. (2002) Episodic memory: From mind to brain. *Annual Review of Psychology*, 53, 1–25.

Tversky, A. and Kahneman, D. (1987) Rational choice and the framing of decisions. In R.M. Hogarth and M.W. Reder (eds) *Rational Choice: The contrast between economics and psychology* (pp. 67–94). Chicago: University of Chicago Press.

Tversky, A. and Koehler, D.J. (1994) Support theory: A nonextensional representation of subjective probability. *Psychological Review*, 101(4): 547–67.

Umino, A. and Dammeyer, J. (2016) Effects of a non-instructional prosocial intervention program on children's metacognition skills and quality of life. *Intern. J. Educ. Res*, 78, 24–31.

Valentine, T., Pickering, A. and Darling, S. (2003) Characteristics of eyewitness identification that predict the outcome of real line-ups. *Applied Cognitive Psychology*, 17, 969–93.

van der Hoort, B., Guterstam, A. and Ehrsson, H.H. (2011) Being Barbie: The size of one's own body determines the perceived size of the world. *PLoS ONE*, 6(5), e20195.

van der Weiden, A., Ruys, K.L. and Aarts, H. (2013) A matter of matching: How goals and primes affect self-agency experiences. *Journal of Experimental Psychology: General*, 142, 954–66.

Van Horn, J., Irimia, A., Torgerson, C.M., Chambers, M.C., Kikinis, R. and Toga, A.W. (2012) Mapping connectivity damage in the case of Phineas Gage. *PLoS One*, 7(5), e37454.

VanVoorhis, C.R.W. (2002) Stat jingles: To sing or not to sing. *Teaching of Psychology*, 29(3), 249–50.

Vitzthum, F.B., Veckenstedt, R. and Moritz, S. (2014) Individualized metacognitive therapy program for patients with psychosis (MCT+): Introduction of a novel approach for psychotic symptoms. *Behavioural and Cognitive Psychotherapy*, 42(1), 105–10.

Vogelaar, B. and Resing, W.C.M. (2018) Changes over time and transfer of analogy-problem solving of gifted and non-gifted children in a dynamic testing setting. *Educational Psychology*, 38(7), 898–914.

Volkogonov, D. (1994) *Lenin. A new biography*. New York: The Free Press.

von Neumann, J. and Morgenstern, O. (1944) *Theory of Games and Economic Behaviour*. Princeton, NJ: Princeton University Press.

Vrij, A., Blank, H. and Fisher, R.P. (2018) A re-analysis that supports our main results: A reply to Levine et al. *Legal and Criminological Psychology*, 23(1), 20–3.

Vrij, A., Granhag, P. A., Mann, S. and Leal, S. (2011) Lying about flying: The first experiment to detect false intent. *Psychology, Crime & Law*, 17(7), 611–20.

Wagemans, J., Elder, J.H., Kubovy, M., Palmer, S.E., Peterson, M.A., Singh, M. and von der Heydt, R. (2012) A century of Gestalt psychology in visual perception: 1. Perceptual grouping and figure-ground organization. *Psychol. Bull.*, 138, 1172–217.

Wager, T.D., Phan, K.L., Liberzon, I. and Taylor, S.F. (2003) Valence, gender, and lateralization of functional brain anatomy in emotion: A meta-analysis of findings from neuroimaging. *Neuroimage*, 19, 513–31.

Wagner, A.D., Schacter, D.L., Rotte, M., Koutstaal, W., Maril, A.M., Dale, B.R., Rosen, B.R. and Buckner, R.L. (1998) Building memories: Remembering and forgetting of verbal experiences as predicted by brain activity. *Science*, 281, 1188–91.

Wagner, A.D., Shannon, B.J., Kahn, I. and Buckner, R.L. (2005) Parietal lobe contributions to episodic memory retrieval. *Trends in Cognitive Sciences*, 9, 445–53.

Wallas, G. (1926) *The Art of Thought*. London: Jonathan Cape.

Walton, D. (2010) A Dialogue model of belief. *Argument and Computation*, 1, 23–46.

Wason, P.C. (1960) On the failure to eliminate hypotheses in a conceptual task. *Quarterly Journal of Experimental Psychology*, 12, 129–40.

Watkins, M.J., Ho, E. and Tulving, E. (1976) Context effects in recognition memory for faces. *Journal of Verbal Learning and Verbal Behavior*, 15(5), 505–17.

Wells, A. (2009) *Metacognitive Therapy for Anxiety and Depression*. New York: Guilford Press.

Wells, A. (2011) *Metacognitive Therapy for Anxiety and Depression*. New York, NY: Guilford Press.

Wernicke, C. (1874) *Der aphasische Symptomenkomplex*. Breslau: Cohn and Weigert.

Wheeler, S. (2020) Learning theories: Three levels of information processing. https://www.teachthought.com/learning/learning-theories-three-levels-information-processing/

Whiten, A. and Byrne, R.W. (1988) The Machiavellian intelligence hypotheses: Editorial (pp. 1–9). In R.W. Byrne and A. Whiten (eds)

Machiavellian Intelligence: Social expertise and the evolution of intellect in monkeys, apes, and humans. Clarendon Press/Oxford University Press.

Wickens, C.D. (1984) Processing resources in attention. In R. Parasuraman and D.R. Davies (eds) *Varieties of Attention.* London: Academic Press.

Wickens, C.D. (2008) Multiple resources and mental workload. *Human Factors,* 50, 449–55.

Wilf, M., Holmes, N.P., Schwartz, I. and Makin, T.R. (2013) Dissociating between object affordances and spatial compatibility effects using early response components. *Frontiers in Psychology,* 4(Article 591).

Willingham, T. and Riener, C. (2019) *Cognition: The Thinking Animal.* Cambridge: Cambridge University Press.

Wimmer, H. and Perner, J. (1983) Beliefs about beliefs: Representation and constraining function of wrong beliefs in young children's understanding of deception. *Cognition,* 13, 103–28.

Windey, B., Vermeiren, A., Atas, A. and Cleeremans, A. (2014) The graded and dichotomous nature of visual awareness. *Philosophical Transactions of the Royal Society B,* 369, 20130282.

Wixted, J.T. (2004) The psychology and neuroscience of forgetting. *Annual Review of Psychology,* 55, 235–69.

Wolfe, J.M., Võ, M.L.-H., Evans, K.K. and Greene, M.R. (2011) Visual search in scenes involves selective and nonselective pathways. *Trends in Cognitive Sciences,* 15, 77–84.

Woollett, K., Spiers, H.J. and Maguire, E.A. (2009) Talent in the taxi: A model system for exploring expertise. *Philosophical Transactions of the Royal Society of London, Series B, Biological Sciences,* 364(1522), 1407–16.

Workman, L., Peters, S. and Taylor, S. (2000) Laterality of perception processing of pro- and antisocial emotion displayed in chimeric faces. *Laterality,* 5, 237–49.

Workman, L. and Reader, W. (2016) *Evolutionary Psychology* (3rd edn). Cambridge: Cambridge University Press.

Workman, L. and Reader, W. (2021) *Evolutionary Psychology* (4th edn). Cambridge: Cambridge University Press.

Yardley, H., Perlovsky, L. and Bar, M. (2012) Predictions and incongruency in object recognition: A cognitive neuroscience perspective. In D. Weinshall, J. Anemuller and L. Vangool (eds) *Detection and Identification of Rare Audiovisual Cues,* 384, 139–53.

Yerkes, R.M. and Dodson, J.D. (1908) The relation of strength of stimulus to rapidity of habit formation. In E. Loftus (ed.) *Eye-witness Testimony.* London: Harvard University Press, 1979.

Yong, E. (2010) Meet the woman without fear. *Discover Magazine.* https://www.discovermagazine.com/mind/meet-the-woman-without-fear

Young, R.M. (2001) Production systems in cognitive psychology. In N.J. Smelser and P.B. Baltes (eds) *International Encyclopedia of the Social and Behavioral Sciences*. Oxford: Pergamon Press.

Zeiler, S.R. and Krakauer, J.W. (2013) The interaction between training and plasticity in the post-stroke brain. *Current Opinion in Neurology*, 26, 609–16.

Zeki, S. (2015) Area V5 – A microcosm of the visual brain. *Frontiers in Integrative Neuroscience*, 9(21), doi: 10.3389/fnint.2015.00021

Zerilli, J. (2021) *The Adaptable Mind: What Neuroplasticity and Neural Reuse Tell Us about Language and Cognition*. Oxford: Oxford University Press.

Ziegler, J.C., Perry, C. and Zorzi, M. (2014) Modelling reading development through phonological decoding and self-teaching: Implications for dyslexia. *Philosophical Transactions of the Royal Society B: Biological Sciences*, 369 (1634) Article 20120937.

Zihl, J., von Cramon, D. and Mai, N. (1983) Selective disturbance of movement vision after bilateral brain damage (p. 315). *Brain*, 106, 313–40.

Zlatev, J. (2002) Meaning = life (+ culture): An outline of a unified bio-cultural theory of meaning. *Evol. Commun.*, 4(2), 253–96.

Zogg, J.B., Woods, S.P., Sauceda, J.A., Wiebe, J.S. and Simoni, J.M. (2012) The role of prospective memory in medication adherence: A review of an emerging literature. *Journal of Behavioral Medicine*, 35, 47–62.

INDEX

Printed in the United States
by Baker & Taylor Publisher Services